RESPONSIBILITY IN MASS COMMUNICATION

RESPONSIBILITY IN MASS COMMUNICATION

REVISED EDITION

by William L. Rivers
and Wilbur Schramm

HARPER & ROW, PUBLISHERS

NEW YORK, EVANSTON, AND LONDON

1817

Contents

1 The Impact of Mass Communication

> Public opinion is a compound of folly, weakness, prejudice, wrong feeling, right feeling, obstinacy, and newspaper paragraphs.
>
> —SIR ROBERT PEEL

It is one of the interesting ironies of our time that many critics of mass communication make their attacks with flourishes that suggest that they have hit upon something new. Those who belabor the mass media for playing up trivia, however, should be told of the critic who in 1591 complained about newspapers that "scarce a cat can look out of a gutter, but starts a half-penny Chronicler." Those who bemoan what they consider the degenerating influence of newspapers, magazines, broadcasts, films, and books should know of the critic who wrote in 1592:

A company of idle youthes, loathing honest labor and dispising lawful trades, betake themselves to a vagabond and vicious life, in every corner of Cities and market Townes of the Realme, singing and selling ballads and pamphlets full of ribaudrie, and all scurrilous vanity, to the prophanation of God's name, and withdrawing people from Christian exercises, especially at faires, markets, and such public meetings.

And yet, even if the modern critics seem to be doing little more than echoing complaints that are centuries old, there are differences worth remarking. The chief one is surely the widespread intensity of the modern attacks. In mid-twentieth-century America, both the number of critics and the bitter vehemence of their attacks set this period apart. In fact, it sometimes appears to those who produce the mass media that *everyone* is an acid critic. Surely this is a reflection of an important fact about modern life: We have become aware of the importance of mass communication. Nearly everyone is convinced that the mass media, good or bad, are central to modern society. As James Reston has written: "The Nineteenth Century was the era of the novelist. The Twentieth is the era of the journalist. A distracted people, busy with the fierce competitions of modern life, must be addressed while they are paying attention, which is usually at the moment of some great national or international event."

Criticism is likely to become more intense. Certainly, its intensity has traced a rising curve in recent years. The roar of approval from conservatives when General Eisenhower attacked "the columnists and commentators" in a speech at the Republican National Convention in 1964 was only more concentrated—not more vehement —than the wrath of the radicals at "the Establishment press" during the 1968 Democratic National Convention in Chicago. Right and left seem equally convinced that the mass media are slanted against them. And, of course, political coloration is only part of the issue. In 1968, the National Commission on the Causes and Prevention of Violence focused an investigation on the media. At about the same time, the eleven-million-member General Federation of Women's Clubs began a campaign to improve the quality of American life by cleaning up mass communication.

The irony of the close public attention to the mass media themselves springs from the fact that never before have the media been so conscious of their need for responsible performance. However well or ill they actually perform, a self-conscious quality is now a heavy overlay on their actions. This can be illustrated in many ways, but it is made graphic by looking at the editorial pages of many newspapers.

The first principle of an editorial page is that it belongs to the editor (and/or publisher). An adage of journalism runs: "The news columns belong to the reader; the editorial columns belong to the editor." In effect, this means that the reader should be able to demand that the news be as fair and impartial as human judgment can make it; but the editorials and the syndicated columns on the editorial page are the editor's territory. He *may not* write or publish libelous matter; he *should not* lie or knowingly publish the lies of others. But he has a right—even a duty, some would say—to present a vigorous viewpoint that reflects his own leanings. This goes for the syndicated columns he prints as well as for the local editorials he writes.

Significantly, though, fewer editors are as concerned today with promoting their own views. Editorial pages over the nation have become much less partisan. An editor who has liberal leanings is likely to be careful to publish syndicated columns that reflect a conservative—or at least a moderate—viewpoint in addition to columns that square with his own ideas. The same is generally true of many conservative editors. One can, of course, find exceptions: the New York *Post* is a liberal paper that seldom gives space to conservative views, and the Chicago *Tribune* seldom gives space to liberal views. But we are discussing *most* newspapers, and it is quite obvious that most editors and publishers are proud that there is a degree of balance on their editorial pages. They view a wide-open Letters-to-the-Editor column as a kind of balance for their own editorials in that writers of letters can refute editorials. They see a balance in the publication of liberal, moderate, and conservative columnists. (Some editors try to achieve a balance of syndicated columns by publishing only moderates, but this is difficult.)

To understand how much the editor has given up, it is necessary to stop and reconsider the premise that the news columns belong to the reader, the editorial columns to the editor. Actually, the brutal truth is that *everything* belongs to the editor. There is no law—and, thanks to the First Amendment, there cannot be a law—holding that an editor *must* publish *anything*. This is a real measure of how much the editor has given up. If he doesn't like the Democratic candidate for President, the editor need not even mention the candidate's name—in editorial columns *or* in news columns. Indeed, one of the foundation stones of this country was the libertarian ideal that every man would speak and write his own ideas. The clash of the myriads of ideas would produce The Truth. Editors have moved far from this ancient ideal, some because they know that single-newspaper towns make it unlikely that there can be a free market place of ideas. To their credit, many publish ideas they consider nonsense. It was all very well, a hundred years ago, to hold that a man who wanted to disseminate his ideas should start his own newspaper. Today the costs of news gathering, production, and distribution make that decision improbable. The point of all this is that an editor *may* do anything he likes with any part of his paper. But so many good editors give their news columns to their readers that we feel we can say to any editor: You *should* present the news fairly, adequately, and impartially. So many of the good editors try to balance their editorial pages that we feel we can say to any editor: Don't you think you should balance the editorial page? The difference between the statement in one case and the question in the other is crucial.

The important fact, however, is that many editors are *trying* to behave more responsibly today than they have ever behaved before—and are being criticized more acidly than ever before. This is not to say that even the best editors deserve our unstinting applause. A man who has the best intentions may be an inept performer, and the weight of this book, which carries evidence of many questionable acts, is one measure of failure. No, this is only to say that many editors are aware of their responsibilities, and in this fact there is hope for improvement.

Much the same point can be made about the other media—radio, television, film, magazines, and books: Whatever the value of the performance of some, however crass their motives, they are aware of their importance in a way that their predecessors were not. One of the notable results of the so-called Age of Communication is that communicators have become self-conscious. This has manufactured an unfortunate by-product in some cases: pomposity by the carload. Yet self-consciousness—awareness of role—also manufactures an entering wedge for the critic. And since critics, if they are numerous and powerful and incisive enough, represent a threat, they can work changes in even the most powerful institutions.

Nearly always, of course, there are opposing critics. The new morality that we can see so starkly in many of today's films and broadcasts and books—especially the frank treatment of sex and drugs—is primarily a reaction to the criticisms of the young, who do not hold with the taboos of earlier times. But if this new morality is a response to the criticism of one group, it is offensive to another. The cheers that greeted the appearance of films like *Bonnie and Clyde* and plays such as *Hair* were mingled with the outraged roars of those who consider such productions the madness of a decaying society. The chief irony will not escape the thoughtful reader: This is not unlike the reaction of the critic of 1592 who was concerned about "the prophanation of God's name."

Surely this teaches us something in addition to the fact that the more things change the more they remain the same. It should suggest that we can understand modern communication only by taking an overview of its slow development and trying to determine what has been learned about its effects.

The story begins about 1450 in Mainz, Germany, with one of those conjunctions of materials, skills, an idea, that turns the course of history. The materials were the wine press, which had been used for centuries in western Europe; cast metal type, which had been invented fifty years earlier in Korea and again, independently, at Mainz; and paper and ink, both of which had been developed many centuries earlier in China and brought to Europe. The skills were calligraphy and block printing, which had been elegantly developed by Asians and Europeans, especially in the medieval monasteries. The new idea was to print from movable type, so that one piece of type might be used interchangeably in many jobs. The result was a machine for rapidly duplicating writing —the writing being standardized into type faces.

That was the beginning of modern communication. The story of the five hundred years of development in communication since that time is a story of man's changing relationship to machines in the communication process. The difference between communication before and after 1450 was simply that man had finally made an efficient machine to duplicate interpersonal communication. It was, of course, a monumental change. Unfortunately, we do not know the first words that were printed from movable metal type. The earliest dated piece of printing that remains is a papal indulgence, struck by Johann Fust and Peter Schoeffer in 1454. The first book was apparently the forty-two-line Bible, which was printed not later than 1456, probably by Johann Gutenberg.

It is significant that at its very birth the new art served the chief power center of the time: the Church. Had the printing press been a different kind of machine, it could have been restricted—as certain other communication devices, like heraldry, or the semaphore, have been—to one master, or one class, or a certain kind of task, or a certain topic. But the peculiar characteristic of machine-duplicated communication was that it could be applied to and became involved with all the public affairs of man—and swiftly. William Caxton was printing in England by 1476, Aldus Manutius in Italy by 1494; Juan Pablos was printing in Mexico City less than fifty years after Columbus first saw the new continent. Everywhere it went, the printing press was involved in the matters that exalted or stimulated or troubled man. It served the parties in power, but it also served all the revolutions of the spirit and the body politic. It was used by the Church, but it also carried the great debate on the Reformation. It circulated the precious books of Aristotle, which had been chained to the library desks of the Middle Ages. It disseminated the extraordinary intellectual output of the Renaissance. It carried commercial news to the merchants of England and northern Germany, and also revolutionary pamphlets—so effectively that anonymous pamphlets are even today the symbol of revolution in some European countries. Without the press there might have been an Enlightenment, but it is doubtful if there could have been a French or an American revolution.

In the vast ground swell of democracy toward the end of the eighteenth century, the press led the people toward their new importance. And just then, shortly after 1800, came the first major improvement in the remodeled wine press. It was a new source of power, a gift of the Industrial Revolution. First steam, then electricity, replaced man's muscles and enabled him to produce more of the same product much faster. The exciting thing about the power press was that it came precisely when it was needed to reach masses of new voters. It offered those who could not read a strong incentive to learn, and thus it was meshed into the growth of public education. Then smart merchandisers discovered that they could sell newspapers for a penny and still make a profit if they sold enough, and if they sold enough they could also lure advertisers, and so we had "mass communication": prices the common man could pay, enormous circulations, profitable advertising, large publishing organizations, the attractive concept of the new machine as the voice and servant of democracy, and the misleading concept of a "mass audience."

By the middle of the nineteenth century, the telegraph and the cable were speeding communication, and the camera and photoengraving were adding a vivid quality. But none of this was fundamentally new, for the Washington hand presses that rode west in the American covered wagons were essentially only a hardier version of the press that Gutenberg had at Mainz in the middle of the fifteenth century. The presses that printed the Gettysburg Address were essentially the same machines, powered by steam. All this was still a part of the great wave of communication that began to break at Mainz about 1450. The accomplishment of that first wave rested entirely on an ability to make swift duplicates of writing on paper.

The first fundamentally new development came late in the nineteenth century. As the first wave of modern communication can be dated back to 1450, the second can be dated, if not to Samuel F. B. Morse and the telegraph, at least to Alexander Graham Bell and the telephone in 1876. The difference between communication before and after 1876 was that man had finally begun to make efficient machines that could be interposed in the communication chain and be trusted to listen and see for him. In a sense, of course, the printing machine had been interposed in the communication chain, but it merely duplicated; it did not communicate directly. It made a product that could be read at leisure, the reader taking the initiative, setting his own pace, selecting from the material as he wished. The second wave of modern communication made a profound change in shifting the initiative, at least in part, from receiver to sender. That is, once the receiver had made his basic choice, the sender was in charge. The machine, or the force behind it, controlled the pace, the repetitions, the emphasis, the timing.

These attributes of the second wave can be seen clearly in the machines which were developed in a quickening stream after Bell's. A few years after the telephone was invented, Thomas A. Edison's phonograph and his movie camera and projector made it possible to store both sounds and moving sights. De Forest's triode vacuum tube, in 1907, opened the world of radio and television.

Most of the new machines which have ushered in the second wave are much faster than the press. They bring tidings more swiftly, answer an argument more quickly. They have about them a sense of reality, a sense of immediacy, that print has never had. They have in their essence an emotional quality that is difficult to achieve in print. These newer media came into being when Western countries were being urbanized, when the work week was being greatly shortened and people began to have more leisure. They came into being at a time when America was on the verge of a striking change from what David Riesman[1] calls "inner-direction" to "other-direction"—from an individualistic work-success ethic and a future-time orientation to a hedonistic present-centered ethic concerned mainly with group relationships and opinions. These new machines—sociable little machines—were exactly what people needed to keep them informed about the people around them. They brought personalities into one's living room, and they transported one into countless other living rooms, not to mention chambers of state. Much more strikingly than print, the new machine-interposed communication extended man's environment and dominated his leisure.

These are the aspects of modern communication which will concern us in this book. But it is important to note that there have been two others. The third wave of modern communication was developing at the same time as the second, but it moved slowly and crested only in the twentieth century. This was communication between men and machines. It developed surely as man became more ingenious at making dials and gauges that would yield information, and instruments on which he could register his wishes. It now seems ordinary, but it would have seemed fantastic only a few decades ago, that a man is able to fly an airplane when ground and horizon are completely invisible, simply by means of messages sent to him by a panel of instruments designed to say how high he is, how fast he is going, where he is heading, whether his wings are level, and how fast his engine is turning. That was fantastic in 1915, and the idea of ships seeing the shoreline or planes seeing the ground quite clearly through clouds and fog was unimaginable in 1935. Yet by the 1940s we had a machine—radar, of course— that operated through an electronic screen and conveyed exactly this kind of information, in exacting detail. The end of radar's development and that of other kinds of communication between men and machines is still in the distant future.

If the third wave of modern communication developed slowly, the fourth is so recent that we are not yet aware of its dimensions—except to know that it is vast. It can be pretty well dated to an article by Claude E. Shannon in the *Bell System Technical Journal* in 1948.[2] Shannon began modestly: "The recent development of various methods of modulation . . . has intensified the interest in a general theory of communication." That is exactly what Shannon provided. The effect of his paper, and of the formulas in it, was to stimulate a great outpouring of developments in communication between machines.

As machines in the nineteenth century came to do the work of man's muscles, so the new machines are able to do some of his thinking. The great computers, which have come into being in the last three decades, and the concept of feedback of information (which made possible such relatively simple devices as thermostats), have become so sophisticated that it is now possible to put a machine in charge of other machines and to build a factory to run itself. We have built machines with qualities thought previously to be man's unique prerogative. Under the name of automation this fourth wave of modern communication has already reshaped industry, and it is beginning to have a profound effect on man's concept of himself and his place in the world.

The next new medium after television may already be technically feasible. Indeed, in a scatter-shot way, it is already operating. A product of the computer age, this new medium looks like a cross between a television set and a typewriter. One of the scientists who is experimenting with it, Professor Edwin B. Parker of Stanford, describes its future this way:

Imagine yourself sitting down at the breakfast table with a display screen in front of you. You touch a key and the latest headlines appear on the screen. Not the headlines that were written last night— or even those of six or seven hours ago. But headlines that may have been rewritten and updated five minutes or just 50 microseconds before you see them on the screen. You type another key or poke a light pen at the appropriate headline and the whole story appears on the screen.

Imagine that you've been "reading" your news-screen regularly and so you know the background of the story and the recent day's events. You want only today's information and you have it by touching just one key. Maybe you haven't kept up and so you want all the background information, the pre-history, the explanation and interpretation. Touching a different key will provide it.

Are you interested in something that hasn't made the major headlines? Like a bill on education being considered in Congress. There may be no major story today, but you still want to find out what is happening to the bill. Perhaps there's something you missed yesterday or the day before that's not front-page news today; the computer has stored it for you. You can have the latest information whether it's on today's or yesterday's story.

Because you grew up before the development of this medium, are you so conditioned to the physical feeling of paper in your hand that you can't enjoy the news without it? You can get up in the morning, go to the console, indicate what you want (perhaps a pre-selected general summary of the news of the day), and have it printed out for you while you are shaving or getting dressed.

There's a person in the news you'd like to know more about. Ask your computer for a biographical sketch. You don't understand the economics of the gold market. Request a tutorial program on the subject. You want the comics? Press the right button. Catch up on the strips you missed while you were on vacation. You want to glance at the want ads or supermarket ads. The computer will present on your screen the comparative meat prices today at the different super-markets.

You're interested in chess. Read the chess column—or play chess with your computer. In 1968, if you're a Grand Master, you won't find your computer much of a match. The best computer chess pro-grams today can win only in Class D tournaments but not in Class C, B, or A or at the Grand Master level. But in five years the com-petition will be much sharper—there'll be a better chess program.

Your child comes home from school with a question about insects or, "What's an atom, Mommie?" If you have an encyclopedia in your computer store, you won't be embarrassed for an answer. For instance, the Systems Development Corporation in Santa Monica has in its computer store the *Children's Golden Book Encyclopedia.* You can ask questions through the time-shared computer and get answers dis-played.

The revolutionary quality of this change should be clear. Think what it means: we will enter a period when the *receiver,* not the sender, decides what information is to pass through a channel of communication. Instead of taking what is available, the receiver orders what he wants.[3]

Let us be clear that we are limiting ourselves in this book to the first two waves of modern communication because the third and fourth are so new. Young as machine-duplicated communication and machine-interposed communication are when measured against the history of human communication, they are old when compared with man-machine and machine-to-machine communi-cation. They are old enough to have acquired an ethic and to be incorporated into philosophies.

We are especially concerned with them, too, because of their reach. The great voice of print was caught up in the ground swell of democracy and the sharply breaking waves of revolution in the seventeenth and eighteenth centuries; and the impressive new technology (the power press, photoengraving, stereotyping, sound and sight recording on film, and transmission by air waves) was caught up in the steep curve of economic growth in the nineteenth and twentieth centuries. As a result, the tiny hand press, the squeaking earphones, the flickering film, have in our time become huge business enterprises: daily newspapers, publishing houses, radio and television stations and networks, and film studios and theater chains. We call these developments mass communication because of their massive product and the enormous audiences they have come to serve.

Significantly, the general tendency of the Industrial Revolution toward larger and fewer manufacturing units has been reflected in newspapers. Even while the national population has nearly doubled since 1920—from 105 million to more than 200 million—and the combined circulations of daily newspapers has more than doubled—from 27 million to nearly 62 million—the number of dailies has decreased by nearly 300. There are signs that a plateau has been reached. Although the giant metropolitan dailies have been dying, suburban papers are enjoying a period of expansion, and during the past twenty years nearly as many new dailies have been established in the suburbs as have died in the central cities. The figures in this table[4] show the trend in relation to the national population:

	Number of Dailies	Total Circulation	U.S. Population
1888	1,442	4,543,713	61,000,400 (est.)
1900	2,120	9,330,930	75,994,575
1914	2,442	25,426,911	96,000,000 (est.)
1920	2,042	27,790,656	105,710,620
1930	1,942	39,589,172	122,775,046
1940	1,878	41,131,611	131,669,275
1950	1,772	53,829,072	150,697,361
1956	1,760	56,147,359	162,000,000 (est.)
1968	1,754	62,000,000	200,000,000 (est.)

The machine-interposed media came along relatively late in the Industrial Revolution and therefore have rather short histories of concentration. They were caught up in the tidal wave of growth almost as soon as they had a marketable product. Motion pictures, in 1920, were already attracting weekly audiences equivalent to nearly a third of the people in this country. Radio, which had thirty stations and 60,000 receivers in 1922, had more than 5,700 stations (commercial and educational) and more than 250 *million* receivers in 1966—and was in more than 98 per cent of American homes. Television reached barely 75,000 homes in 1947, but in 1968 there were 57 million television-served homes in the United States.[5]

Mass Communication Media in the United States

Medium	Number of Units	Circulation and Audiences	Financial Support
Books	1,600 publishers of one or more titles annually; 87 publish 60% of books	28,600 titles, 933 million copies per year	By sales estimated about $1.5 billion annually
Daily newspapers	1,754 dailies	62 million copies a day	70% from advertising; 30% from circulation; total ad income about $4.5 billion
Magazines	2,630 publishing houses	49 magazines have over 1 million circulation each	Advertising and circulation in varying proportions; total ad income over $1.6 billion
Television	617 commercial stations; 156 educational; 3 large networks	55 million receiving sets; 10 million color receiving sets	Advertising mostly (time sales); total ad income $2 billion
Radio	4,100 AM stations; 1,600 FM; 4 large networks	More than 250 million receiving sets	Advertising time sales; total ad income $0.8 billion
Films	6 large studios; numerous independent producers; 16,000 theaters	Weekly attendance about 59 million	Attendance and small local advertising income; estimated $1.5 billion

Dramatic as these figures are, they are merely incidental. For the truth is that in the lifetime of many of us a new system of public communication has developed. The social bulk of these new enterprises can be gauged only in these terms: One hundred years ago, there was no radio, no television, no movies; newspapers were little more than political organs, and magazines and books were the products of limited industries. Only fifty years ago, there was no public radio, no television; motion pictures were barely advancing out of the nickelodeon stage; newspapers almost everywhere were a combination of political organ and yellow press.

What would people have thought a century ago if someone had predicted that it would soon be possible to buy for ten cents a newspaper connected by leased wires and reporters to all the principal cities of the world, no more than minutes removed from a news event anywhere? What would people have thought fifty years ago if someone had told them that soon most homes would contain a relatively inexpensive little box through which one could see and hear the Metropolitan Opera, the Olympic Games, the meetings of the United Nations, war in Asia, and candidates for national political office? What would people have thought if someone had predicted that books bound in paper would soon be purchased in supermarkets along with the weekly groceries?

These developments have made a profound difference in the way we receive information, and in the kind and amount of information we receive. For communicators, they have made a profound difference in the opportunities they offer and the responsibilities they impose.

Perhaps the most striking aspect of this communication complex is its pervasiveness. If we were describing our culture to a visitor from another planet, we should have to report the set of mass communication experiences which come to us throughout all except perhaps the first year or so of our lives. In imaginative language, we might call these the *teach-please* experiences (after Horace) or the *inform-entertain* experiences, because each of them is intended, in some proportion, to teach and please, inform and entertain. Most of a newspaper is designed to inform; most radio and television programs and most films are designed to entertain. A magazine of large general circulation is usually a fairly even combination. Textbooks are mostly to inform; novels, mostly to entertain. Each of these teach-please experiences comes from mass communication, and we should be hard put to name any man-made products except food, clothing, and shelter which are more widely pervasive.

Most of us depend upon mass-communication products for a large majority of all the information and entertainment we receive during life. It is especially obvious that what we know about public figures and public affairs is largely dependent upon what the mass media tell us. We are always subject to journalism and incapable of doing much about it. We can see too little for ourselves. Days are too short and the world is too big and complex for anyone to be sure of much about the web of government. What most of us think we know is not known at all in the sense of experience and observation.

We get only occasional firsthand glimpses of government by catching sight for a moment of a presidential candidate in the flesh, by shaking hands with a Senator (or talking with one while he absently shakes hands with someone else), by doing business with the field offices of federal agencies, dickering with the Internal Revenue Service—all the little bits and pieces of contact with officialdom that are described, too grandly, as "citizen participation in government."

We learn more at second hand—from friends, acquaintances, and lecturers on hurried tours, especially those who have just come from Washington or the state capital and are eager to impart what they consider, perhaps erroneously, to be the real story of what is going on there.

Yet this is sketchy stuff, and it adds only patches of color to the mosaic. The expanse of our knowledge of public affairs must come from the mass media. There simply are no practical alternatives. The specialists are, for the most part, in the same condition as the lay citizen. The professor of political science who devotes six months to studying municipal government in France will develop from the experience a more precise knowledge which he can pass on to his students when he returns to the classroom, and to his colleagues through scholarly articles. But in the context of the vast sweep of happenings over the world, his study is narrow—and by the time he returns to deliver his lectures and write his articles, the contemporary study he made is part of yesterday. Like the layman, he must learn of today through the mass media. Clearly, all of us live in a synthetic world, and the synthesis is fashioned largely from information supplied through mass communication.

This is one of the chief functions of mass communication, then: It *helps us to watch the horizon,* much as the ancient messenger once did. No longer depending on the running messenger or the distant drum, we watch the horizon through news bulletins or on-the-scene broadcasts or advertisements of opportunities.

Mass communication *helps us to correlate our response* to the challenges and opportunities which appear on the horizon and to *reach consensus* on social actions. In a real sense, tribal actions and town meetings have given way to mass communication, which enables us to read the rival arguments, see the rival candidates, and judge the issues.

Mass communication *helps us to transmit the culture* of our society to new members. We have always had teaching at the mother's knee and imitation of the father—and we still have. For thousands of years we have had schools of some kind. But mass communication has entered into this function by supplying text-books, teaching films and programs, and a constant picturing of the roles and accepted mores of our society for both native Americans and immigrants. A large group of immigrants were once asked, "How did you first learn what American life was like?" Some of them had received letters from relatives, but their chief source was the picture magazine. "How did you get your first English lessons?" They answered, "From your movies."

Mass communication *helps entertain us.* The ballad singer, the dancer, and the traveling theater—even the pitchman—have gone on television, radio, and films. The storytellers of old are chiefly in print.

Finally, mass communication *helps sell goods and services,* and thus keeps our economic system healthy. We once listened for the town crier's advertisements, the word-of-mouth tidings of bargains, the bells of the traveling store-wagon—none very different from the practices of tribal times. Now we read the ads in newspapers and magazines, see them on television, and hear them on radio.

Does it make a difference that we now see so much of the world through the mass media? Marshall McLuhan and Harold Innis, the Canadian philosophers and critics of communication, argue that it certainly does. Oral cultures, they say, were time-bound; the people with power were those who could remember the past, its laws and lessons. When man invented printing, he moved into a space-bound culture. There was no longer any need to worry about remembering the past, for its records could now be stored conveniently on paper; the men with power in a media culture are those who know the most about the present and have the facilities to manipulate it. Before the age of printing, man saw the world with all his senses, three-dimensionally, realistically. Through printing, he saw it only with his eyes, and in an abstracted, linear, sequential form. Printed language very probably acts as a filter for reality. It gives some of its own form to life. Television, on the other hand, is a step back toward the oral culture. It merely extends man's eyes and ears, and lets him see reality much as he used to before Gutenberg. This is what McLuhan means when he says that television is "retribalizing" us.

We may now be at one of the great turning points of communication history. With machines that bring us incomparably more information, from farther away, than ever before, we are again becoming accustomed to looking at the distant environment without the interpretive filters of print. For some years now we have become accustomed to seeing our candidates on television rather than merely reading about them. We participated as a nation, by means of television, in the tragic events of November, 1963, and in similarly terrible events of 1968. The Vietnam war is the first war we have seen extensively on television.

For four centuries, until recently, we followed reality from left to right across a printed page. Most of our codes and standards of reporting on the environment have been formed from our experience with print. Are they still applicable to the audio-visual reporting on which we increasingly depend?

The media themselves thus have an effect, and the way we use them, the messages we put through them, also have an effect. Let us review some of the things we have learned about how communication has an effect on people.

We might begin with a homely little scene:

Mrs. A looks suspiciously at her husband, who is deep in a detective story while she is telling him the neighborhood news. She concludes her story abruptly: "And the horse ate up all our children."

"That's fine, dear," he says after a moment.

"Henry, did you hear a word I said?" she demands indignantly.

"No, dear," he says absently, turning the page.

Communication has to clear four hurdles: it must (1) attract attention, (2) be accepted, (3) be interpreted, and (4) be stored for use.

In this sad little story—it might happen to any of us!—the process of informing failed to clear the very first hurdle: It did not get attention. Millions of messages of all kinds die similarly. All of us go through life surrounded by messages, so many more than our senses can attend to or our nervous systems handle that we must defend ourselves by paying attention—or perceiving—selectively.

One way to determine how individuals select information is to think of a "fraction of selection," which might be represented as

$$\frac{\text{expectation of reward}}{\text{effort thought to be required}} = \text{likelihood of selection}$$

The likelihood that a receiver will attend to a message is enhanced when the reward is greater and the effort smaller. This helps to explain why television has made such a dent in movie attendance (less effort is required to enjoy programs at home), why jamming does not entirely stop the listening to foreign short-wave broadcasts (some listeners want very badly to hear them), and why the use of public libraries falls off so sharply after the teen years (the effort becomes much greater). The limitation of this approach is that it implies a rationality that does not always bulk large in the process of selection. Surely much selection is accidental: A person quite often "just happens" to be where he can attend to a given message. Some selection is impulsive. Much is the result of role patterns or habits learned from obscure experience. It is important to remember, however, that over the years a person tends to seek the kinds of communication that have rewarded him in the past—his favorite television programs, his favorite columnists, the advisers he trusts. He has, therefore, a built-in expectation of reward developed from looking in certain places. Beyond that, he tends, other things being equal, to select the cues to information which are close at hand and easy to find in the glut of communication.

Advertisers and other professional communicators try to make their messages appear more rewarding by appealing to the needs and interests of their intended audience—some of the appeals, like the beauties who advertise soft drinks, quite remote from the rewards their users are actually likely to enjoy from accepting the product. They try to lure acceptance by making their messages stand out with large headlines or color or pictures or cleverness or repetition, and by saturating the channels. They also try to present their messages so as to eliminate noise and interference. One technique is to build in redundancy where it is necessary. When points are obscure, repetitions and examples are used to make them clear. In international news cables, important words are often repeated to negate the possibility that they will be garbled in transmission: "WILL NOT—REPEAT NOT—ACCEPT TERMS," the cable reads, and no editor ever upbraids a correspondent for that kind of redundancy.

Once the message has been presented as well as possible, the sender can do little more than be alert to feedback from the receiver. A skilled speaker, for example, can "read" his audience and adjust his communication accordingly. Although it is no longer possible to sharpen the message that has been sent, he can still add to it or correct it. And there is always the next time.

Then it rests with the receiver. If he attends to the message, he must decide whether to accept it. His acceptance will depend largely on the apparent validity of the message and on his judgment of the sender's credibility or prestige. A well-known experiment in attitude change once used a series of messages about the President of the United States which varied from very favorable to very unfavorable. One of them said that the President favored communism. The experimental audience laughed and refused to accept that message because of its lack of face validity.[6] On the other hand, many readers would accept a rather shocking news item in a distinguished newspaper like the *New York Times* because of the *Times's* reputation for accuracy.

A person who accepts a message will interpret it as his stored-up experience and his built-in values dictate, for he can interpret only in terms of the responses he has learned. We tend to interpret new experience, if possible, in ways that fit with old experience and accepted values. This, of course, sometimes leads to distortion—

often to selecting the parts of a message that fit comfortably and discarding the rest.

How this works is suggested by a well-intended communication which went awry when a certain educational administrator was subjected to very serious charges by a local newspaper. A distinguished academic committee investigated and reported that the charges were without foundation. There had merely been, the committee members reported, "a failure of communication" in the administrator's department. They saw this as a vindication of the administrator (after all, what department has not sometimes suffered communication failures?). But the newspaper paid little attention to the acquittal, and trumpeted for weeks the fact that the committee had found a "failure of communication" involving the administrator. Ultimately, the administrator resigned. The chagrined committee members realized that they (the senders) and the newspaper (the receiver) had approached that communication with different purposes. They had thought to explain the trouble and to indicate that it was not serious. The newspaper, however, was out to get the administrator, and simply seized upon that part of the message that would further its purpose.

The process of informing, then, is not at all simple. In fact, it involves so many problems and pitfalls that the constant flow of relatively accurate information in human society may seem almost miraculous. Here is another little scene:

"What do you think T. S. Eliot really meant by 'The Hollow Men'?" asks Miss A, who is a high school senior.

"I don't know," her brother answers. "Why doesn't he write so that there's no question what he means?"

"It wouldn't be any fun if he did," says Miss A.

This exchange indicates the different ground rules which operate when the goal of the communication process is entertaining rather than informing. True, entertaining communication must get over the same hurdles. The message must be presented so as to be interpretable within the experience of the audience; it must appeal to audience needs and interests; and it must, so far as possible, be designed to avoid the hazards of noise and interference. That is, it must gain attention, be accepted, and be interpreted. Feedback is at least as important in entertainment as in informing; in live entertainment it is the crucial element—the artist fits his act to his audience, or he fails—and in media entertainment it is so important that broadcasters spend millions of dollars every year to learn about their audiences. The chief difference lies in the unwritten contract between sender and receiver. In informational communication, the sender is to be a good reporter, and the audience is to bring to the experience a reality-seeking and reality-testing mood. Entertainment, however, requires of the receivers a certain willing suspension of disbelief. Instead of reacting skeptically to anything that checks poorly with their picture of reality, members of the entertainment audience must be willing to go along with a story or a spoof or a joke, or to agonize and rejoice with a character who never lived or never could live. Instead of expecting simple, clear, unambiguous writing, they may be pleased with a certain level of artistic ambiguity and a host of latent meanings.

The entertainer may be expected to be more concerned with form than is the informational communicator. *How* he writes or speaks or moves is expected to give pleasure. He is usually imaginative rather than utilitarian, prizes rich writing over clear writing, and must expertly turn a phrase or build a scene. In short, although informational communication may be artistic, and although entertainment communication may present a picture of reality, the thrust of informing asks for the skill of the reporter, and the thrust of entertaining asks for the skill of the artist.

The receiver of entertainment communication is expected to be willing to identify with one or more of the characters, put himself in their places, feel with them. In poetry and modern painting, he is expected to enjoy ambiguity rather than be frustrated by it. Indeed, there is reason to believe that resolving ambiguities is one of our most pleasurable experiences, perhaps because so much pride is involved. One who understands James Joyce's *Ulysses* certainly develops a measure of pride. One who understands a joke is almost surely pleased, at least in part, because he "got it." (And it may be that jokes which must be explained cannot be funny because the necessity to have them explained robs the listener of his pride.) But it is also true that the question "What did the author mean?" is shunned by most modern writers and many modern teachers in favor of "What did the author mean to *you?*"

Communication can be used to teach as well as inform or entertain. An example of this kind of communication effect comes from

Colombia, where the use of television for in-service training of teachers has been studied by a Stanford research team. It was found that teachers learned much from a televised course on the new mathematics. But when they viewed the course in groups, and discussed each lesson, they learned considerably more than when they viewed alone; and they learned still more when their groups had supervisors who directed the discussions.[7]

Communication used for instruction must leap the same hurdles as any other kind of communication—attention, acceptance, interpretation, storing—but there are other characteristics. Learning is active; it comes from practicing responses. Lectures or textbooks alone are not enough. Most teachers gradually become aware that the progress of their students comes about not so much from what they teach as from what their students go about learning: the skills they practice, the problems they solve, the answers they seek.

For years teachers have built practice and discussion around textbooks. The coming of instructional television provided a stricter test because television could offer everything the classroom teacher could provide except personal interaction with pupils. It could do some things better than most teachers—such as furnishing excellent demonstrations and teaching aids—and make available the best teaching. And indeed it has been found that pupils learn a great deal from television courses. But they learn a great deal more when programs of practice, discussion, and individual activity are built around television in the local classroom.

The messages of instructional communication must be presented so that they encourage the pupil to rehearse the responses he is expected to learn, and active study and practice must be organized. Almost nowhere in the world is one of the mass media being asked to carry the entire burden of instruction alone. In the "outback" country of Australia, where families often live several hundred miles from the nearest town or school, both elementary and secondary education are offered by radio, but the radio lectures are combined with correspondence study, and wherever possible the pupils are brought together in groups of five or six every day to study together under a supervisor. In Italy, where thousands have been taught by television to read and do simple arithmetic, the process does not work very well unless the pupils are brought together to practice their new skills under supervision. In India, rural adult education has been found to result in more learning and more action if rural programs are piped into a discussion forum.[8]

Like entertainment communication, instruction presupposes a kind of contract between teacher and pupil. The teacher contracts to give the pupil a systematic view of useful knowledge, and to give him opportunities to practice what he must learn. The pupil contracts to show a certain level of trust in his teacher's guidance and a willingness to engage in a certain amount of learning activity. Supposedly, he *wants* to learn. One of the teacher's tasks is to maintain this motivation and, if necessary, increase it. If the pupil is not motivated to learn, then, in effect, he does not sign the contract, and the instructional communication is likely to be wasted.

One more example: About twenty years ago a series of delightful cartoons was prepared to make fun of racial prejudice. It was thought that this would provide a method for penetrating the defenses of prejudiced people, and perhaps stimulate them to laugh their way out of their rigidity on the subject of race relations. But the most prejudiced people completely misinterpreted the cartoons, and considered them really to be justifications of their own positions. After looking at one cartoon that showed a woman in a hospital refusing to accept a transfusion unless it was "blue blood," a prejudiced person said, "That's a very good idea. I must warn my doctor to be careful about that if I ever need a transfusion."[9]

Like informational communication, persuasive communication must get the message through, but that is rarely enough. To accomplish any substantial change, persuasion must control a psychological process in the receiver. It must set in motion some psychological dynamics by which the receiver will, in effect, change himself. In the example just given, the communication got through and set something going, all right, but it was the wrong thing.

It is not necessarily difficult to implant new attitudes or encourage new behavior in a new area, of course. If our first contingent of astronauts should return from the moon with an account of dangerous and hostile little green men, we would be easily persuaded to view this new threat with alarm. After all, we do not now have much in our mental files on the subject of moon men. However, if we had long known of the moon men and had long held attitudes toward them, changing the attitudes would be difficult. For when a strong area is attacked directly, the message is likely to be rejected or distorted.

Consider the situation in which persuasion occurs. Unlike entertainment and instructional communication, persuasion involves no contract between sender and receiver. The sender is on his own. He must choose the information and package it to fit his goals. He may attract attention by entertainment (the programs accompanying the commercials), by saturating the perceptual field (big type, loud commercials, parades, rallies), by big names and big events. He can advance arguments, make threats, offer rewards. *Caveat emptor!*

The receiver comes with his defenses up, prepared to be skeptical. He has experienced persuasion before. He asks, "What is there for *me* in this message?" He comes with a set of needs he wants to satisfy. He already has a set of beliefs and attitudes; some are relatively flexible but many he is prepared to defend stubbornly. He comes with a set of personal relationships and loyalties, and he feels deeply dependent on many of them. He comes with a set of perceptions of opportunity and threat in the environment and is not prepared to change them without persuasive evidence. On balance, the persuasion situation is a buyer's, not a seller's, market.

The receiver's needs, his beliefs and attitudes, his personal relationships, and his perception of the environment are all interdependent. A substantial change in one is likely to bring about a change in others. If, for example, the astronauts should bring back a convincing account of hostile moon men, this would substantially change our perception of the kind of threat that exists in our environment. In turn, this might lead us to think of other earthlings as allies rather than as enemies or competitors; to reorganize our goal patterns and our priorities for using resources; to rethink our concepts of the universe and of man's position in it.

The process of persuasion, so far as it is primarily a *communication process* (as distinguished, for example, from the use of force), consists of introducing information which leads the receiver to reappraise his perception of his environment, and through that to reappraise his needs and his ways of meeting them, or his social relationships, or his beliefs and attitudes. Perhaps the closest we have come to the kind of change that might be brought about by discovery of dangerous little moon men is the notorious panic caused by Orson Welles's radio broadcast, in 1938, of a dramatization of "The Invasion from Mars." The more susceptible listeners believed that invaders were actually sweeping all before them. Suddenly, their environmental support seemed to be crumbling, and with it their confidence in law and order and national power. Their need for self-preservation took control, and they fled to the hills.

Although the conscious use of threats to arouse the need for self-preservation can initiate a process of change, this has been shown to be a two-edged sword. In a famous experiment, researchers were somewhat surprised to find that lesser threats concerning tooth decay accomplished more than strong threats to send their experimental subjects to the toothbrush and the dentist.[10] Later experiments showed that when the threat was too unpleasant, and especially when the cure was remote or difficult or uncertain, the whole topic was often repressed—swept under the rug. This may have been one of the reasons why the campaign against cigarette smoking was relatively ineffective. The prospect of lung cancer was so frightening, the cure so uncertain, the entire relation of smoking to cancer so befogged by counterclaims, that it was easier to change an old habit slightly (switching to a filter) and repress the picture of cancer than to make greater changes. (One of the most dramatic changes in product marketing did result from the campaign against cigarette smoking. Nonfilter cigarettes, which had always led the filters in sales, fell well behind.) Apparently, threats must be made in a low key unless one can offer a clear and certain remedy. Advertisers are usually careful to offer a carrot even as they brandish the stick: They suggest the horrors of bad breath, but they emphasize that it can be purged with Little Miracle Mouthwash, and that social joys are then available.

A change process can be triggered by altering a receiver's perception of his social relationships. Every salesman tries to establish himself as a friend of the prospective buyer. Many of the most successful evangelists place a new convert in a group of believers at once so that his decision will be socially reinforced. Many advertisements hold out the implied hope of being able to join an admired group—"men of distinction" or the sponsors of a particular cause or the effervescent "Pepsi Generation."

One of the patterns which the Chinese have been reported to use in attempts at brainwashing involves both removing old social support and providing new support. A military captive is removed from his officers—and thus from his authority structure—and ultimately from his fellow P.O.W.'s—his friendship group. He is allowed to receive no mail from home, and is told that other captives have informed on him. These actions remove the social support for the values and behavior patterns the Chinese hope to change. Then the captive is placed in a small group where other captives are studying communist doctrine and writing "confessions" of their former "errors." He is rewarded and socially supported for every step he takes in the desired direction, and encouraged to build new friendships among converts. Obviously, so radical a change as persuading a soldier to give up his loyalty to his country is not accomplished very often, but the process is strong: (1) it undermines confidence in existing social relationships and (2) offers new relationships that (3) reward one for desired opinions and behavior.

Another tactic is to build cross pressures. If a man can be convinced that two groups he values, or two advisers he trusts, disagree completely on the point at issue, he will be vulnerable to a suggestion that seems to offer a way out of the conflict.

One of the most powerful processes available to persuasive communication is what we might call the strain toward consistency. Human beings strive for balance between what they know and believe and do. Suppose, now, that a persuasive message can push its way into cognitive areas that are relatively lightly defended. And suppose that this new information is out of balance with the present position, but not so far out of balance as to be rejected. For example, suppose it says that some admired individual or group holds a position that is inconsistent with the person's present position; or that a new position is not really inconsistent with his own, but rather a development of it. Then there is some reason to hope that the individual may reorganize and change some of his more strongly held positions in order to attain consistency.

This may help to explain the success of role playing in attitude change. When a young person is encouraged to prepare a prize contest oration or essay that takes a specified point of view toward some controversial topic, he is likely to be under some strain to bring his attitudes into consistency with those he has publicly expressed.

It is important to remember that there are strong defenses against change in any attitudes and beliefs that really matter to the holder. It is necessary to breach those defenses in some way—to implant information that will start a process of reappraisal and reorganization.

The things we have been talking about are true both of mass communication and of interpersonal communication. Mass communication is certainly different in that it is more complicated. Large organizations are inserted into the communication chain, with their own internal communication systems, their own needs to inform themselves, to arrive at and carry out policy decisions, and to accustom their new employees to roles and norms. These organizations operate around machines and therefore can duplicate messages and send them in vast numbers through space and time and to huge audiences. Instead of dealing with a single receiver, or with small face-to-face groups, the mass media have audiences many of whom they never see nor hear from. Feedback is weak. The mass media must decide whether to program for the largest possible audience or for segments of it, and how to divide time and energies to program for different segments.

Moreover, social demands and social controls on the mass media are usually louder and stronger than those on the individual. Any society usually has rather definite ideas of what it wants its mass media to be and do. It may exercise control through law, through executive control, through economic support, or through many informal channels.

On the whole, however, the similarities between the processes of mass communication and interpersonal communication are far greater than the differences. Mass communication faces the same defenses and must leap the same hurdles: attention, acceptance, interpretation, and storing. It requires the same kinds of contracts between sender and receiver for entertainment and instruction. It must depend upon activating the same kinds of psychological dynamics if it is to persuade.

It was fashionable for a number of years to worry about the great and awful power of mass communication because of the enormous number of hours people gave to media entertainment and the size of the media audiences for political information. But the more that scholars investigated the effects of the media, the more they found that the same resistances to change applied there as in person-to-person communication—in fact, rather more strongly. People come to the media, as to other messages, seeking what they want, not what the media intend them to have. Because there are so many media and media units, they have considerable choice. They still have their defenses up; they still defend their strongly held positions. Because of their distance from the media, and the relatively isolated way of reading, viewing, or listening, they tend to put great reliance on their own social groups and their own advisers. Interpersonal channels of information are functioning side by side with mass media channels, and these interpersonal channels are exerting much of the influence on society.

The mass media become especially powerful when those who use them are able to build close and influential relationships with their audience. In the 1930s, Father Coughlin used radio to build a following that can only be described as personal. Many dictators in our own time feel that control of the media is essential to their power and continuing influence. The birthday and "get well" cards that some people send to entertainers they do not know, and even to cartoon and fictional characters, are evidences that personal attachment can build up through the media.

Mass communication media can and do effect change in many cases when they are all in agreement. If one can imagine all those with pivotal roles in all the media agreeing to present the information and develop the psychological dynamics that would persuade the American people to adopt one point of view—toward the war in Vietnam, toward race relations in the United States—then there would be a possibility of dramatic change.

In the absence of such an unlikely agreement, we must consider the power of the mass media not as a tidal wave but as a great river. It feeds the ground it touches, following the lines of existing contours but preparing the way for change over a long period. Sometimes it finds a spot where the ground is soft and ready, and there it cuts a new channel. Sometimes it carries material which helps to alter its banks. And occasionally, in time of flood, it washes away a piece of ground and gives the channel a new look.

Undoubtedly the most important effect of the media is to feed the ground—to deposit layers of information, day by day, hour by hour, so that a base is laid for the knowledge on which we walk. Compared with the occasional great and dramatic changes we can attribute to the media, this slow, continuing, never-ending effect is immensely more powerful and significant.

2 Four Concepts of Mass Communication

> Though all the winds of doctrine were let loose to play upon
> the earth, so Truth be in the field, we do ingloriously, by
> licensing and prohibiting, to misdoubt her strength. Let her and
> Falsehood grapple: who ever knew Truth put the worse in
> a free and open encounter?
>
> —JOHN MILTON

It is obvious from all this that anyone who tries seriously to trace
the effects of the mass media is studying human behavior. It is
equally obvious that one must analyze political theory, for just as
the effects of the mass media are modified, and sometimes muted,
by the receiver of information, so mass communication is shaped
and colored and flavored from the beginning by society. Each
society controls its mass media in accordance with its policies and
needs. The controls may be legal and political (through laws and
censorship), economic (through ownership and support), or social
(through criticism and the giving and withholding of patronage).

It is difficult for a citizen of the United States to think of his
system as controlled. After all, the basic policy springs from the
First Amendment to the Constitution, "Congress shall make no
law . . . abridging the freedom of speech, or of the press," and
from the Fourteenth Amendment, "no State shall make or enforce
any law which shall abridge the privileges or immunities of citizens
of the United States." Together, these seem to rule out control by
the national or the state legislatures. But it is also true that Spain,
a society which has long been strictly controlled, proclaims in its
Charter that "all Spaniards may freely express their ideas." And
Article 125 of the Constitution of the Soviet Union states that "the

citizens of the U.S.S.R. are guaranteed by law (a) freedom of speech; (b) freedom of the press." Obviously, if these basic policies are to have any real meaning, we must look much deeper into the relationship of mass communication and society. We must start with certain basic assumptions that any society holds—concerning the nature of man, the nature of society and the state, the relation of man to the state, the nature of knowledge and truth and moral conduct.[1]

Authoritarianism

Modern communication was born in 1450 into an authoritarian society. The essential characteristic of an authoritarian society is that the state ranks higher than the individual in the scale of social values. Only through subordinating himself to the state can the individual achieve his goals and develop his attributes as a civilized man. As an individual, he can do little; as a member of an organized society, his potential is enormously increased. This means not only that the state ranks the individual, but also that the state has a caretaker function and the individual a dependent status.

Furthermore, individuals within the authoritarian state differ greatly in status. Authoritarian philosophers like Hegel ridicule the democratic belief that "all should participate in the business of the state."[2] Instead, there is a sharp distinction between leaders and followers. Some are held to be leaders because of divine selection, as were the Renaissance monarchs who claimed to rule by divine right. Some are leaders because they are believed to have superior intellect, wisdom, or experience. In any case, an authoritarian state always places a man or a few men in position to lead and to be obeyed; these rulers and their advisers stand at the locus of power.

What is the source of truth in an authoritarian society? It may be an accredited divine revelation, the wisdom of the race, or simply the superior ability of a leader or group to perceive dangers and opportunities. It may be, after a floundering reaction from disappointment with previously accepted truth, an emergent new promise—as sometimes happens when a country turns in desperation to a dictator. Always the source of truth has two characteristics: (1) It is restricted; not every man has access to it. (2) It becomes the standard for all members of the society. To preserve unity of thought and action and to maintain continuity of leadership, the authoritarian state employs all the tools of persuasion and coercion it commands.

Three powerful strands entered into the Renaissance authoritarianism that first played host to modern communication. The first was the doctrine of divine right by which such monarchs as the Tudors and the Stuarts claimed to rule, and which set apart a bevy of hereditary nobles from the rest of the people. The nobles, of course, protected their status in politics and war.

The second strand was the authoritarian tradition of the Roman Church, which had grown powerful in the Middle Ages. The Church considered itself the repository of divine revelation. As shepherd of mankind, its responsibility was to protect this revelation from contamination and to protect its flock from impure doctrine. The Church permitted debate, but not on basic assumptions, and not among others outside the qualified members of its own order. The Church enforced its dictates with imprimaturs, book proscriptions, and even excommunications. In many countries, for some centuries, it could command and usually receive the cooperation of the state in controlling expression.

The third strand was the long history of authoritarian political philosophy reaching back to Plato. For all his idealism, Plato had argued that, once authority in a state is equally divided, degeneration begins. Just as a man must govern his own baser instincts and appetites by intellectual control, so must the leaders of a state keep the material interests and selfish passions of the masses from dominating society. Plato's own theoretical Republic was governed by philosopher-kings. Plato's own teacher, Socrates, while vehemently arguing his freedom to deviate from the laws of Athens, readily admitted that the authorities were entitled to enforce those laws no matter how wrong. Robert MacIver has written, "Plato wanted to 'co-ordinate' the life of the citizens under a strict cultural code that banned all modes of art and even of opinion not in accord with his own gospel. Very politely, in the *Republic,* he would 'send to another city' all offenders against the rigid rules prescribed for the artist and the philosopher and the poet. With equal politeness, in the *Laws,* he would require poets first to submit their works to the magistrates, who should decide whether they were good for the spiritual health of the citizens."[3]

This kind of tradition was carried through to the early centuries of printing, though in quite different ways, by many other philosophers: Machiavelli, who advocated that all else must be subordinated to the security of the state, and that nonmoral actions by political leaders, as well as strict control of discussion and dissemination of information, are justified by the need for security; Thomas Hobbes, the naturalistic philosopher, whose theories of the state and its relation to the individual did much to justify the authoritarian policies of seventeenth century governments; Georg Hegel, who has been called the father of both modern fascism and modern communism, and who gave to authoritarian philosophy its final idealistic touch by saying that the state is the "ethical spirit . . . Will . . . Mind . . . the state, being an end in itself, is provided with the maximum of rights over against the individual citizens, whose highest duty is to be members of the state."[4]

Such sentiments were overriding, but they were no threat to the infant voice of printing in its earliest days because print did not seem to be a threat to authority. When it became certain that print would become a great voice, the authoritarian governments began using their regulatory power. First they controlled access by issuing patents or licenses to printers and publishers, thus assuming the power of determining who could enter the business. Since each licensee had either a monopoly or a grant of vast privilege, he was quite likely to publish what his rulers wanted published.

But there were independent spirits even among the licensees. The rulers instituted prior censorship, which required that all manuscripts or proof had to be examined and approved by government representatives. This was clumsy and laborious, especially when the coming of newspapers made too much to read, and clever journalists outwitted the censors. This kind of censorship fell of its own weight late in the seventeenth century.

Then the rulers threatened punishment *after* printing—such as prosecution for treason or sedition. Although some governments published their own papers, paid and bribed writers for other publications, and subsidized printers—thus setting forth clear guidelines as to what should be printed—for the most part printing establishments in this stage of authoritarianism were permitted to be privately owned.

In a real sense, then, printing during its first two hundred years was chiefly another tool to promote unity and continuity within the state. Printing was to carry wisdom and truth as wisdom and truth were identified by the rulers. Access to the medium was restricted to those who would operate for the "good of the state" as that was judged by the rulers. The people at large were considered incapable of understanding political problems, and communication was therefore forbidden to "disturb the masses." The media were not expected to criticize rulers and political leaders, and, of course, they were not permitted to attempt to unseat authorities. Discussion of political systems on broad principles was permitted; and it was often possible to criticize political machinery without fear of reprisal, but not the manipulators of the machinery.

The basis for communication ethics in such a system is clear. Stated negatively, there should be no publishing which, in the opinion of the authorities, would injure the state and (consequently) its citizens. More positively, all publishing should contribute to the greatness of the beneficent state, which would as a consequence enable man to grow to his fullest usefulness and happiness. Significantly, one need not decide for himself; there is always an authority to serve as umpire. There is always revelation—if one can know it—the wisdom of the race or the past—if one can perceive it—or the guidance of the leader—which is the easiest to perceive and the most common of guideposts in an authoritarian society.

By the second half of the eighteenth century, the tide seemed to be turning away from authoritarianism, but the authoritarian spirit has not died. In many parts of the world today it continues, even though it is often disguised in democratic verbiage by leaders who issue frequent claims of press freedom. A rule of thumb will suggest the vast spread of authoritarian communication: Wherever a government operates in authoritarian fashion, an investigator is almost certain to find some authoritarian controls over public communication. Spain is as good an example as the communist countries. For all the Spanish protestations of freedom, Fernand Terrou and Lucien Solal point out that "the management of the enterprise is subject to a 'power of oversight' and publishing is hemmed in by a network of obligations and restrictions which make it quite unnecessary to lay down special provisions for the formation or operations of the enterprise. . . . The supervision to which it is subjected places it, in relation to the authorities, in a state of absolute hierarchical subordination."[5] The mechanism includes a state organization for management and supervision which is empowered to fix the size of circulation, intervene in appointment of members of the managerial staff, oversee the work of the staff, censor where necessary, and issue rules for journalists.

This and many similar examples suggest that it may be less appropriate today to speak of state intervention in press affairs than of state integration. For in many countries the press is interwoven with public policy and with the administrative machinery of the state.

Broadcasting is a special case. Even in those countries which can boast truly of a high degree of press freedom, the broadcast media are likely to be controlled to some extent. In the United States, the early period of rapid growth of radio was chaotic. By 1933, President Roosevelt found it necessary to study the confused situation of uncontrolled use of the air waves and to recommend legislation. The resultant Communications Act of 1934 created the Federal Communications Commission, which has two overarching responsibilities: the allocation of spectrum space to broadcast services, and licensing stations to serve the "public interest, convenience, and necessity." Since licenses are issued for only three-year periods, the Commission is at least an implied threat of state control. However, sensitive to the tradition of freedom for the other media, the Commission has been slow to use its power. It is difficult to consider this an authoritarian relationship—just as it is easy to see that the broadcast media are much more restrained in criticism of government than are the print media.

In other countries, broadcasting is organized in a wild variety of patterns. In many of the Latin American countries, as in the United States, the pattern is private enterprise. In Great Britain, Japan, Canada, and Australia, private and public broadcasting enterprises operate side by side, the former supported by advertising, the latter by a tax on receiving sets. In these countries, special efforts are made to keep the public broadcasting system free of government political influence. The British Broadcasting Corporation, for example, is a public corporation—neither a private nor a state enterprise—responsible to a board of distinguished citizens. In a majority of countries, however, broadcasting is a state monopoly, and in some of them the fact of an authoritarian relationship to government is clear even though the government itself cannot be described as authoritarian. In Belgium, broadcasting is a public foundation; in France, a public service with its own budget; in Germany, a public establishment operating typically under a large broadcasting council that represents many cultural, religious, and professional organizations, and that appoints a board of governors; in Italy, a ccmpany operating under a concession from the state; in India and numerous other countries, an administrative service that may perform in the interest of the people but can hardly be expected to criticize the state.

Films and books are also in a twilight zone—not necessarily subject to authoritarian control, but seldom really free. Even in countries where the mass media are not subordinate to political authorities, films and books are often censored on moral grounds. In the United States, censorship usually occurs at the state or municipal level; in some other countries, at the national level.

Thus the question of authoritarian systems is complex, and it becomes necessary to consider degrees of control:

1. Countries where control of some or all of the media is complete;
2. Countries where political criticism by some or all of the media is possible, but where censorship operates;
3. Countries where special laws or other discriminatory legislation expose media workers and executives to arrest and persecution;
4. Countries where unofficial methods discourage criticism or opposition from the media.

From country to country, these categories often shift with the tides of politics. But the fact is clear that authoritarianism has been the dominant philosophy behind public communication for more years in more countries than has any other pattern of thought.

Libertarianism

Throughout the sixteenth and seventeenth centuries, a new theory of mass communication struggled to be born, drawing its prenatal strength from the great revolutions of the popular mind and the body politic which characterized western Europe then. It was a time of startling change, succeeding apparent or relative changelessness. First there were the penetrating developments in geography and science, which challenged the traditional knowledge and seemed to vindicate the power of human reason over inherited and revealed knowledge. There was the Reformation, which challenged the authority of the Church of Rome and brought forth discussion and argument at sharp variance with authoritarian patterns. There was the swift new growth of the middle class and of capitalism, both of which challenged the old idea of fixed status and ushered in a world of social mobility. There were political revolutions, like the one in England against the Stuarts, challenging the right to arbitrary rule.

Most importantly, the new theory put its roots down into the kind of intellectual change represented by the Enlightenment of the seventeenth and eighteenth centuries. This was one of the most revolutionary intellectual movements of all time. As Cassirer said, the basic idea of the Enlightenment was "the conviction that human understanding is capable, of its own power and without recourse to supernatural assistance, of comprehending the system of the world, and that this new way of understanding the world will lead to a new way of mastering it."[6] Man, who had already proved that the world is round, who had looked at the planets through telescopes, who had discovered the circulation of the blood, and who had challenged the Church of Rome, was throwing down the gauntlet to all the old custodians of power and wisdom. He was declaring his independence of all outside restrictions on his freedom to use his understanding to solve religious, political, and social problems.

In a sense, the intellectual revolution was chiefly secular, not only because it challenged the authority of the one Church, but also because it tended to transfer the rewards for good conduct nearer to the arena of worldly gains. It is difficult now for us to develop a proper focus on the change in business and economics which was under way during the hundred years between the middle of the seventeenth and the middle of the eighteenth century. At first, a religious ethic was predominant. In 1644, Robert Keane of Boston was nearly excommunicated—not fined or imprisoned, *excommunicated*—for the crime of charging too much interest on a shilling loan, and the minister of Boston proclaimed: "To seek riches for riches' sake is to fall into the sin of avarice."[7] Little more than one hundred years later, such strictures had been buried in a business ethic accompanying a boom in both England and America. Adam Smith was preaching the conventional wisdom of classical economics, including the commandment that government shall never (well, hardly ever) interfere with the market.

The intellectual revolution was even more profoundly secular because it succeeded in transferring the focus of interest from theology to science, from theological argument to scientific inquiry. If it were possible now to graph the focus of attention from the beginning of printing to the beginning of power printing—from 1450 to a little after 1800—the result would certainly be a sharply rising line of secular interest, and a sharply falling line of sacred interest. It is likely that the lines on the graph would cross somewhere in the seventeenth century.

The libertarian theory of communication grew with and from these revolutions of mind and spirit. Much of its doctrine and many of its fighting phrases were the thought of early philosophers. Descartes was one of the first, his sweeping influence deriving from his emphasis on reason as the road to truth. The most influential of the libertarian philosophers in England was John Locke, who was pivotal in intellectual change. Arguing that the center of power was the will of the people, he held that the people delegate their authority to the government and can withdraw it at any time.

One of the earliest of the great antiauthoritarian documents that spoke directly to the question of a free press was John Milton's *Areopagitica*. Based on the premise that men have reason and wisdom to distinguish between right and wrong, good and bad, it is an eloquent argument for freedom from government restriction. Men can exercise their reason to its fullest power, Milton wrote, only when they have free choice. Given a "free and open encounter," truth will triumph over error.

Although Milton's thesis had little effect in his own time, it was revived and expanded in the eighteenth century. John Erskine defended Thomas Paine in a memorable court trial when Paine was accused of grievous error in publishing *The Rights of Man:*

The proposition which I mean to maintain as the basis of liberty of the press, and without which it has an empty sound, is this: that every man, not intending to mislead, but seeking to enlighten others with what his own reason and conscience, however erroneously, have dictated to him as truth, may address himself to the universal reason of the whole nation, either upon subjects of government in general, or upon that of our own particular country.[8]

Erskine's position was instantly caught up by the defenders of the new theory of communication. Jefferson carried it further, contending that, just as the function of government is to establish and maintain a framework within which an individual can develop his own capabilities and pursue his own ends, the chief function of the press is to inform the individual and to stand guard against deviation by government from its basic assignment. A constant victim of press vituperation during his own political career, Jefferson nevertheless maintained that a government which could not stand up against criticism deserved to fall:

> No experiment can be more interesting than what we are now trying, and which we trust will end in establishing the fact, that man may be governed by reason and truth. Our first object should therefore be, to leave open to him all the avenues of truth. The most effectual hitherto found, is the freedom of the press. It is therefore the first to be shut up by those who fear the investigation of their actions.[9]

Here are most of the elements of the new theory: the reliance on reason to discriminate between truth and error, the need of a free market place of ideas in order that reason may work, and the function of the press as a check on government.

In the nineteenth century, John Stuart Mill defined the market place more clearly. He wrote in his famous essay *On Liberty:* "If all mankind minus one were of one opinion, and only one person were of the contrary opinion, mankind would be no more justified in silencing that one person, than he, if he had the power, would be justified in silencing mankind." Why? Mill answered with four propositions: First, if we silence an opinion, for all we know we may be silencing truth. Second, even a wrong opinion may contain the grain of truth that helps us find the whole truth. Third, even if the commonly held opinion is the whole truth, that opinion will not be held on rational grounds until it has been tested and defended. Fourth, unless a commonly held opinion is challenged from time to time, it loses its vitality and effect.[10]

This was the philosophical tradition out of which grew the new theory of mass communication. That theory was foreshadowed in the sixteenth century, envisioned in the seventeenth, fought for in the eighteenth, and finally brought to widespread favor in the nineteenth, when power was added to the printing press and machine-duplicated communication could be brought to a large part of the public. By then, the authoritarian system of communication seemed to be vanquished. Most countries had adopted at least the language of the new libertarianism, although many authoritarian practices remained below the surface—and remain today.

To see what a revolutionary change this is from authoritarian theory, let us ask of libertarian theory the same questions we asked of authoritarianism. The nature of man? According to authoritarian theory, of course, man is a dependent creature, able to reach his highest level only under the guidance and care of the state. According to libertarian theory, he is independent and rational, able to choose between right and wrong, good and bad. In authoritarian theory, the state outranks the man on the scale of values. In libertarian theory, the state exists only to provide a proper milieu in which man can develop his potentialities and enjoy a maximum of happiness. If the state fails in this mission, it can be radically changed or abolished.

This is the essence of libertarian theory: The task of society is to provide a free market place of ideas so that men may exercise reason and choice. In place of more formal controls, libertarianism chooses to trust the self-righting process of truth. This implies that ideas must have an equal chance and that everyone must have access to the channels of communication.

In theory, then, the mass communication system that would result from libertarianism would be private enterprise—privately owned media competing in an open market. Anyone with sufficient capital could start a newspaper or a magazine or a publishing house, and capital demands should not be so severe that viewpoints would be squeezed out.

What kind of mass communication did libertarianism actually bring?

In the United States and Great Britain, the cradles of libertarianism, the printed media did develop very much as predicted. In the eighteenth and early nineteenth centuries, many small, privately owned newspapers represented every shade and variety of viewpoint. It was easy to enter publishing, especially because the many political factions were eager to support journals which reflected their opinions.

After the middle of the nineteenth century, however, support of the press began to come in large measure from advertising rather than from political subsidy. The costs of entering publishing multiplied. Almost from the beginning of broadcasting and film, costs were a major factor. Thus, today, the libertarian theory of mass communication faces a special responsibility: to make a market place which is *restricted* by capital demands a truly *free* market place of ideas and facts.

The ethical responsibility of the libertarian communicator might be expressed by John Locke's phrase, "enlightened self-interest." The degree of enlightenment, of course, varies wildly with individuals. At one extreme might be a Pulitzer, who wrote that "nothing less than the highest ideals, the most scrupulous anxiety to do right, the most accurate knowledge of the problems it has to meet, and a sincere sense of social responsibility will save journalism."[11] At the other extreme might be placed a statement attributed to William Peter Hamilton of the *Wall Street Journal:* "A newspaper is private enterprise owing nothing whatever to the public, which grants it no franchise. It is therefore affected with no public interest. It is emphatically the property of the owner, who is selling a manufactured product at his own risk."[12] Between these extremes are the positions and practices of most publishers, broadcasters, and film makers.

Soviet Communist Theory

Ironically, libertarian England of the mid-nineteenth century provided the freedom that allowed the birth of a new kind of authoritarianism. It was there and then that Karl Marx, a German exile, constructed his general theory of history. His concept proceeds, first, from his dialectic of social change. Growing up in a period of sweeping scientific, industrial, and social change, Marx gloried in the new developments. Indeed, Crane Brinton has written, he tried "to find in change itself the riddle of change."[13] Marx found the answer he sought chiefly in Hegel. This was the famous *dialectic*.

In adapting Hegel's dialectic, Marx turned it upside down. For

Hegel, an idealist, "the idea," the life process of the human brain, made the dialectic work. Marx held that for Hegel dialectics "is standing on its head. It must be turned right side up again, if you would discover the rational kernel within the mystic shell."[14]

Marx concluded from this that productive forces would always change faster than the relationships of the producers—workers and capitalists—thus throwing society out of balance. As he analyzed it, capitalism contained the seeds of its own destruction. It would always be riddled by economic crises and depressions. The rich would grow richer and fewer; the poor, poorer, more numerous, and more desperate. The last stage of capitalism would be imperialism, which would breed wars and more misery. Finally, the working class, unable to contain their misery and frustration any longer, would rise, liquidate the surviving capitalists, take over the means of production, and then build a classless society. Since all society is economically determined, Marx said, the political system, the arts, religion, philosophy, and all other components of culture would change with the economic system.

The goal of this social dialectic was not only a classless society, but also a *stateless* society. Marx insisted that the state is merely a device by which one class controls another. Among the many Marxian paradoxes, this one emerges most notably: an extraordinarily optimistic view of man as being ultimately able to live without government *and* a view of man as a pawn moved by economic forces. And Marxian dynamics requires that man shall be organized into a machine to change society so that society can in turn remake man.

But when the Soviet leaders had the chance to apply the theory, after 1917, they found it incomplete. Marx had never explained how the future was to be run. Instead of being allowed to wither away, the state had to be expanded mightily. Eventually, Stalin explained that deviations from Marxist theory were essential for a time because the Soviet Union was ringed around by enemies and must maintain a strong central government and military establishment for defense.

Soviet leaders found it similarly easy to develop a theory of mass communication even though Marx had written almost nothing about it. By trial and error, and under the force of need, the Soviet theory of communication developed as an integral part of the Soviet state. Far from the concept of the press as a Fourth Estate that would watch and report on and criticize the government, Soviet mass communication became an instrument of government. Since the media were conceived of instrumentally, as tools for the work of the state, private ownership was no more thinkable than private ownership of heavy industry, which was also to do the work of the state. Moreover, inasmuch as the problems of the state were pressing and serious, the mass media must not be used for frivolity. As Lenin wrote, the press should be "collective propagandist, collective agitator . . . collective organizer."[15] This integral and instrumental concept of the mass media, which was shaped primarily by Lenin, is central to the doctrine which lies behind their use.

The developing communist theory held that power is resident in the people, latent in social institutions, and generated in social action. But it can be realized only when it is joined with the ownership of natural resources and the means of production. Freedom is "a lie," Lenin said, "so long as the best printing-works and the largest stocks of paper are in capitalist hands."[16] Another Soviet theorist argued that the press is free "not to trade in news, but to educate the great mass of the workers and to organize them, under the sole guidance of the Party, to achieve clearly defined aims." Those aims were made clear by Lenin in 1918: "We must and shall transform the press into an instrument for the economic re-education of the masses."[17]

How is truth derived for expression in the mass media? In the early years of Soviet power, it was assumed that truth was arrived at through the collective deliberation of the Party. Each Party member was supposed to have full freedom of discussion until a Party Congress reached a decision. As early as the Tenth Congress in 1921, however, Lenin expressed grave doubt about the efficiency of this system. During the 1920s, control passed rapidly from broad discussion and Party Congresses to a small group of top Party leaders. The appropriate behavior of a Party member today, Margaret Mead has written, "is to know the principles of Marxism-Leninism and to apply them as directed by the Line, not to think about them."[18]

It is a mistake, however, to assume that the communist theory of communication does not allow criticism. Lenin himself attached high importance to criticism and self-criticism, and even to exposé. One of the chief functions of the press is to carry criticism from the top—especially from the Party—and from below—from individuals, working collectives, or trade unions. But there is a sharp limitation. Soviet journalists may criticize people, including high bureaucrats, but not institutions. The foundations of Marxism-Leninism are sacrosanct. Thus *Pravda,* the central organ, often carries an article critical of factories, districts, or regions which fail to meet production quotas, and ministries and bureaucrats are attacked for failing to introduce new methods. BRING PARASITES TO ACCOUNT! shouted one headline over an article criticizing shortages. But such negative news was more than balanced by articles headed NEW SUCCESSES ON THE GRAIN FRONT, THE TOILERS OF UZBEKISTAN WILL FULFILL THEIR HIGH OBLIGATIONS, and UNDER LENIN'S BANNER, FORWARD TO THE VICTORY OF COMMUNISM.

Strongly critical articles are nearly always inspired by Party leaders. Some writers who fail to obtain Party approval sometimes stray over the line into *objectivism,* which is presenting events, facts, or ideas without putting them in the proper context of social and class evaluation. This is illustrated by the writings of Viktor Nekrasov, a Russian author who traveled widely in the United States and in Europe, then published articles comparing life in the Soviet Union with life in the West. Nekrasov's articles, which appeared in the literary journal *Novyi mir* in 1962, made it clear that he was impressed by the modern painting and architecture of Italy, France, and the United States. He regretted that the Soviet public was unable to see the experimental films made in the West, and he admitted that he had been embarrassed because he had not been able to read the works of Albert Camus, Franz Kafka, and William Faulkner in the Soviet Union. He reported favorably on modern housing developments in Europe and America, to the detriment of the Moscow development, Cheremushki, which is the pride of Soviet planners. Nekrasov also wrote a balanced assessment of life in the West, depicting positive as well as negative aspects.

On January 20, 1963, the government organ *Izvestia* responded to Nekrasov's reports with a bitter editorial entitled "Tourist with a Swagger Stick." It attacked Nekrasov for failing to point out that the developments he approved were for capitalists rather than for workers: "It is quite incredible how he fails to see the sharp social contrasts and class contradictions in American life, the war psychosis, fanned by the imperialist circles. . . . The crux of the matter is not factual errors, but the thoughtless and untrue generalizations and parallels which lead to bourgeois objectivism and sterile descriptive methods which distort reality."

A similar journalistic sin in communist theory is *escapism*—presenting reports that are not relevant to social reality or political demands, thus distracting readers from serious concerns. Like objectivism, escapism is reproached in all communist states. Acting on the instructions of the Agit-prop Department of the Central Committee of the Communist Party of Czechoslovakia, the Union of Czechoslovak Journalists reprimanded:

> In our press, objectivism and escapism are beginning to appear in the form of servile admiration of the "miracles" of Western technique, in reprinting nonsensical matter from the Western press as, for example, "How many pearls are there in Queen Elizabeth's necklace?" From such contentless materials, no one can clearly tell whom and what class they serve, from what point of view they were written, and why, since the reader does not profit in any way by reading them, they were ever published.[19]

One can quite properly describe communist journalism as an offshoot from authoritarianism, and yet some differences should be clear. Typically, of course, the mass media under the old authoritarianism were and are largely privately owned, except in some countries in the case of broadcasting. These media were and are controlled primarily by patents, licensing, guilds, government pressure, and censorship. Communist media are usually controlled by ownership, by Party personnel in key positions, by directives, review, criticism, and censorship. The essential point is that in the older authoritarian systems the media have typically been part of the business system, and to that extent less exclusively an instrument of government. They have been in bondage to the state. The Soviet media are *in* and *of* the state.

Significantly, the Soviet system has removed the profit motive from mass communication, thus causing the rewards to spring, not from the by-products of prosperity, but from the by-products of orthodoxy and skill. It is largely true, too, that the Soviet system has succeeded in defining the function of mass communication positively (the press is *required* to do certain things), whereas the older authoritarianism defined communication functions primarily in negative terms (the press is *not permitted* to do certain things). Finally, it is obvious that the Soviet media are integrated, planned, used in a way that the older authoritarian media almost never were. The older media were merely controlled; the Soviet media serve the state just as steel plants and infantry do.

Still, the ethical implications of communist authoritarianism are much like those of the older form. There is always an outside check on what is right. For the revealed Will of God, or the wisdom of the philosopher-king, or the will of the sovereign ruling by divine right, the communists have substituted a body of doctrine subject to interpretation by a small group of informed leaders. In neither the old nor the new authoritarianism are individual or human rights made the basis of ethical or responsible acts. The communists speak of collective rights—"the classless society" and "the people's state." There is a continuing emphasis on the good of the state and society and the welfare of the proletariat because, according to communist belief, the improvement of society must precede the development of man, and both are dependent on the material welfare of society.

To understand how communists can describe such a system as *free,* it is necessary to understand their premises, particularly that freedom is for the people, not for the media. The problem is to be free from harmful information, debasing entertainment, false teaching—as defined by the leaders of the people. Indeed, the spokesmen for this system can be acidly scornful about Western media, which, they feel, exist to make money for their owners and advance the political goals of the capitalist class, regardless of the effect on the public.

Social Responsibility Theory

Just as the changing nature of some authoritarian societies has brought forth a new authoritarian theory of communication, so the changing nature of some libertarian societies has resulted in a new libertarian theory. The fact that libertarianism has changed is rooted in human knowledge. Newton's perpetual-motion machine, the universe, running according to immutable laws which rational man can seek out and understand, has been challenged by discoveries about evolution, statistical mechanics, and relativity. John Locke's philosophy of inherent rights and rational man has been challenged by modern philosophy, which is inclined to doubt the existence of any right without a corresponding obligation, and by modern psychology, which has identified many areas of irrationality in man and cast considerable doubt on his ability to distinguish truth from skillful propaganda. Classical laissez-faire economics has been challenged by the belief that interfering with the free operation of the market may enable us to avoid the disastrous troughs of the business cycle; and studies of the robber barons by the muckraking journalists at the turn of the century and analyses of the trusts by journalists, economists, and U.S. Department of Justice attorneys in more recent times cause us to doubt that laissez faire and the common good are the easy equation that classical economists made them seem. In short, our view of man and our view of society are altogether less optimistic than they were in the Enlightenment.

It follows, of course, that our view of mass communication has changed. One of the basic needs of society in the Enlightenment seemed to be to free the press from the state so that it could operate as a check upon government and as a vehicle through which man might discern the truth. For more than half a century now, however, the tendency has been to examine the performance of the press and perhaps to lay some requirements upon it that would be quite foreign to the spirit of libertarianism.

Mass communication has been subjected to a rising wave of criticism in recent decades. Although the first American book extensively attacking the press was published in 1859, the wave really began with the publication of a remarkable series of articles by Will Irwin in *Collier's* in 1911.[20] The scatter-shot criticisms of earlier times became obsolete with Irwin's closely reasoned articles. He argued that the influence of the newspaper had shifted, almost unnoticed, from the editorials to the news columns, that the commercial nature of the newspaper was responsible for many of its faults, and that the press had become so distinctively big business that it was inextricably linked to all the other big businesses. Upton Sinclair's savage *Brass Check* followed in 1919.

George Seldes bitterly attacked in *Freedom of the Press* in 1935, then in a newsletter, *In Fact,* which was published during the 1940s. During the 1930s, newspapers were targets in the general attacks on business, especially in such books as *America's House of Lords* by Harold Ickes and Ferdinand Lundberg's *Imperial Hearst.*

In recent years, although criticism has varied, as always, in degree of responsibility, critics have become more knowing as well as more responsible. The late A. J. Liebling's articles in the "Wayward Press" department of *The New Yorker* (collected in a paperback entitled *The Press*) are shrill at some points, but Liebling was a shrewd and witty critic. Ben Bagdikian's articles in the *Columbia Journalism Review,* which is the only continuingly valuable critical organ journalism has ever had, have from the first demonstrated that Bagdikian realizes the limits of perfectibility in human affairs and yet demands of the press what it should be able to give.

The most cogent single body of criticism was formed in the late 1940s by the Commission on Freedom of the Press. Supported by private philanthropy, staffed by scholars, the Commission couched its assessment in words of attack: "It becomes an imperative question whether the performance of the press can any longer be left to the unregulated initiative of the few who manage it. . . . Those who direct the machinery of the press have engaged from time to time in practices which the society condemns and which, if continued, it will inevitably undertake to regulate or control." Considering the sensitivity of journalists to criticism, and especially the fact that "regulate" has always been a red-flag word, it is not surprising that the Commission's critique was harshly received.

Ironically, most of the Commission's ideas about responsible performance were much like those of the leading journalists: It is the duty of the press (and the Commission meant broadcast as well as print journalism) to provide "a truthful, comprehensive, and intelligent account of the day's events in a context which gives them meaning." The press should serve as "a forum for the exchange of comment and criticism," give a "representative picture of the constituent groups in society," help in the "presentation and clarification of the goals and values of the society," and "provide full access to the day's intelligence." The major mission of mass communication, the Commission argued, is to raise social conflict "from the plane of violence to the plane of discussion."[21]

The general themes of the criticisms of all the media have been summarized by Theodore Peterson:

1. The mass media have wielded enormous power for their own ends. The owners have propagated their own opinions, especially in politics and economics, at the expense of opposing views.

2. The mass media have been subservient to big business and at times have let advertisers control editorial policy and editorial content.

3. The mass media have resisted social change.

4. The mass media have often given more attention to the superficial and the sensational in their coverage of human happenings than to the significant, and their entertainment has often lacked substance.

5. The mass media have endangered public morals.

6. The mass media have invaded the privacy of individuals without just cause.

7. The mass media are controlled by one socio-economic class—loosely, "the business class," and access to the media is difficult for the newcomer; therefore, the free and open market of ideas is endangered.[22]

The change in mass communication in recent years has resulted partly in response to such criticisms. The fact that there has been a change can be shown simply. Consider: The guarantee in the Bill of Rights makes it unnecessary for a newspaper or magazine owned by a devout Democrat, or a devout Republican, *even to mention the names* of the opposition party's candidates for President, Congress, the city council, the school board, and other offices, much less to present their platforms, policies, and programs. The vast range of other political concerns can be treated according to a publisher's whim, or not at all. This is one of the measures of the freedom granted by the U.S. Constitution and embedded in the libertarian idea. And yet the press of the United States is devoid of this degree of bias. (Note that the references in this paragraph are to *newspapers* and *magazines*. It is much less certain that broadcasting has this degree of freedom. In fact, were a broadcaster to oppose political candidates in this way—by ignoring their existence—he would surely be called to account by the Federal Communications Commission. Although broadcasters in the United States enjoy wide latitude, the threat of government action marks one of the differences between the printed and the electronic media.)

Why? The cynic might respond that impartiality—or *seeming* impartiality—in news columns is good business. And certainly this is part of the answer. The need for huge circulation figures which promote huge advertising income to pay the high costs of publishing and return a reasonable profit surely influences some publishers to appeal to a wide readership rather than to a narrow partisan group. Still, they need not go to the lengths that many of them do to achieve this end. There is much more to the change in mass communication than avarice.

As much as by any other factor, the change has been influenced by the journalist's ethic. Taught from the beginning to seek out and report fact, the young journalist takes it as an article of faith that he is not to slant news toward private, personal, or group interest. This ethic pervades the news operation, touching those who are in its orbit—including owners—as well as those who have been schooled in its tradition. It is almost unimaginable today that a publisher or a broadcaster would try to order his employees to present news in a way that squares with his own political leanings. This springs in part from the pervasive journalist's ethic, in part from the growing belief among the owners and managers of the mass media that their right to reach great publics implies an obligation.

Does this mean that we have reached a happy ultimate—that mass communication in the United States always works in the public interest? Not at all. For the mass media are *human* instruments. Whatever the intentions of the journalist—however strong his ethic—he is subject to human biases, prejudices, and ambitions. Consciously in a few cases, unconsciously in others, reporters and editors may be swayed by their own leanings or by what they believe their employers want. And however thoroughly a publisher or a broadcaster may have absorbed the ethic and recognized that his power carries obligations, he also is subject to human limitations. He usually *is* a member, with other publishers and broadcasters, of a socioeconomic class, and this colors his views.

What the change in mass communication amounts to, then, is a struggle for responsible performance. The most useful name for the resulting theory is Social Responsibility Theory. This is not a simple concept, and it is not surprising that some have misread its implications. One student of communication systems, John Merrill, has argued:

This so-called "theory" of social responsibility has a good ring to it and, like "love" and "motherhood," has an undeniable attraction for many. There is a trend throughout the world in this direction, which implies a suspicion of, and dissatisfaction with, the libertarianism of Milton, Locke, and even Jefferson. Implicit in this trend toward social responsibility is the argument that some group (obviously a governmental one, ultimately) can and must define or decide *what* is socially responsible. Also, the implication is clear that publishers and journalists acting freely cannot determine what is socially responsible nearly as well as can some "outside" or "impartial" group. If this power elite decides the press is not responsible, not even the First Amendment will keep the publishers from losing this freedom to government. This would appear to many as a suggestion of increased power accumulation at the national level, a further restriction of a pluralistic society. . . .

Many persons will object to this line of analysis and will say that "social responsibility" of the press of a nation does not necessarily imply government control. The writer contends that ultimately it does, since if left to be defined by various publics or journalistic groups the term is quite relative and nebulous; and it is quite obvious that in the traditional context of American libertarianism no "solution" that would be widely agreed upon or enforced could ever be reached by nongovernment groups or individuals.[23]

The answer to Merrill's argument is simple. Social responsibility is defined by various publishers and journalistic groups; it certainly is relative, and sometimes nebulous; and no solution that would be widely agreed upon and enforced can ever be reached. In fact, the whole point of social responsibility is that it is defined by journalists and enforced not at all. If it were defined and enforced by government, it would be nothing more than an authoritarian system in disguise. Is responsible performance viewed differently by different journalists? Of course. This diversity distinguishes our society from the authoritarians. For, as Merrill truly writes in the paper quoted above, "the Marxist or Communist press system considers itself socially responsible, and certainly it is responsible to its own social system." The difference is that the communist society is monolithic; we live in a pluralistic society. Responsibility in a communist society can be defined, delimited, and enforced. Responsibility in a pluralistic society is never so neat. Some American newspapers and magazines support the Vietnam war; others oppose it. Such diversity in an authoritarian society is unimaginable.

Yet the chief question is whether we have actually departed from libertarianism. Let those who doubt it compare a current American newspaper—almost any newspaper—with almost any newspaper of the early nineteenth century. Freedom of the press at that time, Charles A. Beard has written, meant "the right to be just or unjust, partisan or nonpartisan, true or false, in news columns and editorial columns."[24] Under libertarianism, the media were expected to reflect the world as their owners saw it, to tell the particular truth the owner preferred, to distort, to lie, to vilify, all with the confidence that rational men could discern truth among the falsehoods. No one today has confidence in such belligerent libertarianism. However fiercely a publisher or a broadcaster may shape his editorials about the Vietnam war, or however eager he is to publish and broadcast quotations and news of events which support his point of view, he is usually careful to quote spokesmen for the other side of the question in the news columns and in newscasts.

Increasingly, however, critics are asking whether the market place of ideas is sufficiently open. Legal scholars like Jerome Barron and Harriet Pilpel—both of whom are well aware of the limits imposed by the First Amendment—have been arguing for a right of access to the press. In the June, 1967, issue of the *Harvard Law Review,* Barron argues that the press stifles unpopular and unorthodox views by closing them out. He calls for "an interpretation of the First Amendment which focuses on the idea that restraining the hand of government is quite useless in assuring free speech if a restraint on access is effectively secured by private groups." In effect, Barron is proposing that anyone who has something to say should have the right to say it in the press. Failure of that right he considers an abridgment of free expression. Considering the concentration of mass communication in relatively few hands, and considering also the high cost of establishing a new medium of mass communication, Barron argues persuasively. It *is* a denial of effective expression if a spokesman for a cause hopes to speak to an audience larger than a street-corner crowd and finds the media closed to him. We can agree in principle, and yet wonder how a policy that allowed complete access could operate. The problem is much like the ancient one: We should be ruled by philosopher-kings, but who is to choose them? Until such questions can be answered, we must limp along with the system we have.

If all this suggests that this book is written to celebrate the wedding of freedom and responsibility, it is misleading. This is not a perfect world, and the mass communication system in the United States is far from perfection. We have emphasized the trend toward social responsibility because it is a premise. In a sense, the remainder of this book is a test of the degree to which our mass media are responsible instruments of a diverse society.

3 Freedom and Government

Liberty means responsibility. That is why most men dread it.
—George Bernard Shaw

The chief danger in trying to combine freedom and responsibility is that the mass media may lose sight of their basic responsibility, which is to remain free. This is not mere word play. It points up the fact that the mass media are pressured by governmental and social forces which view responsible performance from special, and sometimes selfish, perspectives. Depending upon where one stands, after all, it is possible to argue that almost any action is responsible or irresponsible.

Consider the apparently responsible act of exposing an unethical official and driving him from office. From the point of view of one who fears that negative publicity will erode public confidence in government itself, it would be far better for the official's colleagues and superiors to judge the quality of his behavior, and perhaps to dismiss him quietly. Thus, from this point of view, the exposé is irresponsible journalism.

Or consider the seemingly simple act of reporting that the pitcher who won twenty games for the local major-league team is holding out for a better contract next season. In such situations, many baseball fans call and complain to the general manager— who may believe (accurately, in some cases) that the pitcher is using the mass media to win the new contract. From the general manager's point of view, the media may be irresponsible, especially if they publish stories on the holdout day after day.

Though these may seem to be extreme notions of responsible performance, they are central, not extreme, to those who are affected. Considering the vast numbers who are affected in one way or another by journalism, it is not surprising that the instruments of mass communication are inundated by far less substantial complaints. Clearly, freedom can be eroded if the mass media are oversensitive to every point of view. For this much is certain: If the mass media should try to heed *everyone's* notions of responsibility, very little would be published or broadcast. In such a circumstance, "freedom" would be an empty word.

Certain kinds of freedom that we expect mass communication to preserve are clearly central to democratic society:

Freedom to know. This is a social right, belonging to all the people, to receive the information we need to organize our lives and to participate intelligently in governing. It is a direct right, and it is shared by everyone.

Freedom to tell. This is the right to transmit information freely and to argue publicly on issues. It, too, is a right of all the people, but it has been institutionalized in the mass media.

Freedom to find out. This is the right of access to sources of public information. Because not everyone can attend a presidential press conference, a Congressional hearing, or a State Department briefing—to name only a few events limited by space and geography—this right has been largely delegated to the mass media. Journalists must represent the public in such cases, and journalists are consequently those who speak up most pointedly against closed meetings and withheld documents.

It is the fundamental responsibility of the mass media today to defend these freedoms against international forces, government, domestic power groups, individuals, and even restricting influences within the media. The defense must be carefully balanced with some sensitivity to the views of outsiders, both because other perspectives may be valuable and because insensitivity could lead to strong controls. How all these forces act and interact with the media suggests the delicacy of the balance.

Government Controls

We speak of "freedom," but it is never absolute. Almost any mass media system is subject to certain basic statutory controls, among them a law designed to protect individuals or groups against defamation, a copyright law to protect authors and publishers, a basic statute designed to preserve the common standard of decency and morality, and another basic statute to protect the state against treasonable and seditious utterances. Almost everyone—including journalists—nods in agreement with such restrictions, believing that even a free system should not permit the instruments of mass communication to defame the innocent, to steal literary property, to outrage the common morality, or to incite treason. And yet it may be that we agree with these restrictions because we have become accustomed to them. Or so it seems when we consider the views of two Justices of the United States Supreme Court, Hugo L. Black and William O. Douglas. They argue that the First Amendment means *precisely* what it says, that freedom of speech and press are absolute, subject to no restrictions. Dissenting in *Ginzburg v. United States* (March 21, 1966), Mr. Justice Black stated: "I believe the Federal Government is without power whatever under the Constitution to put any type of burden on speech and expression of ideas of any kind." Mr. Justice Douglas has argued:

The First Amendment does not say that there is freedom of expression provided the talk is not "dangerous." It does not say that there is freedom of expression provided the utterance has no tendency to subvert. . . . All notions of regulation or restraint by government are absent from the First Amendment. For it says in words that are unambiguous, "Congress shall make no law . . ."[1]

Still, the majority of the Supreme Court has always overridden such arguments. For decades, the Court has cited a decision delivered by Justice Oliver Wendell Holmes in 1919 in the case of a California pamphleteer named Schenck who had been accused of sedition for opposing the draft in World War I. Justice Holmes expressed the unanimous opinion of the Court that the state has a right in wartime to quell free expression: "The question in every case is whether the words used are in such circumstances and are of such a nature that they will bring about the substantive evils that Congress has a right to prevent."[2] Similar reasoning has been used to justify restrictions in many other kinds of cases, especially during the cold war. "Clear and present danger" has become a familiar phrase in court decisions.

A leading constitutional scholar, Leonard Levy, holds that "we do not know what the First Amendment's freedom of speech-and-press clause meant to the men who drafted and ratified it at the time that they did so." Almost certainly they meant to outlaw licensing or other prior restraint of the press. But it may be, as Levy argues, that "the security of the state against libelous advocacy or attack was always regarded as outweighing any social interest in open expression, at least through the period of the adoption of the First Amendment."[3] Morris Ernst and Alan Schwartz have even speculated that "the proponents of the Bill of Rights meant [only] to express their fear of the new Union. They wanted to be very sure that the united nation of 1787 would not butt in on the censor business, a business to be reserved to the separate states."[4] However that may be, the Supreme Court has held during recent decades that the states are no more able to restrict free expression than is the federal government. The concept of ordered liberty was cited by the Court to accomplish what J. Edward Gerald has termed a "judge-made overturn in Constitutional theory by means of which the federal government moved to protect the press against state governments."[5]

The Printed Media

Newspapers, magazines, and books have always enjoyed a relatively privileged position among the media in the United States. Print won its large measure of freedom in the eighteenth century, and although it is subject, with the other media, to laws on libel, obscenity, copyright, and the like, only a few publishers consider these unpleasantly restrictive. The U.S. Post Office Department has sometimes held over the printed media a threat to withdraw second-class mailing privileges. This kind of censorship was ruled unconstitutional when copies of *Esquire* were removed from the mails, but it is by no means certain that the Post Office Department is powerless to censor. The definition of its power must await other court tests.[6]

The hundreds of state and local laws restricting seditious and obscene publications have been subjected to court tests throughout U.S. history. Guidelines are slowly emerging. "Classics" are safe no matter how obscene by definition. The supposed effect on "the average man," not on youths or perverts, is the central factor. No work may be banned merely because of its theme or subject matter, and the prevalence of four-letter words is not sufficient reason for suppression; the work must be read as a whole, and social value and literary merit argue for freedom even though some scenes may be sexually provocative. Workable definitions of "obscene," "indecent," "lewd," "prurient," "hard-core pornography," "community standards," and "prevalent attitudes in the community," however, are still lacking. As for sedition, the courts hold that expression "that falls short of threatening the security of the nation is to go unpunished."[7]

Government encroachment which is protested by many leaders of the print media is that directed at commercial practices. A successful suit was brought under antitrust laws against monopolistic advertising practices of the Kansas City *Star*. In other cases, government has sought to require newspapers to pay newsboys a minimum hourly wage. The papers resisted successfully, arguing that the newsboys were "independent merchants" who actually bought papers from the publisher and sold them to subscribers.

Perhaps the most important commercial case was brought under antitrust laws against the Associated Press. The AP, which is cooperatively owned, had long protected its members by refusing to sell its service to their competitors. The new Chicago *Sun,* competing in the morning field with the Chicago *Tribune,* was unable to obtain AP service, and its suit became pivotal. The fact that the *Sun* supported Franklin D. Roosevelt against the Roosevelt-hating *Tribune* added emotional overtones. Robert Lasch described the struggle:

Almost to a man, the publishers of America interpreted the filing of this action as a foul assault against the First Amendment, and with frightening unanimity exerted all their power to impress upon the public that point of view.

"We see in this, not the end perhaps, but surely the greatest peril, to a free press in America," said the Detroit *News.* From the citadel of its monopoly position in a city of 600,000, the Kansas City *Star* cried: "This is the sort of thing that belongs in the totalitarian states, not in a free democracy." "In the event of a government victory," said the New York Daily *News,* "the press services of the United States will be under the thumb of the White House."

These were not extremist positions. They represented a fair sample of the opinion handed down by the press, sitting as supreme court, long before the government brought its case to trial and won the first round in the United States District Court of New York. The Associated Press proudly published a volume of the collected editorial judgments for the instruction of the country.

The country rode out the storm with equanimity. Dimly or otherwise, the people perceived that the newspapers, once again, had proved unable to separate their commercial privileges from their civil rights.[8]

In retrospect, the press outcry seems a bit silly. The government won the case, the *Sun* got AP service, the White House did *not* put its thumb on the wire services, no newspaper was restrained or censored. The question was commercial: whether a news service could be withheld from some newspapers for competitive reasons.

The dangerous element in all this is that the press puts itself in the position of crying "Wolf!" when it is threatened by a rabbit. It helps neither public understanding of freedom of the press nor public respect for the First Amendment to associate them with problems of newsboys' pay or restrictive membership in a news service. It is not that the newspapers were necessarily wrong in fighting these issues—but there is considerable doubt whether they should have been fought on the ground of press freedom.

Now the press is fighting another battle with government decisions that come much closer to infringing concepts of freedom. Again the antitrust laws are pivotal. The question is whether, as the numbers of large metropolitan newspapers diminish, the remaining giants should acquire suburban papers in the same area. The Department of Justice has stepped into several such acquisitions, objecting that competition is diminished. It is not yet certain that the government will be able to establish guidelines for ownership to which the press must adhere, but magazine and book publishers are watching the developing battle between newspapers and government with keen interest, and some fear that a formula which will prevent wholesale acquisitions and mergers may be established. Obviously, this is a question related not so much to historical concepts of freedom as to the press as a business institution.

Like the other instruments of mass communication, the newspaper is a business enterprise as well as an informative public service. As Zechariah Chafee observed, it is like a combination, in one organization, of a college and a large private business, the one devoted to educating the public, the other to making money for a few owners. This is an awkward combination, and yet it must be maintained. Newspapers must be economically strong so that they can remain independent of the government and report on it; yet we must expect an unusual kind of responsibility from newspaper owners. For the free expression of ideas they have been granted is broad. In *Winters v. New York,* a case involving the right to publish accounts of crime and violence, the Supreme Court made it clear that entertainment is also protected:

> We do not accede to appellee's suggestion that the constitutional protection for a free press applies only to the exposition of ideas. The line between the informing and the entertaining is too elusive for the protection of the basic right. Everyone is familiar with instances of propaganda through fiction. What is one man's amusement, teaches another man's doctrine.[9]

Clearly, government regulation of print is sharply limited when the highest court construes freedom so broadly.

Films

In *The Public Philosophy,* Walter Lippmann distinguishes perceptively between the different degrees of government intervention the different media may expect because of their different natures. In our public philosophy, he writes, freedom of speech is conceived as "the means to a confrontation of opinion—as in a Socratic dialogue, in a schoolmen's disputation, in the critiques of scientists and savants, in a court of law, in a representative assembly, in an open forum." Even in the canonization of a saint, Lippmann points out, the Church listens patiently to a "devil's advocate." This confrontation or debate is the basis of our provisions for freedom of speech. When genuine debate is lacking, free expression does not work as it is meant to work. It follows, then, that the degree of toleration that will be permitted in the mass media will be in proportion to the efficiency with which ideas can be challenged and rebutted.

In the Senate of the United States, for example, a Senator can promptly be challenged by another Senator and brought to an accounting. Here among the Senators themselves the conditions are most nearly ideal for the toleration of all opinions. At the other extreme there is the secret circulation of anonymous allegations. Here there is no means of challenging the author; and, without any violation of the principles of freedom, he may properly be dealt with by detectives, by policemen, and by the criminal courts. Between such extremes there are many problems of toleration which depend essentially upon how effective is the confrontation in debate. Where it is efficient, as in the standard newspaper press taken as a whole, freedom is largely unrestricted by law. Where confrontation is difficult, as in broadcasting, there is also an acceptance of the principle that some legal regulation is necessary—for example, in order to insure fair play for political parties. When confrontation is impossible, as in the moving picture, or in the so-called comic books, there will be censorship.[10]

This is keenly observed. But it does not answer the important questions fully. What legal regulation? Censorship of what?

It is clear that the film industry has strong Supreme Court backing for resisting censorship on all grounds except obscenity. In *Burstyn v. Wilson,* a case that involved the censorship of the Italian film *The Miracle,* the Court extended the protection of the First Amendment to film, ruling that a motion picture might not be legally censored on the ground that it is "sacrilegious." Later, the Court ruled that *La Ronde* might not be censored on the ground of immorality. The Court also reversed Ohio's ban of the film *M,* which had been censored because it might "promote crime," and Texas' ban of *Pinky,* which had been censored because it might incite racial tension.

This does not mean that motion pictures are free in fact. One of the most interesting aspects of the film industry's relations with government has been the submissive attitude of the studios. Darryl F. Zanuck stated in *Treasury for the Free World:*

Let me be blunt. The fear of political reprisal and persecution has been a millstone about the neck of the industry for many years. It has prevented free expression on the screen and retarded its development. The loss has not been merely our own. It has been the nation's and the world's. Few of us insiders can forget that shortly before Pearl Harbor the entire motion picture industry was called on the carpet in Washington by a Senate committee dominated by isolationists and asked to render an account of its activities. We were pilloried with the accusation that we were allegedly making anti-Nazi films which might be offensive to Germany.[11]

Similar pressures have been exerted in every time of tension during the existence of motion pictures, especially during the early

1950s, when McCarthyism was rampant, and, indeed, from the very beginning of the cold war.

But the major battles between the federal government and the film industry have been fought on quite different grounds. Founded six years after the passage of the Sherman Antitrust Act, the film industry nonetheless was long characterized by restraint of competition, with the largest companies seeking monopoly and maximum profits. In 1938, the Department of Justice filed suits against eight film companies on the charge that they were engaged in monopolistic practices and in illegal restraint of trade in producing, distributing, and exhibiting motion pictures. The trial was soon adjourned to permit negotiation between the Justice Department and the defendants. Five companies reached an agreement with government attorneys, but three refused to participate in the settlement by decree. After additional years of testimony, negotiation, and court decisions, the Supreme Court held that exhibition monopoly was a goal of the large companies. The result of this and continued negotiations was that theaters were divorced from production and distribution. Eleven years elapsed between the filing of the first charges and the eventual settlement.

But censorship by states and municipalities has influenced film content more strongly than any federal action. Film makers are sensitive to a long history of conflict with states. For example, a film was banned in Ohio in 1937 because "the picture encourages social and racial equality, thereby stirring up racial hatred. . . . All the above doctrines are contrary to the accepted codes of American life." A documentary film on the Spanish Civil War was banned by the Pennsylvania Censor Board with the suggestion that it would be acceptable if the words "Fascist," "Nazi," "Italian," "Rome," "German," "Berlin," and others were deleted.[12] Such experiences lead to anticipatory censorship, with film makers themselves judging the political winds in each period of American stress and often producing their films accordingly. It is not so much that they fear the results of court action; taken to the highest level, films usually win legal tests. But until they win, the result of banning is, or may be, financial failure.

The cases which the film industry is in danger of losing are those which involve censorship on the ground of indecency. Curiously, in recent years the film industry has been bolder in testing this ground than in testing any other. Two feature films which began playing in theaters across the United States in 1966 illustrate this point strikingly. *Who's Afraid of Virginia Woolf?* was a pioneer in its use of realistic dialogue: "Jesus" or "Christ" is used (irreverently) seventeen times; "God," "God damn," or "Lord" is used forty-four times; "damn," seven times; "hell," three times; "bitch," twice; "bastard," eight times; and "son of a bitch" or "S.O.B.," seven times. In comparison, all other films shown in first-run theaters in the United States prior to *Who's Afraid of Virginia Woolf?* were hesitant and tentative. The other film, *Blow-Up,* was similarly pioneering. Nudity and sexual scenes in other pictures were made to seem hesitant and tentative by comparison; nothing so unabashed had been shown in first-run theaters. A new spirit of tolerance was developing, and soon Americans found a growing number of erotically candid quality films, by American as well as foreign producers, being made available to them.

Broadcasting

The heart of the problem of government regulation lies in broadcasting. This industry experiences most of the kinds of encroachment which are visited upon the other media, and more. Programs are frequently attacked for their "indecency" or their "political content." Broadcasting has long been a subject of anti-trust actions. Congress takes a keen and continuing interest in broadcasting, and from time to time has investigated the industry for alleged communists, for monopoly, for violence in programs, political prejudice in news coverage, and the rating systems which help determine program schedules. The point of all this is that each threat to broadcasting is the stronger because the industry is under the continuing regulation of the Federal Communications Commission.

To understand the atmosphere of broadcasting, one must imagine newspapers, book publishers, and film companies as being required to obtain a federal license before going into business, and to renew it—giving proof of good public service—every three years. Such a requirement would be intolerable, and it would be bitterly resisted as contrary to our concept of free communication and undoubtedly in violation of the First Amendment.

The chief problem, of course, is that there are too few channels, or, more correctly stated, too few *desirable* channels. When broadcasters choose their own, as they did in the early 1920s, they cluster around the same channels, and the air becomes so filled with competing sounds that listeners hear only a cacophony of squeals and distorted programs. Moreover, entertainment broadcasters are not alone in using the air. The military, the police, the transcontinental telephone and teletype, short-wave communication from and between automobiles and trains, the forest service, the rural electric service—all these and many others have a stake. The need for the Federal Communications Commission to lay out the boundaries and guard the fences is obvious.

The necessity for commercial broadcasters to obtain licenses from the FCC creates a peculiar problem for a country that has been grounded in libertarian communication theory. The nub of the problem is how the FCC should select the licensee when there is competition for a channel—and it is especially spirited in television. Vast potential profits ride on the decision, not to mention many thousands of dollars which must be spent on legal fees to prepare for the hearings. The FCC, represented by an examiner, must sit in judgment. The Communications Act has given the examiner an almost hopelessly broad yardstick with which to judge applicants: the standard of operation in the "public interest, convenience, and necessity." The meaning of these words has filled countless thousands of pages of hearings and debates. To define them a bit more carefully, the FCC uses standards which the chief law digest, Pike and Fischer, lists under twenty-five headings:

1. fair, efficient, and equitable distribution of facilities
2. interference
3. financial qualifications
4. misrepresentation of facts to the Commission
5. difficulties with other government agencies, involvement in civil or criminal litigation
6. violation of Communications Act or FCC rules
7. delegation of control over programs
8. technical service
9. facilities subject to assignment
10. local ownership
11. integration of ownership and management
12. participation in civic activities

13. diversification of background of persons controlling
14. broadcast experience
15. new station vs. expansion of existing service
16. sense of public service responsibility
17. conflicting interests
18. programming
19. operating plans
20. legal qualifications
21. diversification of control of communications media—newspaper affiliation
22. diversification—multiple ownership of radio facilities
23. effect on economic interest of existing station
24. "need"
25. miscellaneous factors

The FCC usually finds many differences between applicants in terms of these tests. It tends to prefer an applicant with more broadcasting experience, or with better financial backing, or representing local rather than absentee ownership, or representing more diversification of ownership, and the like. Such judgments theoretically enable the FCC to decide which applicant is better able to serve the "public interest, convenience, and necessity."

Discussing each of these standards would require us to delve into questions of law rather than responsibility. But one standard—number 18, programing—bears directly on the question of freedom. The idea of submitting the programs of a mass communication organization to government inspection is repugnant to most broadcasters. In practice, the Commission has seldom examined programing thoroughly, but the threat remains. In 1946, the Commission frightened the broadcasters by publishing a little booklet entitled *Public Service Responsibilities of Broadcast Licensees,* which called for high-quality programing. It promptly became the subject of bitter objections, which predictably involved freedom of communication.

If it is clear that some standards must be considered so that applicants can be compared, it is equally obvious that the essential standard is programs; all the other judgments are secondary. How far do the people of the United States want the FCC to go in defining program responsibility? No one can be certain. It seems obvious that they are willing to have the Commission consider whether a station keeps the programing promises it makes when applying for a license, enforce its regulation on giving equal time to answer an attack on the air, and compare the programing practices of two applicants, at least in broad terms. For example, if one applicant promises only popular records and wire news, and the other promises network service, educational and cultural programs, wire news and local news coverage, and the like, the Commission should surely concede an advantage to the second applicant. But it is doubtful if the public wants the Commission to pass judgment on what a station says about the government (if a broadcast is actionable in the courts, let the case be tried there). Nor should the Commission be able to pass judgment on a news commentator, or a news broadcast, or a variety program. Somewhere between these kinds of action lies the border line beyond which the public seems to be certain that the Commission should not go.

The appropriate stance for a member of the Federal Communications Commission is probably best represented by Commissioner Nicholas Johnson. He does not try to prescribe *what* political or public-service obligation broadcasters should assume. He does try to require that broadcasters engage in public service. He is forever embarrassing them at license renewal time by reminding them of their own promises to broadcast in the public interest—and demonstrating that their practices have not kept pace with their promises. Unfortunately, few of the other Commissioners are so zealous—or so brave; Nicholas Johnson is a maligned figure throughout much of the broadcasting industry. The majority of the Commission usually upholds the governmental axiom: Regulatory agencies become all too friendly with the industries they are supposed to regulate.

Court action is a less frightening prospect to broadcasters today than is Commission action, and Commission action is in turn less frightening than Congressional action. "If the threat of Congressional action hung over us in radio times, it hangs one hundred times as heavy now that we are in television," one network head has said. This is because the political potency of broadcasting makes it a constant concern of officials, and because of the broad investigative powers of Congress and the constant possibility of restrictive legislation.

Like many other groups concerned with the restrictive power of government over broadcasting, the Commission on Freedom of the Press recommended that the First Amendment be broadened to protect broadcasting as well as the print media. Many Supreme Court decisions have moved in this direction. Yet broadcasting can never be quite so free as print. The practical ideal is for broadcasting to be as free as the press *within the limits* imposed on it by its nature.

Free Press and Fair Trial

All the media are involved in the apparent collision of two important Constitutional provisions. The First Amendment prescribes a free press. The Sixth Amendment prescribes a fair trial. If the press uses the full extent of its freedom to report and comment on the accused, can his trial be fair?

The debate on this question has been heavy in recent years, but the dilemma is historic. It began to reach wide public attention in the 1930s with the trial of Bruno Richard Hauptmann, a carpenter, for the kidnaping and murder of the infant son of Charles A. Lindbergh. Because Lindbergh was America's leading hero—he had become the first pilot to fly the Atlantic alone only a few years earlier—the Hauptmann trial was front-page news for months and was reported in a highly emotional atmosphere. Hauptmann was convicted and executed. Many critics held that news coverage of the trial was so prejudicial that Hauptmann had not been tried fairly. Walter Lippmann sketched the issues cogently:

We are concerned with a situation spectacularly illustrated in this case, but typical of most celebrated criminal cases in the United States, which may be described by saying that there are two processes of justice, the one official, the other popular. They are carried on side by side, the one in courts of law, the other in the press, over the radio, on the screen, at public meetings—and at every turn this irregular popular process interferes with, distorts and undermines the effectiveness of the law and the people's confidence in it.

Because there are two pursuits of the criminal, two trials and two verdicts—the one supposed to be based on the law and a thousand years of accumulated experience, the other totally irresponsible—the self-appointed detectives get in the way of the regular detectives, the self-appointed judges and jurymen and advocates for the prosecution and defense get in the way of the officers of the law, and the official verdict becomes confused with the popular verdict, often in the court itself, almost always in the public mind.

We can examine the problems best, I think, by examining a few concrete instances. Hauptmann was arrested on September 20, 1934, and within a week there was a headline in a New York paper saying that "clues build iron-clad case against Bruno, police claim," and a few days later it announced that "twelve men and women selected at random" by a reporter had decided, according to the headline: "Bruno guilty but had aids, verdict of man in street."

Here we find that the police, unless the newspaper was lying, which I doubt, made an appeal to the public to believe their evidence before that evidence had been submitted to a court of law. That was an interference by the police with the lawful process of justice. It is for a jury to determine whether a case is "iron-clad," and since juries have to be selected from the newspaper-reading public, such a positive statement on the authority of the police is deeply prejudicial. I do not for a moment think that Hauptmann was innocent, but that does not alter the fact that he had a right to be tried before a jury and to be tried nowhere else. Because he was tried in two places at once, thousands of persons came to believe that he was not tried fairly. But in the administration of justice it is highly important not only that the right verdict should be reached, but that the people should believe that it has been reached dispassionately.

In the two headlines I have cited, and you will recognize them as being by no means exceptional, we see the police rendering a verdict on their own evidence and a newspaper establishing a verdict among the potential jurors.

Let us pass to trial in Flemington. It had, of course, to be a public trial. But if it was to be a reputable trial, it had also to be a trial in which the minds of the judge, the jury, the lawyers, and the witnesses all concentrated on the evidence, were as little influenced as possible by excitement or prejudice. The courtroom at Flemington is said to have a maximum seating capacity of 260 persons. On January 2, according to the *New York Times,* the constables on duty admitted to an already overcrowded courtroom 275 spectators without passes. A few weeks later it was learned that attorneys for both sides were issuing subpoenas to favored friends in order to force their admission as spectators in the courtroom, more than a hundred having been issued for one day's session. The authorities permitted the installation of telegraph wires in the courthouse itself, and one of the telegraph companies alone had to have a hundred men on hand. Although it was forbidden to take pictures during the trial, pictures were taken, and the authorities took no action.

Now there is no use pretending that a case can be tried well in an overcrowded courtroom with every actor knowing that every word he speaks, every intonation of his voice, every expression of his face, will instantly be recorded, transmitted to the ends of the earth, and judged by millions of persons.

This brings us to the actual trial of the case outside the courtroom. As a sample from the press, we may take a report in which it is said that Hauptmann on the stand "made senseless denials" and he was described as "a thing lacking human characteristics." This, let us not forget, was during his trial and before the jury had rendered its verdict. We should not delude ourselves into thinking that comment of this sort is of no effect simply because the jury is locked up and is not allowed to read the papers. The witnesses read them, the spectators read them, and no newspaper man needs to be told that the sentiment of a crowd communicates itself more or less to everyone. There is no way to isolate a jury in such a way as to protect it from the feeling of the crowd.

We have next to consider the conduct of the lawyers. They began trying the case in the newspapers almost from the day of Hauptmann's arrest. The counsel for the defense, Mr. Reilly, appeared in the news-reels two days after his appointment and declared his belief that Hauptmann was innocent. A few days after the opening of the trial he announced to the press that he would name the kidnapers and that they were connected with the Lindbergh household. Two weeks after the trial, while the case was set for appeal, he addressed the Lions Club of Brooklyn and denounced the verdict, and the next day he addressed a mass meeting at which, during the course of his speech, the crowd booed Colonel Lindbergh.

Hauptmann himself issued newspaper statements during the course of the trial, the statements being given out by his lawyers. The prosecution also tried the case in the newspapers. On January 3, Mr. Wilentz said at his press conference that Mrs. Lindbergh's testimony would be "loaded with importance"; on January 22, he told a reporter that he would "wrap the kidnap ladder around Hauptmann's neck," and so on and so on.

Finally, we cannot omit the Governor of New Jersey, who, on December 5, 1935, while the case was still pending before the Supreme Court of the United States, let it be known that he was conducting his own investigation. I do not criticize him for that. The governor of a state has a right and, I think, an obligation to satisfy himself that justice has been done in his state. But the governor, who is a member of the New Jersey Court of Pardons, a quasi-judicial body, proceeded to try the case not before the court but in the newspapers. On December 8 his investigators let it be known that rail 16 of the ladder had, in their opinion, been planted against Hauptmann, and the governor was quoted as saying that he thought so, too. He also gave his opinion about fingerprints and was reported as saying that his personal investigator was "convinced that Hauptmann is not the man."[13]

Lippmann has been quoted at such length here not only because this is a classic case, but also because his account makes it clear that the press is far from alone in trying criminals on the front pages. Indeed, as Lippmann emphasized, "without the connivance of the regular officers of the law, the abuses of publicity would have been reduced to manageable proportions." The opposing attorneys "by their public statements violated No. 20 of the Canons of Ethics of the American Bar Association."[14] Nonetheless, the press was blamed. In 1937, two years after the Hauptmann trial, the American Bar Association passed Canon 35, which sought to ban photographers and electronic media (meaning chiefly radio, at that time) from the courtroom. In 1952, when television had become strong, it, too, was banned by Canon 35.

Competition is at the root of the dilemma, and it affects all parties. The police and the judges are public figures who compete for public favor. The opposing attorneys must try to gain every ounce of advantage in an adversary proceeding, and publicity may be an advantage. Elements of the mass media are in competition with each other.

It should not be forgotten that the mass media represent the right of the public to know whether or how its courts are dispensing justice. There are two approaches to this responsibility. One consists in re-examining, re-evaluating all the evidence, and, in effect, conducting a second trial to check the verdict of the court. Such investigations, carried on after the legal trial, have turned up many miscarriages of justice. A reporter for the Miami *Herald* won a Pulitzer Prize in 1966 for just such a process.

The second approach to this responsibility requires checking on the performance of the police, the judges, the other officials, and the lawyers to determine whether they are dispensing justice. This is the more difficult approach, for it surely includes calling officials to account for making comments and leaking facts that should come out in the course of the trial, not in a press conference or interview—and comments and facts are, of course, the lifeblood of mass communication. Journalists, then, not only must refuse to accept some of the proffered news, but must also criticize the officials who offer it. Is this a fundamental obligation? Lippmann thinks so: "It is our duty, I believe, to make it plain to the regular officers of the law that we expect them to administer justice in an orderly way, that we shall attack them if they do not, and then we shall defend them if they do. Then let them choose between the yellow press and the reputable press, and let them find out whose favor counts the more."[15]

Unfortunately, too few journalists have approached their responsibility in this way. Too many have deserved the comment of Judge Philbrick McCoy of the Superior Court of California: "The primary misconception is that the courts are places of entertainment and that criminal trials are conducted for the purposes of satisfying the sadistic instincts of a large part of the public, including the relatively few who can crowd into the courtroom. The more sensational the offense or the defense, the more sordid the story which is unfolded, the greater is the demand for detail."[16]

As a result of sensational and apparently prejudicial reporting, the debate on free press and fair trial has moved far beyond the simple question whether cameras and other modern reporting devices should be allowed in the courtroom. Skirmishes between the bar and the mass media over that issue were elevated to the plane of war as a consequence of events beginning in Cleveland in 1954. The pivotal event was the trial of Dr. Samuel Sheppard. The case had all the elements of high drama: Dr. Sheppard was a handsome young osteopath accused of the brutal murder of his lovely young wife. The family was prominent. There was another woman. A mysterious man was alleged to have been in the house on the murder night.

Many of the patterns of the Hauptmann case were repeated. Hordes of reporters and photographers descended on Cleveland. Information was leaked. Notes were passed to reporters by the accused. Lawyers talked. Self-styled crime experts analyzed the evidence, even added evidence, in public print. Biographies of the accused were published and broadcast. The photographic coverage was extensive. The sex element was played big, and the crime was described in gruesome detail.

There was, of course, wild variation in the way the story was disseminated. As Alan Gould, then executive editor of the Associated Press, pointed out: "You put a crime-and-sex story in the hands of 1,700 editors and you get every color in the spectrum. . . . Some papers are playing it big, with all the trimmings, photos, sidebars, purple phrasing. Others are dead-panning in the writing, but keeping the story on page one. Still others are keeping it inside. There is evidence that a few are ignoring it entirely, or nearly so. To the majority, it's a good news story—but only colossal, as they say in Hollywood."[17]

Dr. Sheppard was convicted and sentenced to life in prison. Then, in 1966, after he had served ten years, the Supreme Court ruled that the "carnival atmosphere" of the 1954 trial had deprived Dr. Sheppard of his Constitutional rights. In an opinion written by Mr. Justice Thomas Clark, the Court held:

A responsible press has always been regarded as the handmaiden of effective judicial administration, especially in the criminal field. Its function in this regard is documented by an impressive record of service over several centuries. The press does not simply publish information about trials but guards against the miscarriage of justice by subjecting the police, prosecutors, and judicial processes to extensive public scrutiny and criticism.

The Court has therefore been unwilling to place any direct limitations on the freedom traditionally exercised by the news media for "what transpires in the courtroom is public property." But the Court has also pointed out that "legal trials are not like elections to be won through the use of the meeting-hall, the radio and the newspaper."

There can be no question about the nature of the publicity which surrounded Sheppard's trial.

Nor is there any doubt that this deluge of publicity reached at least some of the jury. . . . The Court's fundamental error is compounded by the holding that it lacked power to control the publicity about the trial. From the very inception of the proceedings the judge announced that neither he nor anyone else could restrict prejudicial news accounts, and he reiterated this view on numerous occasions.

Since he viewed the news media as his target, the judge never considered other means that are often utilized to reduce the appearance of prejudicial material and to protect the jury from outside influence. We conclude that these procedures would have been sufficient to guarantee Sheppard a fair trial and so do not consider what sanctions might be available against a recalcitrant press nor the charges of bias against the state trial judge.

The carnival atmosphere at trial could easily have been avoided since the courtroom and courthouse premises are subject to the control of court. . . . Bearing in mind the massive pre-trial publicity, the judge should have adopted stricter rules governing the use of the courtroom by newsmen as Sheppard's counsel requested. The number of reporters in the courtroom itself could have been limited at first sign that their presence would disrupt the trial. They certainly should not have been placed inside the bar. Furthermore, the judge should have more closely regulated the conduct of newsmen in the courtroom. . . .

Secondly, the court should have insulated the witnesses. . . .

Thirdly, the court should have made some effort to control the release of leads, information, and gossip to the press by police officers, witnesses, and the counsel for both sides. . . .

The judge should have at least warned the newspapers to check the accuracy of their accounts. . . .

The prosecution repeatedly made evidence available to the news media which was never offered in the trial. Much of the "evidence" disseminated in this fashion was clearly inadmissible. . . . The newspapers described in detail clues that had been found by the police, but not put into the record.[18]

It is clear from all this that the Supreme Court held the trial judge chiefly responsible. But this should not be allowed to obscure the role of the news media. The Court cited the Cleveland *Press* for a vicious series of headlines and news accounts, and among the many prejudicial reports was a broadcast carried by station WHK in Cleveland in which Bob Considine likened Sheppard to a perjurer and compared the episode to Alger Hiss's confrontation with Whittaker Chambers.

The Supreme Court decided that Dr. Sheppard should be retried promptly or granted freedom. A retrial was held in November, 1966, under closely controlled conditions, and Dr. Sheppard was found not guilty.

The chief result of this and similar cases has been much stricter supervision of court proceedings. If that were all, we might consider it a lesson well learned. Unfortunately, local law enforcement officials and judges in many areas were frightened or confused or both, and overreacted. In Phoenix, a judge suppressed the right of the media to report what occurred in open court. In Wake County,

North Carolina, two Superior Court judges issued a rule concerning publicity and due process which suppressed virtually all police news. These and similar actions were fought successfully, but they illustrate a national tendency to take the Supreme Court's decision further than it was intended to go.[19] Ironically, in attempting to preserve the defendant's rights by restraining the press, officials are endangering the Sixth Amendment itself. The reason for the guarantee of a fair trial springs from the bitter experiences of the colonists with Star Chamber proceedings in Europe, where closed courtrooms enabled officials to make capricious decisions.

It is essential to strike a balance between the Star Chamber of old and the People's Courts in certain communist countries today, where decisions are often rendered in an atmosphere of emotion by the voice of the populace. Ideally, the courts and the media will exercise full responsibility to protect both the individual's right to a fair trial and the public's right to know.

The machine-interposed media pose a special problem. Although most people have become accustomed to pen-and-notebook reporters, they are likely to be embarrassed and inhibited in court by the knowledge that every word and action may be carried to a vast audience. Moreover, the presence of machines—especially television and film cameras, flashbulbs and bright lights, and photographers moving around for sharp camera angles—is more likely than the presence of reporters to result in a disorderly courtroom and to distract attention from the serious attempt to administer justice. Finally, unless the court scene is recorded for later broadcast, there is no middleman in the process to exercise judgment as to what should be broadcast. The newspaper reporter, of course, can weigh his material and exercise a sober second thought as to what it means, what should be restrained, and what interpreted. But when the machine media are open channels, they carry everything they see and hear.

Courts, investigative committees, and other public bodies have been keenly aware of these differences. The result has been the exclusion of cameras of all kinds from many such public events, especially court trials.

Some public hearings have been televised. The crime investigation hearings conducted by Senator Estes Kefauver in the early 1950s demonstrated dramatically how television can *enhance the public's right* to know. When a witness objected to having his face photographed, the cameras centered on his hands—resulting in some of the most eloquent news coverage ever made in a hearing room. The hearings which pitted Senator Joseph McCarthy against high-level Army officers and Department of the Army officials were similarly revealing on television. Several important debates in the United Nations have proved the power of television, especially those in June, 1967, when Israel went to war with neighboring Arab nations and the UN was the center of cease-fire efforts.

It seemed for a time that court trials, too, might be opened to the machine media. In Portland, Oregon, a presiding judge made news in 1954 when he permitted photographers to cover a sensational murder trial. He specified that no flashbulbs were to be used, and that the photographers were not to move around the courtroom, but should remain in their reserved seats in the front row of the spectators' gallery. Each Portland paper took more than a hundred pictures, and parts of the trial were also filmed for later television broadcast. No one complained that the trial was disrupted in any way. The judge expressed his pleasure that the photography "was done honestly and decently without interrupting or bothering anyone."[20]

The outlook for more such experimentation was bright. New engineering developments were making it possible to cover hearings, trials, and assemblies without disrupting them. Cameras had been developed which would take interior shots without flashbulbs, and cameramen had learned to restrict their movements as well as their equipment. The bar associations of most states were still opposed, but news photographers and television cameramen found a convincing way to show that their machines could be unobtrusive. In state after state, members of the bar and representatives of the mass media would meet to discuss the issue, and only after the meetings were adjourned would the attorneys be told that cameras had recorded every minute of the meetings.

Then, in 1962, a swindler named Billie Sol Estes, who had already been convicted in a federal court and sentenced to fifteen years in prison, was tried in a state court in Texas on additional charges. Although Canon 35 of the American Bar Association was still in force, it is not law; and Judicial Canon 28 of the State Bar of Texas permitted news photography and radio and television broadcasting at the discretion of the trial judge. Estes' attorneys argued before the pretrial hearing that television, radio, and news photography should be banned from the courtroom. But it was a case that attracted national attention, and the judge denied the motion. Estes was found guilty.

In 1965, the Supreme Court reviewed the case and reversed Estes' conviction. In a decision written by Mr. Justice Clark, the Court held:

These initial hearings were carried live by both radio and television and news photography was permitted throughout. The videotapes of these hearings clearly illustrate that the picture presented was not one of judicial serenity and calm to which petitioner was entitled. Indeed, at least 12 cameramen were engaged in the courtroom throughout the hearing taking motion and still pictures and televising the proceedings. Cables and wires were snaked across the courtroom floor, three microphones were on the judge's bench and others were beamed at the jury box and the counsel table. It is conceded that the activities of the television crews and news photographers led to considerable disruption of the hearings. Moreover, a venire of jurymen had been summoned and was present in the courtroom during the entire hearing but was later released after petitioner's motion for continuance had been granted.

. . . Pretrial can create a major problem for the defendant in a criminal case. Indeed, it may be more harmful than publicity during the trial for it may well set the community opinion as to guilt or innocence. Though the September hearings dealt with motions to prohibit television coverage and to postpone the trial, they are unquestionably relevant to the issue before us. All of this two-day affair was highly publicized and could only have impressed those present, and also the community at large, with the notorious character of the petitioner as well as the proceeding. The trial witnesses present at the hearing, as well as the original jury panel, were undoubtedly made aware of the peculiar public importance of the case by the press and television coverage being provided, and by the fact that they themselves were televised live and their pictures rebroadcast on the evening show.

When the case was called for trial on October 22, the scene had been altered. A booth had been constructed at the back of the courtroom which was painted to blend with the permanent structure of the room. It had an aperture to allow the lens of the cameras an unrestricted view of the courtroom. All television cameras and newsreel photographers were restricted to the area of the booth when shooting film or telecasting. Here, although there was nothing so dramatic as a home-viewed confession, there had been a bombardment of the community with the sights and sounds of a two-day hearing during which the original jury panel, the petitioner, the lawyers and the judge were highly publicized. The petitioner was subjected to characterization and minute electronic scrutiny.[21]

In a 5-to-4 decision, the Supreme Court ruled that Estes deserved a trial without such extravagant coverage by television. Mr. Justice Potter Stewart entered a vigorous dissent: "The suggestion that there are limits upon the public's right to know what goes on in the courts causes me deep concern. The idea of imposing upon any medium of communications the burden of justifying its presence is contrary to where I had always thought the presumption must lie in the area of First Amendment freedoms." The majority stopped short of the kind of ruling that would suggest to judges in lower courts that cameras are never welcome in any trial, but it is clear that the cause of electronic communication lost ground.[22]

Considering the activities of the mass media during the Estes and Sheppard trials, and especially during the wild period immediately after the assassination of President Kennedy, it is not surprising that the outlook for resolving the free press–fair trial issue seems more distant than ever.

The coverage of the Kennedy assassination will be discussed in a later chapter. It should suffice to report here what Erwin Griswold, Dean of the Harvard Law School, wrote in the October 24, 1964, issue of *Saturday Review:* "We all remember the broadcasts of last November 22 and 23. It remains my best judgment that by November 24 Lee Harvey Oswald could not have obtained a fair trial anywhere in the United States and that the Supreme Court would have so held."

Everything points to stronger restrictions on law enforcement coverage by all the media. One might recall the occasions when reporters went wild and judge that restrictions will serve them right. But there should be sober second thoughts: Would a white civil-rights worker arrested in rural Mississippi benefit if reporters for the wire services and wide-ranging papers like the *New York Times* were restricted in reporting what happens to him? The real dangers have been spelled out by Nicholas Horrock, a reporter for the Baltimore *Sun,* who holds that "prosecutors, police and other mechanics of the law enforcement business spend much of their time and effort now in endeavoring to conduct their business with as little public scrutiny as possible." Recalling his days as a cub reporter in New Jersey, Horrock told of the arrest of a Newark Negro for the rape of a suburban housewife. He and a veteran reporter were at the police station when the Negro was brought in at 2 A.M. Said the veteran: "Look around—do you see any lawyers—anybody from the ACLU? Sure you don't. You and I are it."

Government Secrecy

Unfortunately, the subtle struggle over political information is often resolved into a meaningless debate as to whether the Eisenhower Administration, the Kennedy Administration, or the Johnson Administration was most adept at managing the news. Nothing is quite so absurd as thinking of news control by government as a modern phenomenon. The focus may be sharper today, but the truth is that information policy has been at the very center of governing the United States from the beginning.

Patrick Henry set the terms of the historic debate. The government, he said, must keep from the press "such transactions as relate to military operations or affairs of great consequence, the immediate promulgation of which might defeat the interests of the community." The press must prevent officials from "covering with the veil of secrecy the common routine of business, for the liberties of the people never were, or never will be, secure when the transactions of their rulers may be concealed from them."

The great question has always been: Which are the affairs which might "defeat the interests of the community"? The writing of the Constitution was deemed to be one. The delegates to the Constitutional Convention straggled into Philadelphia in May of 1787— their deliberations began nearly two weeks late—but for all the desultory atmosphere they were agreed from the beginning that drafting a new form of government, or shoring up the old one, would be impossible if their speeches were published piecemeal and debated on every village square. They took a pledge of secrecy.

There seemed to be good reason for a secret convention. Had the masses of Americans been able to read some of the more extreme proposals, the convention hall might have been a focus for rioting. Brilliant, ambitious, thoroughly aristocratic Alexander Hamilton, holding that the "rich and well-born" must be given their "distinct, permanent share in the government"; smooth Charles Cotesworth Pinckney politely threatening the withdrawal of South Carolina if the majority carried through its plan to abolish the slave trade; endless compromising on the part of several delegates whose public posture was based on inflexible principle—all this went on behind bolted doors.

One day a delegate carelessly mislaid his copy of the proposals. It was found and turned over to George Washington, the President of the Convention. He seemed to ignore it, but as the meeting was adjourning for the day, he stated grimly: "Gentlemen, I am sorry to find that some one member of this body has been so neglectful of the secrets of the convention as to drop in the state house a copy of their proceedings, which by accident was picked up and delivered to me this morning. I must entreat gentlemen to be more careful, lest our transactions get into the News Papers and disturb the public response by premature speculation."[23]

Until James Madison's notes were published decades later, few Americans had any real knowledge of what had occurred during the Constitutional Convention.

Other powerful leaders were as convinced as was Patrick Henry that the common routine of government business must be publicized. They believed that the survival of the new nation depended upon information that would, in Thomas Jefferson's phrase, "penetrate the whole mass of the people." Madison, who is often called the Father of the Constitution, wrote: "Knowledge will forever govern ignorance. And a people who mean to be their own governors must arm themselves with the power knowledge gives. A popular government without popular information or the means of acquiring it, is but a prologue to a farce, or a tragedy, or perhaps both." Jefferson valued information above the federal structure itself: "The basis of the government being the opinion of the people, the very first object should be to keep that right: and were it left to me to decide whether we should have a government without newspapers or newspapers without a government, I should not hesitate a moment to prefer the latter."[24]

Clearly, the founders considered informing the people to be a function of democracy. But they carefully refrained from setting up an official information system. Instead, the informing function was turned over to the press. In effect, the press—privately owned, beyond official control—was incorporated into the machinery of democracy.

Surely, some of the genius of the American idea flows from the fact that the apparatus of information was made an independent part of the continuing government in a way that ensured its freedom from any particular administration. Officials from the first have had to adapt to the anomaly of an information system that is *of,* but not *in,* the government. This established a natural struggle between the men of the press and the men of the official government. Much of the history of American government pivots on the use of information as an instrument of political power.

Secrecy in government has been an issue from the beginning. One of the most enduring official concepts was established in 1792, when a committee of the House of Representatives was investigating the "St. Clair Disaster," one of the most resounding defeats in battle in American history. Major General Arthur St. Clair's troop, which was camped at the headwaters of the Wabash River, was attacked by Indians and lost six hundred men. The House committee called for the original letters and instructions bearing on the expedition. Washington and his Cabinet rejected the request and replied:

We had all considered and were of one mind 1. that the House was an inquest and therefore might institute inquiries 2. that they might call for papers generally 3. that the Executive ought to communicate such papers as the public good would permit, and ought to refuse those the disclosure of which would injure the public.

Thus was established the doctrine of Executive Privilege, which was most carefully spelled out in a Court of Claims decision:

Executive Privilege provides a phase of release from requirements common to private citizens or organizations. It is granted by custom or statute for the benefit of the public, not of executives who may then hold office. . . . Free and open comments on the advantages or disadvantages of a proposed course of governmental management would be adversely affected if the civil servant or executive assistant were compelled by publicity to bear the blame for errors or bad judgment properly chargeable to the responsible individual with power to decide and act.

Every President has relied on this doctrine to thwart inquisitive journalists as well as members of Congress. But seldom until the Eisenhower Administration did the Executive departments and agencies find it necessary to cite Executive Privilege. It was simply accepted that certain categories of information, vaguely defined, would be disclosed only at the discretion of the President and his lieutenants. Complaints from the mass media and from Congress were relatively perfunctory until it became clear that the Eisenhower Administration was one of the least voluble in history. Then on May 17, 1954, President Eisenhower wrote a letter to his Secretary of Defense commanding that Defense officials not testify before Senator Joseph McCarthy's investigating subcommittee as to "advisory conversations or communications or any documents or reproductions concerning such advice." The letter was applauded by most journalists, who had become convinced that Senator McCarthy's sensational fishing expeditions for communists in the federal government were injuring the country.

The journalists did not realize the extraordinary use other Executive departments and agencies would make of this letter. Representative John Moss, chairman of the House Subcommittee on Government Information, found that nineteen major federal agencies were relying on Eisenhower's letter to the Defense Department to claim an Executive Privilege that would allow them to conceal information.

There was more during the Eisenhower years to frustrate journalists. Ironically, a law passed in 1946 which had been designed to make available more information was being used to conceal it. This was Section 1002 of the Administrative Procedure Act, which holds that "all matters of official record" in the federal government must be made available for publication. Eisenhower's subordinates took advantage of three exemptions:

1. Any function of the United States requiring secrecy in the public interest.

2. Any matter relating solely to the internal management of an agency.

3. Information held confidential for good cause found.[25]

Obviously, any official whose chief aim is to conceal information can find a hiding place for it behind these ill-defined exemptions. Together, the doctrine of Executive Privilege and the Administrative Procedure Act enabled federal officials to withhold a startling range of information.

Some members of Congress were as disturbed by government secrecy during the Eisenhower Administration as were spokesmen for the mass media. They began in 1955 to work for an amendment to the Administrative Procedure Act. It was a laborious process. Representative Moss's Subcommittee on Government Information held 173 public hearings and investigations and issued seventeen volumes of hearing transcripts and fourteen volumes of reports, all of which documented widespread secrecy. By 1966, both houses of Congress had passed an amendment to the public-information section of the Administrative Procedure Act. But by the time the amendment became law, *nine* exemptions had been added:

1. Specifically required by Executive order to be kept secret in the interest of national defense or foreign policy.

2. Related solely to internal personnel rules and practices of any agency.

3. Specifically exempted from disclosure by statute.

4. Trade secrets and commercial or financial information obtained from any person and privileged or confidential.

5. Inter-agency or intra-agency memorandums or letters which would not be available by law to a private party in litigation with the agency.

6. Personnel and medical files and similar files the disclosure of which would constitute a clearly unwarranted invasion of personal privacy.

7. Investigatory files compiled for law enforcement purposes except to the extent available by law to a private party.

8. Contained in or related to examination, operating, or condition reports prepared by, on behalf of, or for the use of any agency responsible for the regulation or supervision of financial institutions.

9. Geological and geophysical information and data (including maps) concerning wells.[26]

Although it is clear that these exemptions are better defined than those in the original public-information section of the Administrative Procedure Act, there are many more of them. In the early stages of constructing the new law, journalistic groups—especially Sigma Delta Chi—were enthusiastic supporters. V. M. Newton, Jr., chairman of the Sigma Delta Chi committee on freedom of information, wrote bitter letters of protest in 1961 and 1962, when the first five exemptions were added to the bill. He pointed out that the language of the law was too broad and that the five exemptions were "nothing more than an open invitation to the federal bureaucrat to withhold legitimate information of government from the American people." He reacted even more strongly when the four additional exemptions were incorporated into the bill which became the new law:

> Here again we have a lot of vague and undefined language, and here again, too, it would take no particular sleight-of-hand juggling for any federal agency to fit any or all of its information into these nine exemptions. Furthermore, the nine exemptions extend official government secrecy, by Federal law, over wide areas of Federal government which were not so encompassed in the original Administrative Procedure Act, and they were endorsed by the nation's major journalistic groups. And how exemptions No. 8 and No. 9 mysteriously got into the amendment never has been explained.
>
> I suspect that old Texas touch, which has been so evident in Washington since 1963. Nevertheless, under these two exemptions, our bankers and our oil millionaires will enjoy the privileges of secrecy by Federal law in their dealings with Federal Government, again with press approval. And under exemption No. 6, our Federal bureaucrat can now bask, by law for the first time in federal history, under "personal privacy." What more could he ask?[27]

It should be said immediately that not all journalists agree with Newton. As is suggested by the fact that journalistic groups approved the new law, some believe that the specific qualities of the exemptions will limit concealment. Others, among them a great many Washington correspondents, are not much concerned with freedom-of-information laws of any kind. A former correspondent, Julius Duscha, speaks for most of these with "Good reporting solves freedom-of-information problems." Over the years, public-affairs reporters have developed important sources within government, have learned to take advantage of ambitions and jealousies among officials, and have persuaded a great many officials of the importance of the public's right to know. These facts have helped establish a "credibility gap" for more than one President, for the efforts of a high official to mislead reporters are usually thwarted by subordinate officials who tell the truth, often with the understanding that their names will not be used. Most important, of course, is the fact that any democratic government must maintain at least a façade of conducting the public business in public. As Abraham Lincoln said, "In this and like communities, public sentiment is everything. With public sentiment, nothing can fail. Without it, nothing can succeed."

This aspect influences the other branches of the federal government, not to mention the many state, county, and municipal governments. For we have been discussing a problem of the Executive establishment that applies equally to other governments. Congress itself, which is so zealous in its efforts to open up the Executive departments and agencies, must be pressured to bring more of its own activities into the public arena. One can agree, for example, that many of the meetings of such committees as Senate Foreign Relations and House Foreign Affairs should not be publicized because of the national security, and yet wonder why quite so many committees are so often devoted to closed sessions.

In sharp contrast to the federal government, which seems to have been moving toward more secrecy in recent years, many state governments have been opening meetings and records that were long closed. During the decade from 1955 to 1965, when Congress was laboring to bring forth its heavily qualified amendment to the Administrative Procedure Act, the legislatures of twenty-eight states were quietly adopting simple, unqualified laws opening their records and meetings. Thirty-seven of the fifty states now have meaningful open-records laws, and twenty-nine have open-meeting laws. The Florida law is fairly typical: "All state, county, and municipal records shall at all times be open for a personal inspection of any citizen of Florida, and those in charge of such records shall not refuse this privilege to any citizen."[28]

It is necessary to remember, however, that there are occasions when the public interest is not served by full disclosure. The most difficult problem is deciding when secrecy serves the public interest.

Secret Meetings

It is fairly common in some areas for a city council, a county commission, or a school board to thresh out its business in closed, or "executive," sessions, then to convene a public session and transact its business formally—perhaps merely announcing its decisions. The news media argue that the reasoning and procedures leading to decisions are as important to the public's participation in government as are the decisions themselves. To understand and evaluate, the public needs full disclosure.

The Freedom of Information Committee of Sigma Delta Chi has indicated, however, that it clearly recognizes that occasional executive sessions can serve the public interest:

1. Is the star-chamber session actually one in which public officials are discussing things which belong in the public prints? For example: Premature publicity on a city council's plan to condemn private property for a street or parks project might artificially inflate the price of property under consideration. The council members feel an obligation to the taxpayers and hope to arrange a good deal for them. If the proposition they are considering is actually on the up-and-up, they would not hesitate to tell the newspaper about it for background purposes. But do they have the assurance that the newspaper is as interested in acting with patience and restraint in the public interest as it is in obtaining a story and printing it—regardless of its implications?

2. Are public officials given enough protection against inaccurate, adolescent, or outright malicious treatment of "sensitive" information? Do competitive pressures by two or more newspapers force reporters to betray confidence after they have been admitted to executive sessions of public officials? Are the stories the reporter writes published as written? Or are they jazzed up to his embarrassment and to the humiliation of his news sources?

3. When news and information is withheld or suppressed, does the newspaper enter its complaint on sound ground and with clean hands?

(a) Does the paper have a consistent and generally unimpeachable record of having tried to cover the area of news in contention with intelligent, knowledgeable, and trustworthy reporters? Or is it asserting its traditional rights to information through personnel who are demonstrably unfit to treat it with perspective, balance, and comprehension?

(b) Does the paper burden the source of information by spasmodic attention which demands time-consuming explanations of the obvious, the only alternative being a distorted and possibly damaging report?

(c) Is the information sought and published in an objective manner, or is it treated as an instrument of editorial policy preconceived by the front office?

4. Are objections to the suppression and withholding of information asserted and argued personally by responsible people in a manner that is considerate, logical, and convincing? Or do the objections take the form of personal recrimination, arbitrary criticism, or reckless insinuation?

5. Are newspapers alert enough and consistent enough in their insistence upon "all the news that's fit to print"? Or do some of them invite indifference to release of news through neglect of offices upon which they are supposed to keep a sharp eye? Are not some newspapers guilty of encouraging news suppression that they may promote a certain candidacy, a pet project, or protect a special set of friends?[29]

Obviously, these pointed questions spring from actual cases. And although they fall far short of arguing for secret meetings, these questions suggest that the newspaper (and, indeed, all the mass media) must make certain that its house is in order before challenging public officials. Challenge they must, the committee argues, largely because of "the impulses of political self-preservation which naturally rule most persons in public life."

Secret Records

Harold Cross has pointed out that so-called "public" records and proceedings are of many different degrees of appropriateness for publicity and differently related to the public's need and right to know.[30]

1. Some records, though kept by public officials in public offices, are not really public at all. For example, it could hardly be argued that the public interest would be advanced by opening diplomatic correspondence or FBI files to the press and the public. Tentative understandings or approaches are features of diplomacy

that should not always be publicized—perhaps too often are. On the other hand, both press and public have the clear right, for example, to demand that their governmental representatives should not make secret agreements, as distinguished from tentative approaches and understandings.

2. Some records and proceedings, though "public," are not open to public inspection. Among these, in some states, are the records and hearings in juvenile courts, and in certain public-assistance cases. So far as such records as public assistance are concerned, the purpose in restricting them is apparently to defend the recipient's right to privacy, and to maintain the general morale of the community. It has been suggested that there is a distinction between the news gatherer's right to examine the records and his right to publish. He has a clearer right to check for graft and malpractice, and to publish what he finds, than he has to publish a list of names which would accomplish nothing but further to destroy the self-respect of unfortunate people.

3. Some "public" records and proceedings are open to inspection or attendance, but restricted to persons who have a particular status, qualification, or purpose. For example, corporate tax reports in certain state offices, reports of automobile accidents, records of vital statistics, and records of salaries paid sometimes fall under this heading. Here the news gatherer is on firmer ground in insisting on his right to know. His responsibility is obviously to be discreet when deciding whether the public good of publishing a particular fact exceeds its public harm in invading the privacy of an individual. But he should certainly insist that his status as representative of the public's right to know does give him a special status for examining these restricted records. And he has every right to fight the recent tendency toward regarding the financial relationships of government and individual citizens as "privileged" material, unavailable to the public.

4. Finally, there are some records which are public, ostensibly unrestricted, yet withheld at official discretion. For example, city books are officially open, but in practice are open only at the discretion of the officials concerned. Here the news gatherer's right and responsibility are usually quite clear. He should take whatever legal steps are required to open the records.

Secret Judicial Proceedings

A Hartford, Connecticut, crime wave was solved by the arrest of eight high-school students. They were secretly arraigned at night, and the proceedings were withheld from the newspapers. The judge made the somewhat unguarded statement that the names were kept secret because "the boys were from a good part of town and came from fine parents." This aroused wide resentment in areas where people realized that they were considered "not quite so good." Furthermore, many rumors circulated as to the identity of the youths.

Finally, one of the Hartford papers, noting that the boys had not been arraigned in juvenile court, where the proceedings were legally secret, took legal steps to secure the release of the names. It published the names. Then the boys were turned over to juvenile court, and the further proceedings were closed to publicity. It became known that the youths were suspended from school for the remaining six weeks of the school year; but, as far as could be found out, no other penalties were applied, although the cases involved car theft, safecracking, and burglary. Several years later, one of the youths, twenty years old and in military service, strangled a girl in Texas while on a date.

This case illustrates most of the problems that concern mass communication in the area of secret trials. In the first place, the responsibility for publishing or not publishing rests in some cases on the government side, in others on the communicator's side. Proceedings of juvenile courts, and of a few other courts, are for the most part withheld from the news. Yet when a juvenile is brought before another court, his name is ordinarily not privileged. Some papers have the rule of publishing all the names of juvenile violators that can be obtained. Some refuse to publish names when the violators are under eighteen. Some publish the names only when the offense is unusually grave.

But the point is that it is a very difficult decision because no one knows for sure whether it is for the public good to withhold or to publish such information. If it were clear that the fear of publicity would deter youths from committing crimes, then the responsibility of the news-gathering media would be clear: they would be obligated to search out and reveal all they could of such cases. But it is not clear. If fear of being known were really a deterrent to crime, juvenile delinquency would have ceased long ago, and our prisons would not be so overcrowded as they are. There is no indication whatsoever that the Hartford paper's publication of the names of the teen-age criminals kept one of them from becoming a murderer—or, on the other hand, any proof that the secrecy of the juvenile court proceedings kept others of the youths from going on with a life of crime. It is an area of bewildering uncertainties, and one in which the news gatherer must make the best decision he can on the best evidence he can find.

Therefore, it may be well to look at the arguments on both sides. On the side of the freest publication, we have two main points.

The first is that the public has a right to know what is going on. If the public knows the extent and nature of juvenile crime, it is in a position to seek out the reasons for it and to do something about it. This is a telling argument, although it has been argued in turn that the public can understand the delinquency problem perfectly well without knowing the names of offenders and their precise offenses.

The second argument is that fear of publicity will deter youths from committing crimes. Publicity will act as a punishment for those who have committed crimes. Furthermore, publicity will shame their parents into bearing their full responsibilities in these cases. It is necessary to admit that there is very little proof for this argument. Psychiatrists, juvenile judges, probation officers, and social workers feel, for the most part, that it is not a cogent argument, that, in fact, publicity would in many cases actually be no penalty and would have the worst possible effect on the rehabilitation of the youth.

They contend that children should not be treated like mature adults. Publicity, which would be thoroughly in order for mature criminals, would work against the rehabilitation of the child. For example, publicity may result in the child's being ostracized by his peer group, and even by his family, thus making rehabilitation almost impossible. Furthermore, publicity may magnify the seriousness of the offense and thereby make it harder for the child to return to normal behavior. On the other hand, while publicity may ostracize one child, it will glorify another. Many of the most dangerous of these juvenile offenders are children who are trying to gain some kind of recognition within a group or a gang. Publicity gives them the kind of attention they crave and encourages them to more spectacular feats to enhance their new reputations. For this reason, many cities have established the policy of working with parents rather than bringing juvenile offenders into court. So it is argued that publicity is the worst possible device for ending juvenile delinquency, and the purpose of an antipublicity policy is to nurture the possibility that young boys and girls will become happy, useful citizens.

These are the grounds, then, on which the editor and the broadcaster must determine responsible conduct. They want to guard against what J. Russell Wiggins of the Washington *Post* calls "sweeping this whole problem of youth in crime under the community rug." They must decide, in close consultation with their consciences and with the most expert advice they can obtain, what they can do, and what the courts, schools, and homes can do, to reduce delinquency and save young people for useful citizenship.

One thoughtful, public-spirited editor, Robert W. Sink of the Champaign-Urbana (Illinois) *Courier,* addressed this column to his readers:

(Says the sheriff): "Suppose I do arrest them. You won't print their names. They've suffered no disgrace, and they can go right back and do the same thing all over again. . . ."

The sheriff is right, of course; we don't print the names of lawbreakers unless they are 18, or over. This is the newspaper's own rule. It is just a rule we have decided to adopt.

Because it is a rule of our own choice, we can select the exceptions, and in the last five or six years we have made two that I can recall. One concerned a teen-age burglar. When the police finally caught him, he confessed some 60 burglaries. We decided that this young man had lost his amateur standing and should be treated by professional rules. We printed his name.

The other exception was more recent and concerned one of the more monumental successes in juvenile vandalism. Nobody complained in either instance.

In general we adopted the rule because some very solid citizens convinced us that in the majority of cases the damage to the youngster might outweigh the social benefits of printing his name. First offenders, it is argued, should be given the opportunity to profit from the experience of an arrest, without having the public stigma of lawbreaker placed upon them.

Sheriff Hedrick thinks these kids need the public disapproval of their neighbors. He also thinks that in some cases it would help to protect the neighbors.

"Let me give you a different kind of example," he explains. "There's one 15-year-old boy that we've picked up twice for burglaries. In addition he's confessed breaking into a house and stealing a billfold. The neighbors ought to know that this kid does things like that, so that they can take the necessary steps to protect their property. But if the papers won't print the name, they don't know who it is, and there's no penalty on the boy. He isn't deterred by the disapproval of his friends and neighbors because they don't know about it."

What do you, gentle reader, think about this? We don't think all teen-agers are like this, so don't write us a letter just to say so. There are plenty of law-abiding kids. We don't think prohibition is the answer, either. As an answer this is begging the issue.

Do you think we should drop our rule about printing the names of youngsters 17 and under when they are caught violating the law? Or should we print their parents' names? (One office wag suggested that we should print stories saying: "Driver of an automobile registered in the name of John A. Civicleader was arrested for parking without lights at 2 A.M. Tuesday on the Lincoln Avenue Road.")

It's something you have to make up your minds about, too.[31]

Security Information

This country has long had a tradition of clamming up in time of war, then releasing information quite freely in peacetime. During the cold war, habits of secrecy and censorship developed for war have tended to spill over into peacetime. This has been especially notable since the beginning of the undeclared war in Vietnam. Thus the news media find themselves bombarded on one side by highly articulate spokesmen who warn that communist spies are everywhere, and that security must be tightened; and on the other side by equally articulate spokesmen who say that our security program is excessive, that it is not only destroying freedom of speech and of the press, but also covering up inefficiency and malpractice, and slowing the development of science and technology by classifying everything in sight.

No editor, broadcaster, or film maker questions the right and responsibility to withhold, for the public good, information which might help this country's enemies more than it would help the generality of the American people if it were released broadly. Moreover, no one outside the security system can be certain just what is being withheld or make a valid judgment on the wisdom of the policy. We have learned just enough to be aware that the "Classified" stamp cloaks important information—and a few items that would only be embarrassing to officialdom for political reasons. The responsibility of the mass communicator, who represents the people's right to know, is clearly not to try to break the secrecy but to question carefully the way secrecy is administered, and what it covers.

In practical terms, a news medium is clearly being irresponsible and worse when it does what a proud and prosperous newspaper was accused of doing during World War II—publishing information on a Pacific battle in such form as to reveal to the Japanese that the U.S. Navy had broken the Japanese code. It is just as clearly being irresponsible when it does not oppose restrictions like this one in a Department of Commerce bulletin on advisory censorship:

> Information falling within the scope of this program includes *unclassified* technical data on: advanced industrial developments, production know-how, strategic equipment, special installations.

James S. Pope appropriately called this "a blunderbuss to shoot down all intelligence about our mobilization" and said it showed "little awareness of the dangers of public ignorance at a time of crisis."[32]

The Adversaries

We have said enough to make it clear that the relationship between the government official and the journalist is like that between opposing attorneys. It is an adversary system. And although the journalist and the official may be perfectly good friends—indeed, too friendly in some cases for the cause of dispassionate reporting—their perspectives differ so vastly that tension at some point is almost inevitable.

How this works is suggested best by a letter Edmund G. (Pat)

Brown wrote to his successor as Governor of California, Ronald Reagan:

There's a passage in *War and Peace* that every new Governor with a big majority should tack on his office wall. In it young Count Rostov, after weeks as the toast of elegant farewell parties, gallops off on his first cavalry charge and then finds real bullets snapping at his ears.

"Why, they're shooting at me," he says. "Me, whom everybody loves."

Nothing worse will happen to you in the next four years. Learn to live with that; the rest is easy.

As you must have noticed by now, the press fires the first real bullets at new governors. And the hardest lesson to learn is that it is futile to fire back. Never get into an argument with a newspaper unless you own it. A newspaper fails to get in the last word only if it goes broke in mid-debate.

Publishers in California generally will be more tolerant of a governor before he raises taxes, much as a young man will take more nonsense from a fiancee whose father is rich. But you will be amazed at how easily even a friendly publisher's tolerance is strained by trivial matters—a freeway route through his backyard; a rollback in government construction in his city; failure to follow his advice on the appointment of a judge.

. . . There is also not much I can tell you about the weekly news conference that you haven't already learned. You will find that while both surgeons and reporters operate with professional detachment there is only one real difference between them. Surgeons make more money for cutting you up.

But their motives are the same—to make sure everything is running properly. And in the case of the press, they operate with a proxy from the voters. For the voters, news conferences are as close to a first-hand accounting of what happened to their money as they ever get. . . .

Invest as much time preparing for these inquisitions as you can spare, but don't feel bad if you are caught off-guard. I can still hear a voice from the back of the room asking: "Governor, do you think lobbyists should be required to wear little green buttons on their lapels?" Maybe you would have a ready answer for that. I didn't.

Harrowing as they are, news conferences do provide a chance for correspondents to bore in, a practice that philosophers find a healthy thing for the democratic process. Few governors take any comfort in that.

One last word about dealing with reporters. If you don't want it in the papers, don't do it.[33]

One of Brown's opponents, Richard Nixon, was far less philosophical about the government-press adversary system. Indeed, when Brown defeated him for the California governorship in 1962, Nixon's parting address to the reporters who had covered the campaign was a kind of classic of political savagery. To understand it—and thus to understand another dimension of the adversary relationship—it is necessary to sketch Nixon's earlier jousts with the mass media.

Many journalists had watched Nixon during the early high points of his political career, which included, in 1950, a successful campaign for Senator during which his opponent was smeared as a communist sympathizer. Few were able to forget the Nixon Fund, an arrangement whereby California business interests helped pay his Senate expenses. When this was disclosed during the 1952 presidential campaign, with Nixon as the Republican nominee for Vice President, he made an emotional appeal to stay on the ticket with this climax: "Let them [the members of the Republican National Committee] decide whether my position on the ticket will help or hurt. And I am going to ask you to help them decide. Write or wire whether you think I should stay on the ticket or get off." But in 1958, when a reporter disclosed that 80 per cent of the State Department's mail was opposed to having the U.S. defend Quemoy and Matsu against the Chinese Reds, Vice President Nixon denounced the official who had released the information. He called the official a saboteur and ridiculed the notion that important issues should be decided "on the basis of what random letters say the people will support in the light of the minimum and often misleading information available to them." Many correspondents agreed with the latter idea and thought at the same time that Nixon changed his convictions as easily as he changed his clothes.

Sharply aware that the correspondents were chiefly responsible for the nickname "Tricky Dick," Nixon decided when he was running for President in 1960 that he would avoid them throughout the campaign. The abrasive attitude of Nixon and his entourage toward the journalists who accompanied them may have symbolized the worst mistake of the campaign. Nixon had proved before—notably in going through intensive interviews with Earl Mazo of the New York *Herald Tribune* and Stewart Alsop of the *Saturday Evening Post*—that he could present himself winningly to searching examination. Moreover, the reporting of a presidential campaign is not limited to fashioning news stories from speech notes. It calls for fleshing out a man, highlighting the color and flavor of a personality who is in quest of the nation's highest office, and this is a practice that works to the advantage of any personable candidate. By avoiding the reporters, Nixon made their work difficult and negated a source of his own strength.

As the campaign progressed, some of the correspondents who had followed John F. Kennedy from the beginning had become his friends, many were his devoted admirers, and nearly all diverted themselves by singing cutting songs about Nixon and the Republicans as the Kennedy entourage made its way across the nation. On the Nixon side, the correspondents became fond of composing malicious parodies of his speeches for their private amusement: "GUTHRIE CENTER, IOWA—Vice President Nixon said today farmers should eat their way out of the farm problem. . . ."

Nixon kept his feelings about the battles with the reporters within a small circle of friends for two years (although his belief that partisan journalism had cost him the 1960 election was reported by Fletcher Knebel in the Minneapolis *Tribune*). Then, the day after Brown defeated him for Governor of California in 1962, Nixon's fury burst forth. It was a curious scene to be played by a political figure who had once admitted that he keeps his true emotions in tight control by wearing a façade in time of stress. It sprang from impulse. His staff had decided that Nixon should not face the reporters, who were gathered downstairs at the Beverly Hilton Hotel in Los Angeles awaiting a concession statement. Instead, Press Secretary Herbert Klein was to read a statement to the press while Nixon left the hotel. On the way out, however, Nixon made a new decision. Even as Klein was reading the statement, Nixon pushed his way to the platform, his face working. For the next seventeen minutes he alternately frowned and smiled grimly while indulging himself in a monologue so heavy with venom, courage, and self-pity that Klein was stunned.

Nixon slashed at Brown: "I believe he is a good American, even though he feels I am not." He attacked President Kennedy for cutting off White House subscriptions to the hostile New York *Herald Tribune:* "Unlike some people, I've never canceled a subscription to a paper and I never will" (forgetting that on two occasions of high anger he had canceled subscriptions to the Washington *Post*).

Nixon's most savage criticism was aimed at the reporters. He was harsh about the coverage of the gubernatorial race, beginning with "Now that all the members of the press are so delighted that I have lost," ending with the plea that the mass media "put one lonely reporter on the campaign who will report what the candidate says now and then." He attacked the Los Angeles *Times* by name. (The *Times* had long been a Nixon ally, but it opposed his gubernatorial candidacy.)

It was nonetheless clear that Nixon's fury did not spring from the gubernatorial contest alone; he was lashing out at what he considered hostile treatment throughout his career in public life:

And as I leave the press, all I can say is this: For sixteen years, ever since the Hiss Case, you've had a lot of fun—a lot of fun—you've had an opportunity to attack me and I think I've given as good as I've taken. It was carried right up to the last day.

You won't have Nixon to kick around any more, because, gentlemen, this is my last press conference.

As Nixon stepped down from the platform, he muttered to Klein, "I gave it to those goddamn bastards right where they deserved it."

Not long after that, Nixon moved from California to New York. In 1964 he campaigned vigorously for Republican nominee Barry Goldwater—holding many press conferences along the way—and four years later he was elected to the presidency on the Republican ticket. Nothing was more easily predictable than that President Nixon's relations with the press would be abrasive.

Although former President Johnson never made his animosity quite so explicit, general public consciousness of the adversary relationship between journalists and public officials reached its height during his presidency. Everyone is reluctant to use the word "lie" about a President. As Walter Lippmann commented: "In order to avoid the embarrassment of calling a spade a spade, newspapermen have tacitly agreed to talk about the 'credibility gap.' This is a polite euphemism for deception, rather like the habit of our Victorian grandparents, who spoke of limbs when they were too shy to speak of legs." Nonetheless, a savage joke began to make its way around the country in 1967: "Do you know how to tell when Lyndon Johnson is not telling the truth on television? Well, when he goes like this"—finger beside nose—"he's telling the truth. When he goes like this"—pulling an ear lobe—"he's telling the truth. When he goes like this"—stroking chin—"he's telling the truth. But when he starts moving his lips, he's *not* telling the truth." The knowing laughter that greeted the joke everywhere was testimony to the widespread recognition of an issue the mass media had developed.

As often happens, James Reston summarized the problem most acutely. In a column published in the *New York Times* in July, 1966, Reston wrote:

The Johnson Administration may finally get over its agony in Vietnam—it may even achieve its military objective in the end—but it will probably never regain the confidence it has lost in its judgment and veracity.

With the bombing of targets on the outskirts of Hanoi and Haiphong, it has now done almost everything it said or indicated it would not do except bomb China, and the end of this melancholy chapter in American history is not yet.

The Johnson Administration said it was not seeking a military solution to the war, and it is now seeking precisely that. It said it was there merely to help a legitimate Government defend itself, and it has ended up by supporting a military clique that is not a Government, is not legitimate, and is not really defending itself.

Even when allowances are made for the uncertainties and moral ambiguities of warfare, the guile of this Administration, exercised in the name of high and even noble principle, is hard to match. It was not going beyond the 17th Parallel in Vietnam but it went beyond. It was merely going to respond to enemy attacks on its bases, but it went over to the offensive. It was not going to get involved in a major war on the Asian land mass but it did.

The President was not even faithful to his bad resolves. He said he would not negotiate, but then offered to do so, and spoiled that by refusing to negotiate with the major elements of the enemy he faces. He has not merely misled his enemies but his friends. His old colleagues in the Congress have not forgiven him yet for tricking them into support of a blank check defense of all Southeast Asia under circumstances they could not possibly oppose. And even in this last adventure in Hanoi and Haiphong, we are told officially that the bombing of targets there is not an "escalation" of the war.

The result here is an atmosphere of uncertainty and suspicion. The hawks are as confused as the doves about what is coming next. There is now not a single major nation in the world that supports Mr. Johnson's latest adventure in Hanoi and Haiphong. Even Prime Minister Wilson of Great Britain, whose economic policy depends on Mr. Johnson's continued support of the pound sterling, felt obliged to make a public statement against the bombing.

This question of confidence in the good judgment and good faith of the United States Government is really more important than anything else. The specific arguments about bombing and or not bombing the oil refineries are not vital. Honest men can obviously differ about the wisdom of the decision. Nevertheless, the fate of Vietnam or the United States does not hang on any of these specific arguments.

But a great deal does hang on whether the American people can trust the pronouncements of their Government, whether they can remain united on purposes they understand and respect, whether our allies believe Washington really wants a compromise settlement in Vietnam, or merely an enemy surrender on Washington's terms.

Such attacks do not find officialdom defenseless. In addition to the obvious power of high officials to make their views known—especially through the mass media—by 1967 the federal government was spending more than $400 million a year on public relations and public information. The Executive branch, in fact, spends more on publicity, news, views, publications, and special pleadings than is spent to operate the entirety of the Legislative and Judicial branches. All together, federal expenditures on telling and showing the taxpayers are more than double the combined costs of news gathering by the two major U.S. wire services, the three major television networks, and the ten largest American newspapers.[34] All this dwarfs the similar efforts of state and municipal governments, but they, too, are convinced of the need for engineering consent.

All this suggests why the civics-lesson picture of American government that shows the official acting and the reporter recording his action is too simplistic to be very useful, and why a responsible relationship of media and government in a society like ours is not likely to be stated precisely and finally in terms of logic. Rather, it must evolve out of interaction and thoughtful review, let us hope by men of good will on both sides.

4 Freedom and Society

The market is the place set aside where men may deceive each other.

—ANARCHUS

Many a businessman who inveighs against managed news and the rapacious federal bureaucracy might be shocked to hear that he himself is a serious threat to free communication. Yet it would be difficult to prove that the machinations of government officials are more injurious. Just as the official is usually able to rationalize almost anything he does as a contribution to the public good—after all, he is likely to believe in his own policies and programs—the businessman rationalizes *his* machinations as good for the community. He is likely to echo the thought of the businessman turned public official who said, "What's good for General Motors is good for the country."

It is not business alone which should be called to account. Many elements of society injure free communication, some of them quite unwittingly, and we shall call attention to them. But so much of the business of America is business that it deserves the first and strongest focus.

Class Allegiances

Mass communication is big business, and it is run by big businessmen. This has led to speculation outside the industry, and soul searching within it, as to whether a mass communication system that has become a big business can fairly serve all the economic groups in society. Is the class allegiance of mass communication injurious to freedom? William Allen White, one of the greatest editors and publishers, answered harshly:

Too often the publisher of an American newspaper has made his money in some other calling than journalism. He is a rich man seeking power and prestige. He has the country club complex. The business manager of this owner is afflicted with the country club point of view. Soon the managing editor's wife nags him into it. And they all get the unconscious arrogance of conscious wealth. Therefore it is hard to get a modern American newspaper to go the distance necessary to print all the news about many topics.[1]

Robert Lasch, another journalist, wrote:

In real life industrialists and department store managers do not pound on the publisher's desk and demand favorable treatment. They do not have to. An owner who lunches weekly with the president of the local power company will always grasp the sanctity of private ownership in this field more readily than the public-ownership ideas of a few crackpots. With the best of will, he may tell himself that his mind is open. Yet, as a businessman whose concerns are intimately bound up with those of other businessmen, he has a vested interest in maintaining the *status quo*.[2]

Virginius Dabney, a Richmond editor, has written:

Today newspapers are Big Business, and they are run in that tradition. The publisher, who often knows little about the editorial side of the operation, usually is one of the leading business men in his community, and his editorial page, under normal circumstances, strongly reflects that point of view. Sometimes he gives his editor a free hand but far oftener he does not.[3]

Significantly, these quotations are not from social scientists or professional critics but from respected journalists.

Consider the abortive crusade of the Chicago *Tribune* against illegal truck licenses. For a time, the *Tribune* was so proud of the work by its reporter, George Bliss, that special advertising acclaimed his digging. Then McCormick Place, a monument to the memory of Colonel Robert McCormick, publisher of the *Tribune,* burned down. Restoring McCormick Place required state funds— which meant dealing with the official whose office had jurisdiction over truck licensing. Suddenly, the crusade stopped. The newspaper put Bliss on "other assignments."

This is, of course, one of the most pernicious kinds of class control—the interlocking of other businesses with mass communication. The *Tribune* was not acting as a responsible newspaper.

The problem is not limited to newspapers. Some magazines are bigger businesses than newspapers. Most radio and television operations are large business units, and their executives are nearly always among the business leaders in their communities. Motion pictures have long been characterized by extraordinarily large incomes for top executives and star performers. Thus the possibility of class bias permeates the media, and through entertainment as well as information. In the case of entertainment, we are concerned because popular art may not reflect adequately both the wishes and the needs of the general society. In the case of information, we are concerned because the media may not reflect reality.

An incident in the career of Fred Friendly, long one of the leading documentary broadcasters, suggests the danger. When Friendly was producing a news quiz called *Who Said That?* for NBC, the sponsoring oil company dictated a black list which the broadcasting company accepted. The list of objectionable guests included Norman Thomas, Al Capp, Oscar Levant, Henry Morgan, and several members of Congress.

Later, when CBS produced *The Business of Sex,* an exposé revealing the use of call girls in sales campaigns, organized business wrathfully threw its full weight into the fight to repudiate the program.

Let us be clear about the dangers. The owner of an agency of mass communication is entitled to order whatever policy he wants, so long as it is legal. He might have trouble if he were to decree a policy that would drive away his audiences, but that, too, is his privilege, as long as he can afford it. On the latter point, there is not much evidence that audiences become exercised about *editorial policy*—about the particular stands a newspaper, a magazine, or a broadcaster may take in the columns devoted to opinion. The New York *Daily News,* which is the American newspaper with by far the greatest circulation—more than two million daily, more than four million on Sundays—addresses a wholeheartedly Republican editorial page to an audience made up largely of

Democrats. The readers are interested primarily in the breezy, and largely unbiased, news columns.

The cause for concern springs from those instruments of the mass media which allow their opinions to slop over into the news columns of newspapers and magazines, and into the supposedly unbiased news programs on radio and television.

There was a time, and not so long ago, when this was a much more nagging problem than it is today. To determine whether the newspaper correspondents of the 1930s were free to report the truth as they saw it, Leo Rosten talked with them and won their confidence. Then he used some of their statements in a questionnaire that all the correspondents were to fill out anonymously. Among the statements was: "My orders are to be objective, but I *know* how my paper wants stories played." More than 60 per cent of the correspondents answered, "Yes," indicating that they, too, felt subtle pressures designed to make them slant their dispatches in the direction of the publisher's leanings. Another statement ran: "In my experience, I've had stories played down, cut, or killed for 'policy' reasons." Slightly more than 55 per cent wrote, "Yes," a clear indication of blatant pressure. In most cases, the correspondents were bending to the prejudices of Republican-minded publishers. There were hardly any other kind.[4]

The political commitment of the mass media is still decidedly Republican. Until 1964, one could have predicted confidently even before the national political conventions that the newspapers which endorsed the presidential candidates would endorse the Republican, whoever he was, over the Democrat, whoever *he* was, by about 3.5 to 1. That was the ratio in 1960, and that had been the average ratio in the preceding seven elections. In 1964, Johnson won the support of more newspapers than Goldwater, 445 to 368. But that was an unusual election in many respects. *Life* and the *Saturday Evening Post,* both of which the Republicans were accustomed to counting on as surely as the dawn, went Democratic. It is doubtful, however, whether so many newspapers and magazines would have supported Johnson had the Republicans nominated a more conventional figure than Goldwater.

Nonetheless, the new breed of publisher is as different from the abrasive old publishers of the past as smooth Henry Ford II is different from cantankerous old Henry I. Most of them are even-tempered businessmen who are more concerned with the balance sheet than with whether liberalism and internationalism are the devil's progeny out of Franklin D. Roosevelt. Many have become convinced that responsible journalism pays off. The new era is probably epitomized by Samuel Newhouse, who collects Democratic and Republican papers like stamps and cares little where they stand as long as they remain solvent.

Certainly, strong political partisanship has been fading. In the Hoover-Roosevelt election of 1932, only 5.8 per cent of U.S. dailies were independent or neutral. The figure was 5.1 per cent in 1936. During the next five elections, independence and neutrality traced a steep curve: from 13.6 per cent in 1940 to 31 per cent in 1960. The figure was up to 59.5 per cent in 1964, but one wonders whether that was because some publishers were fearful of both candidates.[5]

What these changes of the past three decades mean to the Washington correspondents is apparent in the new answers to the questions posed by Rosten in the 1930s. Newspaper, magazine, wire service, and radio and television correspondents were asked whether it is still true that "My orders are to be objective, but I *know* how my boss wants stories played." Less than 10 per cent replied, "Yes." Asked whether their stories had been played down, cut, or killed for "policy" reasons, slightly more than 7 per cent replied, "Yes." These are slender figures, especially in contrast to those of the 1930s—and especially in view of the fact that the correspondents are predominantly Democratic and liberal while their employers lean to Republicanism and conservatism.[6]

These are encouraging changes, but they should not be taken to mean that class allegiances and the political and economic allegiances they foster are disappearing. A notable article by Ben Bagdikian in the *Columbia Journalism Review* demonstrated that E. I. Du Pont de Nemours & Co., of Wilmington, Delaware, maintains tight control over much of the news appearing in its two papers, the *Morning News* and the *Evening Journal*. Bagdikian reported that H. B. Du Pont, chairman of the board of owners, ordered suppression of editorial comment on an important controversy which involved the paper professionally but which happened to be in conflict with a personal political project of his own family, and, among other pressures, a director of the paper wrote to an editor saying that a news report of a political rally should have been rewritten to make it "useful to the Republican Party . . . at the polls in November."[7]

More typical are incidents like this:

> On my first newspaper . . . I was city editor when we had trouble with the mayor's wife. She was a temperamental woman; and once when the automobile she was driving collided with another car, she drove away in a huff without stopping to give her name as required by law. But someone got her number, reported it to the police, and we printed the story in our morning newspaper.
>
> . . . The afternoon newspaper owned by the same company published an entirely different version of the same trivial incident, omitting the fact that the mayor's wife had driven off without stopping. After our morning staff reported for work, who should walk into the city room and go into a huddle with the police reporter but the publisher. Naturally we listened as he tried to explain the story to the reporter who had covered it. He wanted a little correction run the next morning, saying that the mayor's wife hadn't driven off. "But how can I say she didn't when she did?" the reporter asked as innocently as you please. To give the publisher due credit, he did, on that occasion, have the grace to blush and walk back into his counting office.

It is important to point out that orders of this kind are very infrequent. Many a journalist has spent decades working for newspapers, magazines, or radio or television news operations without once hearing an *order* to distort the truth. Policy control is most often indirect. "Newspapermen are quick to get the idea of what the boss wants," A. J. Liebling wrote, "but those who get it first have usually had similar ideas right along. The publisher chooses some staff members as his instruments and ignores others (or, if they are obstreperous, gets rid of them)."[8] The same can be said of the other media. Rewarding some behavior and not other behavior, providing an example in highly rewarded employees, selecting judiciously for key assignments—all these are methods that may lead to distortion when perceptive employees translate them into messages.

There are two important defenses against class allegiances and the biases they foster. The first is for media executives to become more conscious of their own positions. Although we cannot expect them—or others, for that matter—to free themselves from their natural allegiances and to eradicate their class biases, we can point out that decisions made without consciousness of bias are the most dangerous kind. As a step toward freeing the media from class bias, we are suggesting an awareness of *unconscious* class bias. More than one publisher who is sensitive to his own standing in the community has adopted a policy of leaning over backward to avoid distortions. Others in all the media can do the same.

The second defense is probably much more powerful. It is a growing feeling of professionalism among journalists throughout the mass communication system. Modern executives who might be disposed to order that news be suppressed or distorted are often restrained by the knowledge that their subordinates consider themselves professional newsmen first, employees second. It is a brave or myopic publisher who will challenge the newsman's ethic—and an unusually spineless newsman who will back down when so challenged. To the extent that a sense of professionalism continues to grow among journalists the power of class allegiances will fade.

Control Through Support

On May 23, 1962, Donald I. Rogers, business and financial editor of the New York *Herald Tribune,* told a group of conservative businessmen that they were voluntarily paying hundreds of millions of dollars to support their "most vicious and most effective enemies." Rogers' pitch was simple:

You do it through your advertising budgets.

Let's consider the newspapers in our Nation's Capital. There are three daily newspapers in Washington—two of them conservative and sympathetic with the business point of view. These are the old and respected Washington *Star* and the Scripps-Howard afternoon paper, the *Daily News.*

The third paper, the Washington *Post,* is the journalistic flagship of the New Frontier. It rallies behind anything that is advocated or even suggested by Kennedy, Schlesinger or Heller. It is all out for increased government spending. It is in favor of Federal urban renewal. It has fought effectively for Federal aid to education for years. It has trumpeted and pleaded for the President's medicare program tied in with social security. It endorsed with praise the President's tax bill, and urged immediate passage.

Think of anything, anything at all in the way of legislative proposals that you fellows have opposed and have urged the National Association of Manufacturers to block, and you will find that the *Post* is trying to get it enacted.

So, when businessmen place their advertising in Washington, where do they place it?

They place 600,000 more lines per month with the liberal, welfare-state-loving *Post* than in the *Star,* and the poor old conservative *News* runs a poor—a very poor—third.

The latest figures in *Editor & Publisher,* the newspaper trade journal, show that businessmen even increased their support of the *Post* this year over last year, as though in indorsement of the *Post*'s militant support of liberals, and, just to make sure there's no mistaking the point, they decreased their support of the *Star.* . . .

The picture is no different here in New York. We find that the greatest amount of advertising placed by businessmen goes into the liberal *Times,* which supports most of the welfare-state program and at most only gently chides the Administration from time to time.

The influential conservative New York papers, the *Herald Tribune* and the *World Telegram & Sun,* get very sparse pickings indeed from the American business community which they support so effectively in their editorial policies.

. . . For some time the only network-wide-sponsored newscast on TV was the Huntley-Brinkley report, which won an Emmy award. On that show the liberals get the breaks and the conservatives do not. . . .[9]

One can quarrel with Rogers' conclusion that businessmen should put their advertising money only into conservative publications and programs, and yet emphasize that the facts he cites are basic to a real understanding of advertising. It certainly is true that conservative business supports influential liberal publications and programs. The point is that business supports them not because they are liberal but because they are influential. It will be important to keep this basic point in mind as we discuss the kind of control that springs from support. The point is emphasized by events following Rogers' speech. By 1967, the Washington *Post* had increased its lead over the *Star* and the *Daily News* in circulation as well as in advertising. The *Times* had become so dominant in New York that both the *Herald Tribune* and the *World Tele-gram & Sun* were dead.

A first principle is that advertising stands in different focus with different media. The advertising support of motion pictures is almost negligible; it is local and therefore has no relation to the making of entertainment films. Advertising support of the printed media is considerable—often at least two-thirds of the total income of newspapers and magazines—but it is quite separate from the news, editorial, and feature columns. In theory, an advertiser buys space for his message but has nothing to say about the content of material which will appear beside it—or elsewhere in the paper or magazine. He may be able to specify that his ad appear on the sports page, for example, where it will be seen by those who read sports news, but he has nothing to say about what appears in the sports columns.

In broadcasting, advertising support is total. The advertiser on radio and television seldom buys merely a segment of time; he buys a program, or a segment of time in or adjacent to a particular program. If he buys a spot advertisement, the advertiser has nothing to say about program content. If he sponsors a program, he may have everything to say, although the networks have in recent years been exercising their own power of veto.

The advertiser's influence was probably greatest in the heyday of radio, when a very large percentage of all sponsored programs were prepared by advertising agencies for their clients, and the networks were chiefly in the position of supplying time and channels. The networks and stations had the right of refusal, but the hand of the advertiser was clearly visible. This was the period when insistent and repetitive commercials began to fill the air.

With the coming of television, the center of gravity began to move back to the broadcasters. Most programs are made by the networks themselves or by program-packaging houses. Much of the nation's film-making talent has been siphoned off into program-packaging and commercial-packaging firms. The result is that the broadcaster is more often in the position of selling a program than in selling time for a program.

With the increasing costs of prime-time shows—from 6 to 8 million dollars a year for a half-hour weekly series running in any period from 7:30 P.M. to 11 P.M.—many sponsors are now going into "scatter plans." These are minutes of commercial time distributed in and around many shows.

Whatever the medium, principles should govern the relationship of advertiser to media. The most important is that information and opinion should be free of advertiser control—except, of course, advertising information, which should conform to acceptable standards of accuracy and reliability.

Second, no matter who produces the programs or suggests the talent and authors, the media should be free of advertising control that would militate against well-balanced program services.

Third, the media should be free of any advertising control that would prevent high quality.

Fourth, the amount of advertising should be in some equitable proportion to the amount of information and entertainment.

These are broad and lofty principles. How do they apply in practice?

The typical way of exerting control is to withdraw, or threaten to withdraw, advertising support. Consider these incidents:

General Motors signed a contract with CBS to sponsor a series of documentary programs. The first program was announced as "The Vice Presidency: The Great American Lottery." Convinced that this would be an attack on Richard Nixon, who has always been a favorite of many GM executives, General Motors canceled its sponsorship of the entire series.

Threatening to cancel all theater advertising, theater owners in a small town demanded that the editor treat them more "fairly." Specifically: (1) cease to publish news of other towns' closing theaters on Sunday; (2) cease to publish letters to the editor complaining of the quality of pictures currently being shown; (3) support candidates for city offices who were opposed to increasing the cost of theater licenses. The advertising involved provided a considerable amount of the paper's weekly income. The editor compromised.

A certain newspaper supported editorially the right of labor to organize in the plant of an advertiser who was engaged in a bitter fight with unions over that question. Advertising was withdrawn. The paper is said to have lost $200,000.

In cases like these, the only responsible action for a newspaper editor, a magazine editor, or a broadcaster is to check the accuracy of his information and the fairness of his handling, then to carry the information his audience needs. His primary obligation is to his public. And it is from his public that his strength is drawn. If his public is interested and faithful, it will always be profitable to advertise in his medium. Most of the great newspapers and magazines have lost advertisers by refusing to knuckle under, and the advertisers have come back. And although advertising income has been lost in the meantime, the publication has demonstrated its independence and its usefulness, and in the long run has made money by establishing its integrity.

The only possible stance in such cases is fierce independence. The attitude of the medium should be that the advertiser is not doing anyone a *favor* by advertising; it is in his best interest to advertise in a respected medium. A financial reporter for a large metropolitan newspaper reports a case that illustrates the proper approach:

A large corporation withheld for twenty-four hours the announcement of a dividend increase on its common stock, thereby enabling company officials to profit substantially on the resulting market fluctuation. An enterprising reporter discovered the story. It was big news, but the company was a big advertiser. The reporter wrote the story and submitted it to his boss, the financial editor. The managing editor was consulted. All three agreed. The story was published as the reporter had written it. In addition, the newspaper ran an editorial criticizing the company's "reprehensible behavior."

A high corporation official called the reporter into his office and claimed that the story was unfair. The reporter said the executive protested strongly and threatened to pull out advertising. "I told him," the reporter said, "what an interesting story the threat would make for the next day's paper. The advertising stayed."

Another interesting case involved a possible violation of a release date:

The *Wall Street Journal* obtained details of new General Motors models some time before the information was to be released. When the *Journal* published its story, GM canceled $11,000 worth of advertising. The *Journal* was not intimidated.

We do not know whether the *Journal* obtained the information legitimately or was violating property rights in publishing it. This the *Journal* had to decide as responsibly as it could. Having decided that, the editors of the *Journal* rightly judged that the obligation to an important advertiser was subordinate to the obligation to their readers. One of them wrote:

> Would they wish us to print only the banking news approved by bankers, only the steel news approved by steel officials, only the real estate news approved by real estate agents? If our readers thought that every story were censored by the industry or the company which it is covering they would not long have confidence in it. Nor would the situation be any better if we ourselves undertook to censor the news by our ideas of what is "good for business." If we reported only "good news," readers would not find the paper of value even in their own field.[10]

Because they are primarily local, newspapers tend to have more direct and intimate contact with their local advertisers than a magazine has with its national advertisers. But magazines do experience such problems. And broadcasters, both network and local, have them in legion.

From the beginning of World War II until 1961, when he became head of the United States Information Agency, Edward R. Murrow was the pre-eminent public-affairs broadcaster. His *See It Now* was generally regarded as the best series of documentaries ever produced on television. Yet *See It Now* twice lost sponsors because no advertiser wanted to be connected with the controversy the program generated.

Just before the death of *See It Now,* Murrow pleaded with CBS Board Chairman William Paley, "Don't you want an instrument like the *See It Now* organization, which you have poured so much into for so long, to continue?"

Paley replied, "Yes, but I don't want this constant stomachache every time you do a controversial subject."

Columnist Drew Pearson was once better known for his radio news programs than for his newspaper work. But he lost sponsors because no company wanted to be involved in the public mind with the attacks made on Pearson.

Just as any advertiser has a right to decide whether to buy space in a newspaper or magazine, so he has an implicit and explicit right to decide whether to sponsor a program. An advertiser should, of course, put his money where it will do him the most good. The danger, in a medium like broadcasting, is that advertisers who assert their rights force the broadcaster to surrender some of his freedom to serve the public. Only the most responsible broadcaster will continue to offer unsponsored programs.

Should the broadcaster avoid controversial programs? To do so is to ignore the responsibility to explore public problems. Should he shape each program to deliver the widest possible audience? To do so is to fill the air with variety shows, situation comedies, soap opera, giveaways, sentiment, and violence.

It is not just coincidence that the advertisers who put the most money into broadcasting—soap and cigarette manufacturers, for example—are aiming at general audiences. They want to reach as *many* people as possible, *any* people, because a large proportion of any audience will buy soap and cigarettes. This means that such advertisers are not much interested in supporting documentary programs, symphony concerts, and serious drama, for programs of this kind restrict their audiences by their nature and quality. The biggest money in broadcast advertising derives from serving the broadest interests of the broadest public.

This is what makes the position of the broadcaster so difficult. Unlike the publisher, who brings in substantial sums from subscriptions and newsstand sales, the broadcaster has no second source of support. He is always serving two masters, advertiser and public. His service to his audience is restricted by what the advertisers will support.

This problem becomes even stickier when one considers what broadcasters call "adjacencies," which are represented by this case:

A television network dropped an unsponsored educational program and a sponsored educational program with a comparatively small audience, both for the same reason: Advertisers were unwilling to buy time next to these programs. The advertisers (or the agencies) believed that an unpopular program decreases the audience for programs on each side of it.

Thus even the network which tries to absorb unsponsored time, and the few advertisers who are willing to support minority programing, find that the large-audience advertisers exert control. One of the most dismaying aspects of quality programing, and of the plans that responsible broadcasters make to increase it, is the adjacency problem. *Hallmark Hall of Fame* has won many national awards, but its relatively small audience causes other advertisers to avoid a time slot before or after it.

The stickiest problem of advertiser control is in news programing.

Sponsors always insist, through their advertising agencies, that the star of the show read some of the commercials. Many an actor who was sniffy about commercials in the early days of television now reads them and is paid handsomely. Some newscasters will read commercials; others will not.

News should be as objective as possible. Even the tone of voice should reflect the care and objectivity of a dispassionate reporter. But commercials are sales messages whose purpose is to persuade and manipulate. The separation of reporting and selling should be maintained on the air as it is in print. Not only should the advertiser have no control over broadcast news, there should not be even a suspicion of control. Ideally, neither newscasters nor commentators would be sponsored. That would put the responsibility for reliable news squarely on the broadcaster, where it belongs. But news is expensive to gather and produce, and since so many broadcasters believe that it must be sponsored, it is simply up to the broadcaster to nurture the most responsible reporting possible.

We could cite other cases to show other facets of control through advertising—and many heartening examples of fierce independence on the part of publishers and broadcasters. But it is more important to state a basic concern. We are less disturbed by individual cases of advertiser control—damaging as some are— than by the apparent lack of publisher and broadcaster control over misleading advertising. Publishers and broadcasters who are scrupulous about truth and accuracy in news columns and on news programs seem much less concerned with truth in advertising. Although many reject advertising that is obviously false, only a few apply rigorous standards; most seem to believe, at least tacitly, that there should be a double standard. Yet the same public is affected by advertising messages. And the public should be the first concern of the mass media.

When, during the 1960s, Esther Peterson was Special Assistant to the President in Charge of Consumer Affairs, she tried to promote truth in packaging and in advertising. Manufacturers and advertising agencies were not alone in fighting her program. Opposition to her appeal for "full disclosure" of information to consumers seemed to be the first concern of a great many publishers and broadcasters. One of the most shocking speeches during the melancholy period until Mrs. Peterson resigned as Special Assistant to the President was delivered by Herbert R. Mayes, who was long one of the most respected magazine editors. He attacked Mrs. Peterson caustically in a speech entitled "Freedom of Information in the Market Place," argued that consumers don't read package labels anyway, and defended misleading advertising by saying, "I am not opposed to a little misinformation here and there, when it makes one feel good and does scarcely any harm."[11]

Publishers and broadcasters who really hope to serve the public will do well to hold advertisers and agencies to the Advertising Code of American Business, which was developed in 1964, endorsed by more than 300,000 individuals and corporations, and promptly forgotten by too many of them:

1. *Truth.* Advertising shall tell the truth, and shall reveal significant facts, the concealment of which would mislead the public.

2. *Responsibility.* Advertising agencies and advertisers shall be willing to provide substantiation of claims made.

3. *Taste and Decency.* Advertising shall be free of statements, illustrations or implications which are offensive to good taste or public decency.

4. *Disparagement.* Advertising shall offer merchandise or service on its merits, and refrain from attacking competitors unfairly or disparaging their products, services or methods of doing business.

5. *Bait Advertising.* Advertising shall offer only merchandise or services which are readily available for purchase at the advertised price.

6. *Guarantees and Warranties.* Advertising of guarantees and warranties shall be explicit. Advertising of any guarantee or warranty shall clearly and conspicuously disclose its nature and extent, the manner in which the guarantor or warrantor will perform and the identity of the guarantor or warrantor.

7. *Price Claims.* Advertising shall avoid price or savings claims which are false or misleading, or which do not offer provable bargains or savings.

8. *Unprovable Claims.* Advertising shall avoid the use of exaggerated or unprovable claims.

9. *Testimonials.* Advertising containing testimonials shall be limited to those of competent witnesses who are reflecting a real and honest choice.[12]

Until publishers and broadcasters require stricter adherence to these lofty prescriptions, the public can be excused for doubting the truthfulness of advertising—and for imagining that the news columns and news programs, like the ads and the commercials, bear only a general relationship to the truth.

In recent years, the media have been pervaded by volumes of disguised advertising. Radio and television have for so long been guilty of opening the air waves to "plugs" on both news and entertainment programs that it is often difficult to decide whether a guest star on a television variety program is on hand to perform or to promote his opening show at the Boom-Boom Room. In the print media, disguised advertising has grown to the point that it has been given a name—advertorial. An example appeared in the November, 1967, issue of *Reader's Digest.* A special section advocating brand-name drugs over the generic versions of the same drugs was paid for by the Pharmaceutical Manufacturers Association, but only a small box at the end identified it as originating with the PMA. The U.S. Post Office Department charged that the supplement violated second-class mailing regulations. The Federal Trade Commission's Bureau of Deceptive Practices was prompted to warn that publications must clearly label advertisements that "use the format and have the appearance of news or feature articles."

Control Through Favors and Manipulation

Martin Mayer, author of *Madison Avenue, U.S.A.,* distinguishes interestingly between advertising and public relations:

Advertising, whatever its faults, is a relatively open business; its messages appear in paid space or on bought time, and everybody can recognize it as special pleading. Public relations works behind the scenes; occasionally the hand of the PR man can be seen shifting some bulky fact out of sight, but usually the public relations practitioner stands at the other end of a long rope which winds around several pulleys before it reaches the object of his invisible tugging. . . . The advertising man must know how many people he can reach *with* the media, the public relations man must know how many people he can reach *within* the media.[13]

How PR men reach journalists was sketched persuasively in Ben Bagdikian's "Journalist Meets Propagandist."[14] Drawing on his own research and on Senate committee hearings, Bagdikian disclosed that a dismaying percentage of the material used by the media is either inspired by public-relations efforts or supplied by public-relations agencies. Working largely through the syndicates which supply editorials, pictures, news, features, and film to all the media, sophisticated PR men have been able to plant their items so widely that Bagdikian concluded:

It may be time for the executives of great news organizations to reconsider the role of public relations in the news. Public relations is useful, but it has taken over some editorial functions. That it would try to do this is inevitable and it must be said that public relations men are far clearer in their objectives than are editors and publishers. The PR men are bound to further the interests of their clients and they, at least, are doing what they are getting paid to do. They don't have the responsibility of editors and news executives, who arrogate to themselves a crucial and exalted position in American democracy and who insist that they exist and are paid primarily to protect the readers' interests in a fair presentation of significant news.[15]

Shaken by Bagdikian's report, which was written in 1963, a great many executives began to reconsider the role of public relations. It was a process that began much earlier, when one of the standard ways to reach people within the media was to hire them to work in public relations in their spare time. In 1949, the St. Louis *Post-Dispatch* and the Chicago *Daily News* had revealed that fifty-one Illinois newspapermen were secretly on the state payroll. Some seemed to be working for their pay, others were not. The implication was clear that these journalists were being rewarded for political services. Five years later, the Providence *Journal-Bulletin* reported that ten newspapermen were being paid for part-time work by the Massachusetts state government and that twenty-six others were working part-time for various horse and greyhound racing tracks.

The action of the press itself in these cases was questionable. It was some time before the wire services circulated the story of the Illinois case. Then, however, there were many expressions of indignation from newspapers generally. The employees of chain newspapers and some others were fired, but many of the fifty-one were publishers or owners, who simply defended themselves somewhat lamely and continued publishing. In the Massachusetts case, there was little publicity and surprisingly little editorial comment. Fortunately, the trade weekly, *Editor & Publisher,* asked in an indignant editorial why the newspapers generally seemed so unconcerned:

> Why? Is it because editors figure the practice of outside payments is so prevalent in the newspaper business that it is no longer news? Is it because they don't want to "stir up the animals" in their own backyards? Certainly the Illinois and Boston exposés create suspicion that similar situations exist to varying degrees in other metropolitan centers. . . . Periodic exposés of the Illinois and Massachusetts variety do not do the newspaper business any good. They leave readers with the impression that the same thing might exist locally. Only the newspapers themselves can find out if that is true, take steps to correct it, and let readers know what has been done in their interests.[16]

In our view, the editorial was far too delicately phrased. These incidents were shocking, even scandalous. Our whole concept of mass communication rests on the assumption that the media can be trusted to be our eyes and ears in places where we cannot go, and especially to probe into government and public enterprises. In Illinois and Massachusetts, the public was being asked to believe that a journalist could write fairly and objectively, and criticize where necessary, when government and other news sources were paying him under the table.

Fortunately, responsible newspapers have made such practices nearly impossible. They have accomplished this, first, by paying their newsmen enough to remove the necessity of outside employment in most cases; reporters who make $15,000 a year working for metropolitan papers are now fairly common, and great reporters for the great papers can make as much as $25,000 a year.

Many columnists are high in the affluent society. Second, responsible newspapers are properly negative about allowing newsmen to accept any outside employment that may inhibit responsible journalism. When a Philadelphia daily discovered early in 1967 that one of its reporters was accepting money from news sources, the editor promptly fired the reporter and wrote one of the strongest editorial attacks in the paper's history.

The Associated Press, which dismissed an employee in Boston because he had received money from one of the race tracks, has stated a stern policy: "We deem it wholly untenable for any staff member to receive anything of value from any news source, irrespective of its character or purpose and also irrespective of whether the individual is actually in a position to benefit or disadvantage the news source."[17]

If such stern policies applied throughout the world of journalism, there could not have been the curious juxtaposition of items that appeared in January, 1967. One was a column by Hearst columnist Bob Considine which attacked those who were attacking automobile manufacturers. The real problem with auto safety, Considine wrote, was with the drivers, not the manufacturers. At about the same time, the Detroit *Free Press* published a news story reporting that Considine was in Detroit for two days to appear in and narrate a motion picture for Ford Motor Company.

Favors

For too long a time, "anything of value" was a stricter requirement than most of the news media would adopt. Christmas presents were commonly given to newsmen by public-relations agents, and commonly accepted. Free tickets (to circuses, theaters, concerts, and the like) were used by reporters who were covering the events and by others who were not. Free transportation was often given and accepted.

These cases from earlier days may suggest just how widespread such practices were:

A famous heavyweight champion said that in his early days he paid 5 per cent of his purses to reporters to help publicize him. It was apparently an accepted practice.

A sports editor said: "I've been worrying about how much I should accept from the athletic department of the university. Free tickets to the games? Extra tickets? Entertainment? Travel? Gifts at Christmas time? Where do you draw the line? When do you build up such an obligation that you aren't any longer free to criticize?"

A city editor in a small town reported: "Our paper accepted free season tickets to the movie theaters for ten of the editorial and advertising staffs. By tacit agreement we were supposed to publish a pre-written story about the new films when the program changed. And when one of the reporters wanted to start a column of movie criticism, the advertising manager said that was contrary to the agreement with the theaters."

Although athletes no longer pay sports reporters and columnists for publicity—indeed, many stars have begun *charging* for interviews—the dilemma of the sports writer is complex. One bright young writer, David M. Rubin, sketches this picture:

It is a sad fact that what little stimulating criticism of the sports scene exists can be found wholly in the print medium. Radio and television commentators are infected with Coué's disease. They still claim that "day by day in every way" each player in the league is getting better and better, which is rubbish, of course. The electronic sports reporters have become vassals of sponsors and club owners, but that is another story.

The concept of an adversary relationship is a valuable one in explaining the tension which exists between the good news reporter and his information source. In governmental affairs the politician hopes to bury some stories and push others, while the newsman avoids press releases and pursues what he feels to be the relevant facts. This game is played against the background of the public's *right* to know a certain minimal amount about governmental operations. Many believe that except in the area of national defense, nothing is sacrosanct.

But how deep is the public's right to know in sports? Not very. Outside of the score or the winner, the sports fan cannot *expect* any other information. He takes, gratefully and rapaciously, what he is given. The editor of a metropolitan or suburban daily can adopt a *noblesse oblige* attitude without fear of criticism. No one has to be told that sports coverage is superficial. It's been that way for so long that the clever lead, the cliché quote, and the contrived ending are taken for granted.

There are three good reasons for the sorry state of sports reporting, all of them related to the ethics of the business. First is the "phenomenon of the unreportable." On the national political scene, a Washington correspondent soon discovers that there are stories which one doesn't write: legislators tipsy on the floor of Congress; unauthorized junkets; minor conflicts of interest. Hiding such information, however, does not seriously distort political coverage nor encroach on the public's right to know.

But in sports, it is just such "unreportable" information that often determines who plays and who doesn't, who's traded and who isn't. For example, a professional football team, in need of a good runner, mysteriously cuts a powerful fullback. The coach says he "didn't quite fit into our picture," or "his pass blocking was deficient." In reality the player may have been a hotheaded troublemaker or a homosexual, upsetting to team morale. A seemingly healthy baseball player languishes on the bench while his team stumbles into last place. Why isn't he playing? "Can't seem to work his bat into the lineup," says the manager. In reality he thinks the player is too thickheaded to be trusted on the field, and everyone associated with the team knows it, except the fans.

Game plans, the very stuff of football and basketball, are also unreportables. John Scali of ABC news is the center of attention, and rightfully so, when he plays a part in the Cuban missile crisis and keeps the hottest story of the decade under his hat for reasons of national security. But the week before USC meets Ohio State in the Rose Bowl, a Cuban missile sports event, every writer in Los Angeles knows John McKay's game plan, and every scribe in Columbus knows Woody Hayes'. But no one else does. The public is fed only a steady stream of trivia and injury lists (often distorted to lull the opposing coach into a false sense of security). The great early-week strategy battles, where the game is won or lost, never find their way into print.

Other unreportables which should also have a place in comprehensive sports reporting are team morale and individual failure stories. Both are assiduously avoided, although there is no lack of team spirit and personal triumph stories.

A second factor is the position of the reporter as rooter. A man who covers a team day in and day out for months is rooting for the success of that team. He is like a fan, a very privileged fan. Newsmen covering championship teams often receive a World Series or Championship Game ring otherwise reserved only for team members and owners. The sports writer is friendly with players and their families. He has no desire to upset any applecarts. Is it any wonder that he loses his sense of objectivity?

Related to this is a problem which has begun to bother more knowledgeable sports editors. The sports writer provides free publicity to the owners of sports entertainment. A news blackout would be serious, although not fatal, to a team. Thus the management occasionally confuses matters and looks upon the writer as "part of the family" and "interested in keeping the club healthy and happy." This can create serious conflict of interest problems and misunderstandings.

Finally, and most important, is the relationship a sports writer must cultivate with the head coach (in a team sport) or the individual star in golf, tennis, or bowling. There are few other quotable sources on a day-to-day basis. A head coach rubbed wrong can make things quite uncomfortable for an antagonistic writer. He can deny access to players or assistant coaches, to practice fields and locker rooms. This is a serious handicap for gathering what news there is.

The problems in dealing with head coaches are complex. Most fear bad publicity more than they seek good publicity, and they are furious if any item finds its way into print which can be tacked up in a locker room and used to fire the opposition. They also employ their own local reporters as smoke screens to confuse the opposition. Is Jones hurt or isn't he? How confused is the pitching rotation? How strong does he think we are? Much of this goes on with the consent of the rooting reporter.

There are basically two coaching types. The "cliché-coach" moderates everything he says, never offends anyone, fears every opponent, and has said the same things in the same ways for twenty years, AND BEEN QUOTED EACH YEAR IN THE PAPER. The "confider-coach" uses newsmen as a crying towel, pouring out his frustrations and problems on a friendly shoulder. None of this, naturally, is printable, so after hearing the spine-tingling, inside dope, the reporter must get a few quotes for attribution.

So we come to the great paradox of sports reporting. The man at the center—be he manager, coach, or superstar—is of necessity the writer's number one news source; and he is also the worst. Add to this the "reporter as rooter" and the "unreportable phenomenon," and one can understand why sports reporting is superficial in the United States. With no baseline for the public's right to know sports information, there is little the fan can do about it.[18]

The problems on the news side are less vexing, as is suggested by a case reported by a public relations counsel:

Control of the media through favors used to be really critical when PR was just getting started. Finally, the newspapers cracked down on their staffs. Now they sometimes let the auto editor drive courtesy cars and movie reviewers accept free passes, but most of the time the reaction is like the one I got the first time I offered concert tickets to certain members of the Fort Worth *Star-Telegram* staff. Editor Jack Butler answered my letter with a check for two tickets. City Editor Bill Hitch said he had to refuse because of the paper's policy. Later, at the Press Club, I told him that if I'd had any idea that a city editor could be bought for $5 (two tickets at $2.50 each), I'd have been in there long before. He was amused, but it is a good policy, anyway.

This is more than a good policy; it is the only policy for a responsible newspaper. The management which insists that newsmen accept nothing—not even courtesy cars and movie passes—establishes its journalistic independence clearly and positively.

We have been talking primarily about the new standards for responsible newspapers. Unfortunately, a few do not deserve to be called responsible. Somewhat the same point can be made about broadcast news operations. Generally, the news departments of stations and networks are separate from the other departments. Strong traditions of independence were established early in some cases and are as unyielding as those of any newspaper. In others, management has become aware in recent years that professional journalists must handle the news—not announcers who switch from mouthwash commercials to foreign policy. But there are still too many stations which make no clear distinction between news and commerce. The station manager of WIBR in Baton Rouge, Louisiana, said proudly, "Every man who goes on the air here, whether he's spinning records or announcing the news, is a salesman."

There is another danger in broadcast news. Like the newspaperman, the broadcast journalist works in the same building with advertising men, and the product of the journalist is dependent upon the success of the advertising man, and vice versa. But the broadcast journalist also works in the atmosphere of show business, which has long been characterized by exchange of favors. "Plug" and "payola" were coined in the world of entertainment and are still familiar words there. Only the strongest professional sense can prevent the broadcast journalist from slipping into the comfortable ethic of show business. Fortunately, most are able to resist.

It is important to emphasize what is a growing problem for journalists in every medium. An ethic of independence has been firmly established for the general reporter. But the specialist—and specialization is increasing rapidly—is especially susceptible. Sports and vacation editors are often invited to inspect new fishing lodges and resort hotels, many of which are elaborately expensive—but free to the journalist. Nika Hazelton's "Feeding the Food Editor" offers another aspect:

At the recent Food Editors' Conference in Boston, a five-day event organized by the American Association of Newspaper Representatives, the ladies who write the food columns in the nation's newspapers (there are very few men) started their labors with the following dinner: Clams Normande; Turtle Soup with Sherry; Breast of Pheasant with Bread Sauce and Wild Berries, Deviled Ham and Pate Dressing; Wild Rice and Pinon Nuts; Braised Celery; Tomatoes with Pureed Lima Beans; Salad of Endive, Boston Lettuce and Walnuts with White French Dressing; Brandied Pumpkin Ice Cream in Pumpkin Shells; Muster Day Ginger Cookies and Coffee. The whole thing was washed down with Corton Charlemagne, a white Burgundy of the very highest class, and a Romanee St. Vivant, an equally noble red Burgundy. To honor the site Boston Baked Beans and Brown Bread were also served.

The editors were limbering up for a schedule of demonstrations, trips, dinners, drinks, parties and gifts from the nation's leading food manufacturers that can only be called awesome.[19]

The same writer broadens the scope with this:

An editor with a healthy circulation is besieged by public relations firms to go to Peru to inaugurate a new flight, look at olives in Spain, tour the Champagne country, and eat and drink at the most expensive restaurants. A good deal of this wooing is low-pressure and legitimate. Nevertheless, the system is insidious enough. Few people are so callous as to ignore or chastise somebody who's just given them a lovely outing to a sauce manufacturer's island, or a splendid booze bash.[20]

It might seem that the newspaperman and the broadcast journalist should simply decline all such invitations. Many do. But the depth of the problem is suggested by the fact that the vacation editor's trip to the resort, the food editor's five lavish days in Boston, and the flight to Peru will almost certainly enhance each specialist's knowledge of his field. The business reporter who fails to attend the expensive press parties staged by Management Consultant John Diebold, for example, may congratulate himself on his ethics for passing up a $15-a-plate luncheon at the most expensive restaurant in Manhattan, but he may also miss important news or background information; the luncheon is part of an all-day seminar.

Perhaps the only solution is to try to promote the kind of professional attitude exhibited by Percy Hammond, one of the great drama critics. One evening during the 1920s he found himself covering an opening night and was scheduled to leave immediately afterward for a week end at the country estate of the producer of the play. When the curtain came down on the last act, the producer walked over to Hammond and asked, "How long before you can write your review and be ready to leave?" Hammond replied, "About an hour. It won't take me long to slash up *this* turkey."

Manipulation

Early in 1966, *Newsweek* unearthed a confidential memorandum from an old government hand to Vice President Hubert Humphrey. It was a period during which Humphrey's popularity, as reflected by the polls, was going down while that of his potential rival for the Democratic presidential nomination in some future year, Robert Kennedy, was soaring. The memo, entitled "You and the Media," ran:

Your character and personality are being shown to the people in only one way: through the spoken and written word. You are always thought of . . . primarily as a talker and writer. . . . Other facets of yourself ought also to be considered for public understanding. They also ought to add up to a totality approximating your complete self.

You might consider two streams of concern that run strongly through your life:

(a) The reverence and love of life:—the people, family, staff, the wounded, the sick, the hungry, the poor, the dispossessed, the victims.

(b) The defense of life:—the fatherly, brotherly and personal concern that life be preserved, defended, shielded. . . .

These two tumbling courses run steadily down through the stream of your life. . . . During the next years, they will sweep you into a position of even graver consequence to the world. But they must be given a public portrayal that is more honest and open and rounded than the picture of the talker-writer. . . .

The missing elements of yourself must be put back in the picture. They are you in physical action: moving, acting, visiting, climbing, worshiping, hunting, fishing, sailing, boating, hobbying, reading, studying, thinking, sitting, gazing, looking, working, shirt-sleeving, gardening, flying and cooking.

Doing these things will automatically broaden the selection of clothing and the flat image of the correctly dressed gentleman will be enriched by views of the hard-nosed worker, the rough-and-ready woodsman, the cool and steady sailor, the overalled miner, the unstuffed-shirt statesman.[21]

It is impossible to know whether a thousand other memoranda which might more sharply convey the spirit of manipulating images are now reposing in the files of public men. In this age of image building, it seems likely. This memorandum to Vice President Humphrey, however, suggests the method. It is a method that was described precisely by Daniel Boorstin in *The Image* well before the Humphrey memorandum was published: "Now the language of images is everywhere. Everywhere it has displaced the language of ideals." Boorstin is chiefly concerned with what he calls "pseudo-events"; in fact, the subtitle of his book is "A Guide to Pseudo-Events in America." For him, a pseudo-event has these characteristics:

"It is not spontaneous, but comes about because someone has planned, planted, or incited it. Typically, it is not a train wreck or an earthquake, but an interview."

"It is planted primarily (not always exclusively) for the immediate purpose of being reported or reproduced. . . . Its occurrence is arranged for the convenience" of the journalist. "Its success is measured by how widely it is reported."

"Its relation to the underlying reality . . . is ambiguous."

"Usually it is intended to be a self-fulfilling prophecy." That is, to say that something is true, or to act as if it were, leads to the general belief that it is true.[22]

If the Humphrey memorandum should be put into operation, it would be a classic pseudo-event. His posing as a rough-and-ready woodsman and a cool and steady sailor would certainly not be spontaneous; nor would either pose be struck for any other reason than to be reported. The relation of the pose to the underlying reality would be ambiguous. And although Humphrey would not be likely actually to *become* a woodsman or a sailor, or to remain in the overalls of a miner for very long—he is, after all, a talker and a writer—we know enough about images to be able to predict that he would seem to have the qualities of all these people, which is the aim of the enterprise.

It is not enough to say that something of this sort has been occurring from the beginning of political life. It is true that Machiavelli advised centuries ago that "the mass of mankind is always swayed by appearances." The modern point is that image making has become a vast and calculated enterprise of dimensions that any journalist must consider carefully. The transformation of Ronald Reagan from a moderately pleasing actor in B movies to Governor of the largest state in the Union and contender for the Republican presidential nomination was not at all spontaneous. Much of his success can be traced to Spencer-Roberts, a public-relations firm which specializes in political campaigns. Like its famous predecessor in California campaigns, Whitaker and Baxter, Spencer-Roberts does much more than merely try to get the best possible space in newspapers and the best possible time on radio and television for a candidate or an issue. Today, many such firms help select the issues, and in some cases have a commanding voice in picking the candidates—then present carefully wrought images. Polling organizations travel ahead of candidates to determine which issues will appeal to particular sections, and speeches are shaped accordingly.

Now there is nothing illegal about all this. We are concerned not on the grounds of law, or even ethics, but because our theory of communication presupposes a free market place of ideas and confrontation in a free and fair debate. We wonder whether candidates and interest groups with sufficient money to hire skilled public-relations practitioners may some day gain such a crushing advantage that there will not even be the semblance of a free market place.

The journalist cannot reverse the trend toward public-relations counsels and propaganda techniques, but he must at least be aware that these are among the great forces in modern public life. He can be more than a common carrier to transport whatever the expert manipulators give him. He has an obligation to see that all pertinent sides of a question get an airing, and perhaps an equal obligation to report what he can learn about the manipulators.

This is not to suggest that an air of antagonism should envelop reporters when they approach public-relations men. There is nothing wrong with a candidate or an interest group hiring expert public-relations counsel. Indeed, it is unlikely that journalists could perform half so well without the press official or the news bureau officer at hand to supply information when policy makers are busy. Many a reporter would waste valuable time in gathering news in a large organization without the guidance of a press officer.

Still, there is always a potential element of danger when the give-and-take between a news source and a news gatherer is replaced by a relationship between an expert news manipulator and a reporter. We can only hope that the news gatherer will be equally expert at *his* job, and aware of the modern techniques of image building and manipulation. For a journalist to be more than ordinarily suspicious these days is a step toward reporting the news behind the façade.

Control Through Pressure Groups

When Bill Sanders, who had been the editorial cartoonist for the Greensboro, North Carolina, *Daily News,* moved to the Kansas City *Star* in 1963, it was fairly predictable that some Missourians would express their displeasure. Sanders is a liberal cartoonist who ranks with such deft satirists as Herblock, Mauldin, and Conrad, all of whom can flay with pictures. The *Star,* like most newspapers, serves a varied audience which includes a great many conservatives who would prefer that a cartoon somehow say, "On the other hand . . ." No one was quite prepared, however, for the thunderous drumfire of harassment that centered almost immediately on Sanders, and then moved to the executive levels. For a long period, Sanders' home telephone would start ringing at about 8:00 P.M. and ring at five- to ten-minute intervals until midnight. "Stupid," "Nigger-lover," "Communist," and "Pinko" were only a few of the epithets that Sanders and his wife endured night after night. Letters of protest flooded into the *Star* offices. The telephone stopped ringing at the home of Sanders and started ringing at the home of the *Star* editor, Richard Fowler. The John Birch Society and its sympathizers tried to organize a mass cancellation of 10,000 subscriptions.[23]

It was a classic but not unusual campaign. Let a newspaper or a magazine express unequivocal views on almost any subject, in cartoons or editorials, and a violent response is as certain as the dawn. This has always been true to a degree, but violent pressures today seem different in kind. Editors who once considered the attacks of pressure groups part of the game have become concerned. William Burroughs, board chairman of the *Orange Coast Daily Pilot,* pointed out that there is nothing new about attacks on the press: "Ultra-leftists have been trying it for years. Now it is the ultra-rightists. The difference is that the ultra-rightists are making more yardage." Leonard Finder of the Sacramento *Union* has said: "There has developed, in the opinion of some of us, at least, who have experienced it, an organized movement for the purpose of coercing the press to accept the viewpoints of particular groups, especially particular minority groups. So in the end it becomes a question of freedom of the press."

The pressure groups use every available channel. They organize attacks like those on Sanders, and sometimes succeed in depriving newspapers and magazines of subscribers and advertisers. They send committees or executive secretaries to call on the publisher and other executives. Some of the pressures are subtle: personal influence and friendly contacts at clubs or other social and business occasions. They use favors, parties, entertainment. They use threats.

Nonetheless, newspapers and magazines are somewhat less susceptible to pressure groups than are broadcasting and films. Motion pictures are especially vulnerable. The total product of the American feature film industry is not represented by tens of thousands of items, as newspapers are, with their many news stories, features, editorials, and pictures, and as broadcasting is, with its many programs. Instead, a few hundred major films draw fire from pressure groups. Films are national rather than local, their point of origin is usually Hollywood, and thus they are easy to attack at the source. Moreover, films have only one source of support, their audiences.

The strongest pressure on entertainment films has long come from the Roman Catholic Church, especially its Legion of Decency. We should emphasize that its attacks are not necessarily dangerous to freedom. As long as it controls only its own members, it is merely exercising church counsel and discipline. It becomes dangerous when it tries to determine what the larger community should do. In practical terms, there should be no objection to an effort of a religious organization to keep its own members from seeing a film, but when that organization tries to prevent a theater owner from showing a film or when it pickets a theater to try to prevent others from attending, questionable pressure group activity is clear.

Forever Amber was given a C rating by the Legion of Decency, meaning that it was condemned. Cardinal Spellman declared in a letter to all pastors in his diocese: "I advise that Catholics may not see this production with a safe conscience." Cardinal Dougherty, in Philadelphia, gave an ultimatum to the Fox Theater: It must withdraw the film within forty-eight hours or be faced with a boycott of that theater and of all other theaters in the diocese thenceforth showing a film from the same studio. The studio cut and revised the film in consultation with the Legion, then made a public apology. The picture's rating was changed to B (morally objectionable only in part).

Catholic organizations are not alone, as Hortense Powdermaker has pointed out:

Complaints pile into the MPAA (Motion Picture Association of America) office from individuals and organizations. The Women's Christian Temperance Union complained bitterly . . . over the number of Oscars going to pictures or actors portraying alcoholics. . . . The State Department, interested in carrying out a Good Neighbor policy with Mexico, asked that 152 feet of film be reshot because it had shown some mass scenes with a number of children barefooted. . . . The burlesque of a United States Senator was protested. . . . Negro organizations protest stereotyping. Jews protest the making of *Oliver Twist*. Protestants complain that Catholic portrayals are more favored than Protestant ones. . . . Parent-Teachers' organizations protest violence. . . . Members of various occupational groups, doctors, judges, lawyers, policemen and many others, remonstrate against the way they are portrayed.[24]

If the protests were all heeded, Miss Powdermaker concluded, it would not be possible to make a picture with a villain in it! A good many of the protests are heeded, although in recent years, with the economic pressure of television reducing audiences for bland films, movie makers have become increasingly bold.

Much the same kind of pressure operates in broadcasting, which has its network headquarters in New York and is therefore easy to get at. Pressure groups working on the centers of broadcasting have two threats, which are often made explicit: they can exert influence on the advertisers who are the sources of broadcasting's support, and they can exert influence on Congress to pass stricter laws regulating broadcasting and on the FCC to use its regulatory powers more rigorously. The government threat may be the stronger—broadcasting, after all, lives only by virtue of government-assigned channels—and a powerful pressure group knows the lines of power in Washington. But fear of the advertiser is also strong. Advertisers want pleased audiences, not audiences which may turn some of their displeasure about the program toward the sponsor's product.

Such pressures are subtle and many-sided. The feedback from the audience is so slight that broadcasters must make pivotal judgments on the basis of comparatively few letters or telephone calls. "Twenty-five letters will often set a network on its ear," a prominent broadcaster has said. "One telephone call will do it, if it comes from a sufficiently important source. One editorial in the Hearst press can be very bothersome." Some subjects are, of course, more delicate than others. Religion is one. Loyalty is another. General morality is a third. How these combinations work is illustrated by a revealing incident:

The playwright George S. Kaufman remarked on a pre-Christmas program over CBS, "Let's have one Christmas program on which no one sings 'Silent Night.'" This may seem a relatively innocuous remark, and it was made in a spirit of levity, yet it blew up a storm. It was at least obliquely related to religion. Certain religious groups picked it up and complained. The issue was attractive to sentimentalists, who complained that the network was attacking fundamental American values. To make things worse, Kaufman had been the subject of certain rumors (which start very easily in the entertainment industries) about his membership in or association with Communist-front groups. Some highly placed and articulate persons linked the irreligion to a political bias and cried "Commie!"

An advertising agency is said to have picked up the complaints and put on its own pressure about a "Commie atheist" performer.

There was talk of letters to members of Congress and to the FCC. Therefore, although only about two hundred letters had been received, the network found itself in a real crisis. Even then, it might have been possible to solve the problem with a good-natured apology on the next week's program. But by that time Kaufman was adamant. The network issued a formal apology.

Although there is nothing basically wrong with pressure groups conveying their ideas and recommendations to the mass media, their tactics are often reprehensible. Perhaps they feel that less vehement protests will be useless. If so, it is clearly the duty of the media to consider protests and suggestions seriously. The only element of responsibility involved here is that the particular wishes and recommendations of the pressure groups should be considered in relation to the general public good. It is seldom possible to please all groups equally, and it is usually injurious to try. Broadcasting especially seems to need to develop the will to resist.

5   Truth and Fairness

If the end does not justify the means, what does?
—JOSEPH FLETCHER

In the zeal to resist the favors and manipulations of public relations, government, special interests, and individuals, there is a sharp danger that the most powerful instruments of mass communication will run over them. The problem is one of balance. The newspaper, magazine, radio station, or television operation which is most aware of the need to resist blandishments and pressures may develop such a feeling of independence that it becomes infected by what Senator J. William Fulbright has called "the arrogance of power." In establishing their independence, leading journalists are sometimes insensitive, especially to individual rights. The need for standards of truth and fairness is clear.

What are these standards? The codes of the various media—sketched in a later chapter and reprinted in the Appendix—have made some effort to state them. But codes necessarily deal in generalities; and the more they get into specifics, the more quickly they go out of date, and the more likely they are to be limited to what should not be done rather than to what should. Standards of responsible performance in these areas, as in the others we have talked about, must evolve out of decisions and practice reviewed against a concept of the public good.

Codes give us some help in defining the public good as seen by responsible media men. Where else can we seek guidance in defining that elusive concept? We can go to the material that was a chief source of the codes: the laws, rules, and regulations, and the unwritten laws and customs, the values and beliefs, of our society. These, of course, change as society changes. Laws evolve with each decision of a court; values and customs often change very swiftly. As one example of the rate of this change, consider what happened when similar picture stories appeared in *Life* in 1938 and 1965. In 1938, *Life*'s editors took extraordinary precautions before publishing "The Birth of a Baby." They showed the story in advance to responsible officials, wrote to all subscribers to warn them that the story was scheduled, and placed the story in the middle of the magazine so that parents could remove it easily. Still, there was a continental furor. The story was banned in Canada, in Pennsylvania, and in Boston and thirty-two other cities. The 1965 story, which was heralded by a cover picture, was potentially more explosive. Entitled "The Drama of Life Before Birth," it showed the development of a living human fetus. A few readers wrote in to say that the pictures were "disgusting" or "repulsive." But the difference was pointed up by Managing Editor George Hunt: "The response was as emotional as it was in 1938, but it was different in character—more broad-minded and philosophical, more interested in being informed, less bothered by taboos."[1]

Does this mean that it is necessary to make decisions without standards—to decide each new situation on its merits without guides from the past? This approach has actually been recommended as the New Morality, a so-called philosophy with only one principle: anything goes if you say it does. But this is not the kind of new morality we see around us, and it is not what Joseph Fletcher, the most-quoted philosopher of the New Morality, says in his book *Situation Ethics*.[2] He makes clear that the codes of the law, the principles and maxims of the society, are to be respected. But there is only one norm or principle, according to Fletcher, that is binding and unexceptionable: love. "Love is for people, not for principles," he has written; that is, "it is personal—and therefore when the impersonal universal conflicts with the personal particular, the latter prevails in situation ethics."[3] For the New Morality as for the older ones, for the philosopher as for the mass media employees, public good and personal responsibility must be defined jointly out of the public philosophy and law, as one understands those, and out of one's personal concept of values and ethics. These, along with some knowledge of how similar questions have been decided by other responsible persons, are what an employee of the mass media takes with him into each new decision.

It is in this context that we are going to discuss some of the responsibilities of the mass media for truth and fairness.

Accuracy

To understand the journalist's problems, we must remember these facts: Most book publishers spend from six months to a year bringing out a volume *after they have the manuscript in hand.* The average daily-newspaper staff publishes the equivalent of a sizable book every day. A radio or television station is likely to broadcast in words the equivalent of a book a day. A weekly magazine may publish the equivalent in type of a small book; many monthlies publish the equivalent of a large one.

From this perspective, using the careful process of book publishing as a base, we can better understand why so many small, nagging errors appear in the mass media. Indeed, book publishers, who know the care that must be used in publishing, sometimes wonder that the timely media make so few errors.

This is not to say that we should simply marvel that the media do so well. Mass communication is a human enterprise, and human errors are inevitable, but accuracy is still the first responsibility. Most of the great newspapers spend large sums to try to purge their columns of errors, but a small one, the Rochester *Democrat and Chronicle,* has developed an elaborate system that all the media should imitate. Entitled "A Code of Intolerance," the system is designed to improve writing as well as to reduce errors. Wilbur Lewis, assistant to the managing editor in charge of staff training, explains:

Our system is simple. Each day the paper is combed for inaccuracies and lifeless writing. Every miscue, with carbon, clipping, and occasionally with original copy, is stapled to separate reports from writer and editor. The reports are filled out in personal confrontation.

Naturally, the resulting information has helped to correlate types of errors, who causes them, and why.

The first reason is gambling, which does considerable violence to precision.

Ignorance of the language or the facts and attempting to bluster through with inadequate preparation press hard for second place.

The deadliest and most persistent disease we have isolated is "kako-logic hypnosis," a gift term from an erudite colleague, which translates freely into "fixation owing to word habits." The ailment has a mesmeric effect which reality cannot break.

An example is "pantomime." After the fifth or sixth time we found it spelled "pantomi-N-e," we queried half a dozen staffers. All but one spelled it with the mysterious "n." Somewhat similar results emerged in "apertif" for "aper-I-tif," "m-O-latto" for "m-U-latto," and "m-O-mento" for "m-E-mento."[4]

Spelling errors were not all. Instead, they symbolized what many a purist holds: that those who are careless about small matters may also be careless about significant matters. Lewis continued:

The paper convicted a bookseller of violating the obscenity code when he had merely appeared in court.

It reported that the city owed Monroe County more than a million dollars; the reverse was true.

It identified Pierre Salinger as J. D. Salinger, author of *The Catcher in the Rye*.

In a much shorter period than we care to admit, *Democrat and Chronicle* copyreaders shifted the site of a political campaign, wedded a bride to her father-in-law, dumped a man into Lake Ontario instead of Irondequoit Bay, elected the wrong man village fire chief, pushed an engaged girl into wifehood, killed a budget when it was increased, and paralyzed a man who suffered only minor injuries.[5]

But the result of checking painstakingly for such errors and holding accountable those who made them was to reduce inaccuracies by 40 per cent. As Lewis points out, errors are endemic to a newspaper. Although they cannot be cured, they can be reduced to minor disabilities.

The Dangerous Need to be First

"There are scoops and scoops," said R. A. Farquharson of the Toronto *Globe and Mail*, "but the trend which has put the emphasis on being first, right or wrong, has been, I think, the most dangerous single road to irresponsible newspaper work."[6]

The danger was probably highlighted best during the tragic period of the Kennedy assassination in 1963. Each of the hundreds of journalists who covered the assassination wanted to be first with the facts. The results are highly questionable.

Let us be careful to make the problems clear. The chief problem may be suggested by the fact that the most recent precedent was six decades in the past. The President is shot. The natural movement is toward him; this much is certain. But the President is dead—bewilderment reigns. Does the reporter stay near the body to glean the details of death? Or does he try to attach himself to the police who seek the assassin? Or does he attempt to divine the next movements of the new President and move with him? And whatever his decision, what should be his manner, what are his rights and privileges, what is the priority of information in tragedy's hierarchy of values?

Above all, where in the midst of chaos does the reporter find incontrovertible fact? This is the most important question, for one who reviews the journalistic record of the assassination period can recognize the inevitable difficulties, award many high marks for enterprise and diligence, and yet be left with the inescapable conclusion that the press reported many more facts than there actually were.

Item. The rifle was found by a window on the second floor of the Texas School Book Depository. Or it was found in the fifth-floor staircase, according to another report. Or it was hidden behind boxes and cases on the second floor. Ultimately, all reports agreed that it had been found on the sixth floor.

Item. The rifle was first reported to be a .30-caliber Enfield. Then it was a 7.65-mm Mauser. But it was also an Army or Japanese rifle of .25 caliber. Finally, it became an Italian-made 6.5-mm rifle with a telescopic sight.

Item. There were three shots. But some reports mentioned four bullets: one found on the floor of the President's car, one found in the President's stretcher, a third removed from Governor John B. Connally's left thigh, and a fourth removed from the President's body. There was even one report of a fifth bullet found in the grass near the side of the street where the President was hit. Finally, there was general agreement that there were only three bullets.

So far, the mistakes seem to be of no great moment—small discrepancies fairly quickly resolved. But when these conflicting reports were coupled with some of the more mystifying details, the pivotal importance of absolute accuracy became evident.

Item. The first reports of the President's wounds described "a bullet in the throat, just below the Adam's apple," and a "massive, gaping wound in the back and on the right side of the head." The position of the President's car at the time of the shooting, between seventy-five and a hundred yards beyond the Texas School Book Depository, explains the head wound. But how can one account for the bullet in the throat?

Item. The shots were fired between 12:30 and 12:31 P.M., Dallas time. It was reported at first that Lee Harvey Oswald dashed into the house at Oak Cliff where he was renting a room "at about 12:45 P.M." Between the time of the assassination and the time of his arrival at the rooming house, Oswald was reported to have (1) hidden the rifle, (2) made his way from the sixth floor to the second floor of the building, (3) bought and sipped a Coke (lingering long enough to be seen by the building manager and a policeman), (4) walked four blocks to Lamar Street and boarded a bus, (5) descended from the bus and hailed a taxi, and (6) ridden four miles to Oak Cliff. How did he accomplish all this in fourteen minutes?

Item. Oswald was only an average marksman in the Marines. Yet gun experts who were meeting in Maryland at the time of the assassination held that, considering the rifle, the distance, the angle, and the movement of the President's car, "the assassin was either an exceptional marksman or fantastically lucky in placing his shots." The Olympic champion marksman, Hubert Hammerer, said upon being interviewed in Vienna that *one* shot could have been made under the conditions described, but he considered it unlikely that anyone could have triggered three accurate shots within five seconds with a bolt-action rifle. How did Lee Oswald do it?

All this is the stuff of conspiracy theories. Given a mass of conflicting and mystifying detail about the actions of an accused assassin, it is natural to seek an easier explanation. One is that Oswald was not the assassin—but so many of his actions were suspicious. Another is that he had an accomplice—"No one remembered for sure seeing Ruby between 12:15 and 12:45," one report ran—and the mind leaps to the desired conclusion. Small wonder that the Warren Commission's findings are unlikely ever to receive anything approaching total belief.

It is a curious fact that the most involved of the conspiracy theories sprang from those who are usually the sniffiest about journalistic reports, the academicians. Some of them know that the press goes to the authorities for quotations on matters of moment. Deep down, they are likely to suspect authority more than they suspect the press. Thus it was that a political scientist and a historian, Jack Minnis and Staughton Lynd, wrote "Seeds of Doubt," which appeared in *The New Republic*.

This was by far the most remarkable article to appear during the assassination period. Without ever actually saying that someone was suppressing information and rearranging evidence, Minnis and Lynd seemed to be saying nothing else. Their article was a catalogue of conflicting press reports from the time of the first news up to mid-December, and it broadly hinted that the authorities were making changes as they went along in order to bring inconvenient facts into line with indisputable evidence. The tone was typified by the section dealing with the speed of the President's car:

All early accounts of the assassination put the speed of the President's limousine at about 25 miles per hour, but now it has slowed to 15 miles per hour (*Life,* November 29), "no more than half the 25 miles per hour first estimated by authorities" (*Newsweek,* December 9), and 12 miles per hour (*U.S. News and World Report,* December 9). The latter magazine comments: "If President Kennedy's car had been moving even 20 miles per hour, the experts say, it might have made the lead time too difficult a problem for the sniper."

Assessing the Minnis-Lynd article and an accompanying sidebar that speculated about the throat wound and the whereabouts of Jack Ruby at the time of the assassination, one horrified reader commented, "What can it all mean, except the insinuation that Oswald and Ruby *were* connected and that Oswald's death was part of a mysterious conspiracy in which both were engaged and which the authorities are trying to hush up?"

As it turned out, the structure of the Minnis-Lynd article came crashing down only a few days after it appeared. The President's throat wound, it was finally determined, had not been caused by the entry of a bullet but by the exit of a fragment. Oswald had not made his trip in fourteen minutes but in thirty, having arrived at Oak Cliff at 1:00 P.M. rather than at 12:45. The exceptional marksmanship is perhaps best explained by Gertrude Himmelfarb: "But why . . . assume that each of the shots found its intended mark? It would appear that not three out of three but one out of three achieved its purpose (the first inflicting no serious injury and the second hitting Governor Connally). To know how extraordinarily successful or lucky an assassin is, one would have to know how often he was unsuccessful or unlucky." As if to confirm this diagnosis, it was later reported that Oswald had once shot at General Edwin Walker, and missed.

In the end, one must conclude that the press performed in its best tradition. The *news* of the assassination was made up almost entirely of authoritative reports. After all, reporters did not say that a bullet entered the President's throat; they quoted Drs. Malcolm Perry and Kemp Clark of the Parkland Memorial Hospital in Dallas. The Dallas police first identified the rifle as a .30-caliber Enfield and a 7.65-mm Mauser. A Secret Service man said he thought the weapon was a .25-caliber Army or Japanese rifle. The housekeeper at the Oak Cliff rooming house said that Oswald had come dashing in at about 12:45. And so on.

But the central question is whether the best tradition of the press is good enough. To blame a quoted authority is not a defense of the press but an explanation of two errors: the authority's for making a mistake and the press's for publishing it. The lesson of Dallas is actually an old one in responsible journalism: reporting is not democratic to the point where everything posing as fact has equal status.

It must be said immediately that some errors were inevitable. Governor Connally said that the car had just made the turn at Elm and Houston Streets when the firing began. Mrs. Connally said that the car was nearing the underpass, 220 yards from the turn. Both could not be right—in fact, the consensus of observers indicates that both were wrong—but where can a reporter find better authorities than those who were in the car at the time?

Putting aside the discrepancies that are never likely to be resolved, one must ask whether the reporters were too eager to satisfy the hunger for detail and to beat the competition. It is one thing to report certainties such as that the President has been shot and is dead, and quite another to quote a seeming authority—the nearest Secret Service man, a flustered housekeeper—whose speculations breed suspicion. Is the press responsible for the lingering conspiracy theories that surround the assassination? Certainly not entirely, but the impression is strong that a dark part of the cloud which covers events of November 22, 1963, grew from the many efforts to be first with the facts.

Except in time of war, the problem of firstness is seldom important in the newspaper world. Few newspapers issue extras today. The chief pressures are on the wire services; a beat of two or three minutes by the Associated Press or United Press International may determine which service is used by the hundreds of newspapers, radio and television stations, and networks and syndicates which subscribe to both. The broadcasting networks, too, feel the pressure of time.

Someone once defined journalism as "literature in a hurry." News gatherers deal with such explosive material, whether nuclear or social, that the emphasis on getting it right is paramount; getting it first is not nearly as important.

The Problem of Quotations

For a proper perspective on quotations, it is necessary to go back in time. As recently as fifteen years ago, it was thought that since so few of us speak literary prose—or even grammatical prose—journalists should clean up a speaker's grammar. Even the U.S. Congress gives its members the privilege of correcting their statements before the *Congressional Record* is published, it was reasoned, and the President's words during his news conferences could not then be published verbatim without his permission. This case from the early 1950s suggests the attitudes:

A new mayor, whom a local paper has opposed, sounds illiterate when he is quoted directly, although he is forceful and effective. The paper's policy has been to quote directly whenever possible. The city hall reporter inquires whether he should (1) abandon direct quotations when the mayor is speaking, (2) clean up his grammar, or (3) quote the mayor exactly as he speaks and let the people see what they elected.

When this case was presented to twenty-six newspaper editors and publishers, sixteen said they would instruct the reporter to clean up the grammar, and six said they would abandon direct quotations in this case. One said that he would quote the mayor exactly as he talked, and the others said the decision would depend upon other factors. "Some of our best government officials never got an A in English," said one editor. "Why hold them up for ridicule?"

A reporter on a metropolitan newspaper advised:

I'll change a man's quotes when I write the story. How much I change them depends on the circumstances.

If his grammar is bad, I'll correct it if the changes do not alter the substance of the story.

If it moves the story, I'll rejigger the order of his statements. I often condense a number of quotes just to get the nut of the man's message.

The only thing about a man's quotes that is really sacred is his point of view. If you conserve that, almost any other change is perfectly proper. But on controversial or technical topics you've got to be careful and keep the quotes as close as possible to the original statement.

Let's face it. Unless you have shorthand—which every reporter should have and very few do—you cannot possibly get down accurately everything a man says. But you can listen carefully and avoid misinterpreting.

Many newsmen would still agree with the sixteen editors and publishers who voted to clean up the mayor's grammar, and the general attitude of the metropolitan reporter is shared by many others today. Yet it seems to us that, well-meaning as these policies are, they have been outpaced by the instruments of mass communication. How is any newspaper to justify publishing elegant prose from the mayor while radio and television are broadcasting the seedy actuality of his speeches?

We suspect that the old attitudes are dangerous for another reason. The reporter who becomes accustomed to making a few changes here and there where change doesn't seem to matter may unconsciously make other changes that matter a great deal. Truth is the habit that must be ingrained. Does this mean that the reporter is a vacuum cleaner, reporting everything a high official says? Consider this case:

Phil Ault, executive editor of the Indio (California) *Daily*

News, was working in the London Bureau of United Press toward the end of World War II. A flash announcing the surrender of the Japanese came over the wire, and Ault rushed to the British Foreign Office to get a reaction from the official spokesman. Then he wrote a lead for his story, using the man's own words: "LONDON (UP)—A British Foreign Office spokesman, informed that Japan had surrendered, replied, 'Oh, goody.' "

Ault showed his story to another correspondent, and they agreed that publishing it would set the Anglo-American alliance back several miles. He threw it into the wastebasket.

It seems to us doubtful that the effect on the Anglo-American alliance was the pivotal issue here, although we agree that the story should have been junked. There is a difference between speaking to a friend or an acquaintance and speaking for publication, especially in the case of a high official.

The Accuracy of Pictures

Unfortunately, one of the most widely known aphorisms is "Pictures don't lie." In fact, some pictures tell the truth, some tell part of the truth, some mislead, and some lie terribly. The antiunion magazine which covers a union meeting pictorially by showing all the bulging-bellied cigar smokers the photographer can find would have trouble persuading any objective observer that the truth was being served. News photographers and television cameramen are among the first to admit that *what* they picture and *how* they picture it determine whether their pictures reflect reality. Are the pictures typical of the event? Are they natural? Did the photographer or cameraman pose the subjects? Or did the subjects, noticing the cameras, behave unusually because of them? These are among the many questions that must be answered before one can determine whether pictures are truthful.

A photographer of artistic pretensions visited a state park in search of scenics. Glancing down, he saw an interesting arrangement of dead leaves and rocks along a stream. It occurred to him that the scene would be more attractive if he moved two leaves and added another. But then he began to wonder if it was ethical to modify the arrangement he found.

Thirty graduate students who considered this case could not discern an ethical problem. The work, they held, was artistic, and the fact that the photographer wanted to picture reality should not preclude his arranging anything so innocuous as dead leaves. The instructor answered with another case:

At a photojournalism clinic, a veteran press photographer advised: "Always carry a broken tricycle in the trunk of your car. Then if you come to a fatal accident involving a child, you can use the trike to provide foreground interest."

The students were unanimously critical, arguing that the photographer was clearly fictionalizing. It seems to these authors that the students were clearly right in opposing this falsifying of emotions—and that the rearrangement of the leaves is different only in degree, not in kind. One of the most damaging aspects of photojournalism is that too many of the men who make pictures for the mass media treat the truth casually. They become accustomed to arranging pictures and do not know when to stop. The time to stop is at the beginning—with the innocuous little scene of the leaves.

The whole cast of mind that allows arrangements and rearrangements develops habits that lead to such incidents as this:

A news photographer got an excellent picture by throwing a flashbulb into a crowd. Many people were frightened. The photographer was brought before the editor for praise or discipline. He defended himself by saying that there *was* excitement in the crowd, but it wouldn't show without some special stimulus. Throwing the bulb into the crowd resulted in a "truer" picture, he thought, than he could have obtained otherwise.

The photographer's point is similar to the kind of argument made for writers of fiction who attempt to present a "truth that is truer than reality" by changing and embellishing real events. The fiction writer is justified. The photojournalist is not.

The pitfalls of picture journalism are sharply explored by Henry Fairlie:

Not only is the core of television the public and the spectacular, but there is an important sense in which television has a vested interest in disaster. From the point of view of a good story, both newspapers and television prefer covering a major strike to negotiations which prevent a strike. But it is possible for a newspaper reporter to make negotiations almost as exciting a story as a strike itself; by word of mouth he can collect a picture of the comings and goings which are the essence of negotiation and, by his words in print, vividly describe them. But what can television do with negotiations? It can only show pictures of people arriving at a building and people leaving it. However colorful they may be—and the modern business executive is not normally colorful—this does not make exciting viewing.

Violence is the stuff of television, and the question of how to deal with it is the most important one confronting the medium.

To be sure, the same question confronts newspapers, but the impact of violence—whether a boxing match, a riot, or a massacre—is much greater in a moving picture than in a still picture or in descriptive prose. Violence is movement—the raising of an arm, the smashing of it on someone's head—and movement is what television cannot help emphasizing.

In covering violent situations, three distinct characteristics of television conspire to intensify both its special problems and the special temptations to which it is exposed. There is, first, the limitation of time. The lead news story in a newspaper such as the New York *Times* may take twenty minutes to read; in a popular newspaper or a tabloid, as many as ten. There simply is not this time available in television news. In the reporting of all news, this means concentrating to the point of distortion. In the reporting of violence, it means concentration on the violent incident to the exclusion of the whole event.

. . . There is, secondly, television's tendency to produce self-generating news. The problem arose most notably during the disturbances in Watts; but it has arisen, again and again, whenever there have been similar disturbances in other cities. However spontaneous the original outbreak of violence, an external provocation is added once it has occurred. That provocation is the presence of television cameras in the middle of the trouble spots.

This is especially true on the night after the original outbreak. Then, as dusk gathers, television cameramen and reporters move into the streets looking—literally looking—for trouble, and the crowds begin to play up to them. Their presence is very different from the presence of newspaper reporters, who either roam around, hardly distinguishable, or lounge in bars until they hear that action has broken out somewhere down the block. Television, merely by its presence, helps to create incidents and then itself remains part of the happening.

. . . Finally, in this matter of violence, there is the size of the screen: the limitations which it imposes, the temptations it offers. At the end of last summer, television news showed some alarming pictures of white men and women in the Chicago suburb of Cicero screaming abuse at some Negro marchers. Their hating faces—a dozen of them, perhaps—filled the screen. They looked as if they were a representative sample of a much larger crowd. But anyone who was there knows that these particular whites were only a small part of the crowds in the streets; and that the crowds themselves were only a small part of the total white population of Cicero. To this vital extent, television that night distorted badly.

. . . However paradoxical it may seem, the only immediate answer to most of the problems of television news lies not in pictures but in words. Given the powerful impact of the pictures, the words covering them must supply the corrective. Most television reporting just describes the pictures, and by doing so, reinforces them. But the object of words in television news should be to distract from the pictures, to say: "It was not quite so. This was not the whole story." Pictures simplify; the object of words should be to provide qualification and complication. Pictures involve; the object of words should be to detach the viewer, to remind him that he is not seeing an event, only an impression of one.[7]

Fairlie's points are keenly observed. The most obvious failing of television news is the inevitable distortion that grows from looking at a slice of life in a way that suggests that one is seeing the whole of it. It is a failing that television shares with the other media, but the immediacy and the shattering impact of television place upon its journalists a special responsibility. The problem, of course, is that television news is the child of show business as well as of journalism. The showman does not present a comedian with anything like this announcement: "The comedian who is about to appear is a funny fellow when he's on stage, but he's dour and sour at all other times." By the same token, the show business aspect of television news will hardly permit the television journalist to say that the violent scene he is showing must be judged in a broader context —that the news front that day was actually pretty quiet. Does one expect television journalists to say during a political convention that the whole proceeding is quite dull? No, the show business ethic is paramount. And yet Fairlie's point remains: presenting action as though nothing were tranquil is a species of distortion.

It was inevitable, given the character of the medium, that news would be considered by some broadcasters as little more than a commodity. Several broadcasters with a fine sensitivity to the central demands of journalism had long been warning that star newscasters were allowing their personal business enterprises to color their news judgments. These warnings were given increased focus as a result of Chet Huntley's attack, in the course of one of his Huntley-Brinkley television broadcasts, on the Federal Meat Inspection Act—without disclosing his own financial interest in the meat industry. When, however, Congressman Neal Smith of Iowa complained to the Federal Communications Commission Huntley's special interest in the meat industry become widely known. The FCC reprimanded NBC. To NBC's credit, the reprimand was reported on the Huntley-Brinkley television program —by David Brinkley—and the company began to require that employees make known their financial interests. This is an improvement, but broadcast news remains such a tangle of showmanship, commerce, and journalism that there is reason for concern as television devotes ever more attention to commentary.

Another problem with television news reporting that industry leaders must face is brought on by the bravery of cameramen. It can be stated simply: Should a mother be shown the death of her son? Such a question is posed by the intrepid reporting of the Vietnam war: correspondents and cameramen are so close to the action that they can focus sharply on combat, and transmission is so rapid that home television screens show the action shortly after it occurs. Granted, parents have long been exposed to pictures of their dead and wounded soldier sons in newspapers and magazines. But it must be obvious that the immediacy of television multiplies the effect. The question is clear: What is the obligation of television to a thousand mothers who may watch their sons fall in battle?

The Problem of Headlines

"Let me compose a newspaper's headlines, and I do not care who expresses its opinions," L. N. Flint once said. There is wisdom here, for a great many "readers" of a great many news stories do not go beyond the headlines except to read of matters that especially interest them. Moreover, a newspaper's headlines are its showcase. Many a reader glances over them as he would over a table of contents.

The process of building this table of contents is one of the most demanding. The journalist must fit whatever headline he composes into an arbitrary letter count, which is usually very short. If the headline is in two or more lines, he must usually balance them for length. Within these arbitrary restrictions, he must try to give the reader not only an accurate idea of what is in the story, but also, by the position of the headline and its size, an indication of the story's relative importance.

Even beyond that, the headline writer tries to compose a headline with an action verb—if possible in the first line—on the theory that this makes the story seem more interesting. He tries to avoid passive verbs; they supposedly make a story seem dull. In fact, the headline writer is under a constant pressure to create bright and interesting headlines.

The obvious question is whether we are not in bondage to a system that makes it difficult for us to represent stories accurately and usefully. If so, why do we not make fundamental changes—perhaps using label heads or the magazine-like heads which are not so restricted? The concern with this problem is suggested by the observations of R. A. Farquharson, the Toronto editor we quoted earlier:

Headline writing is a difficult, technical job, and because of the typographical limitations it is exceedingly easy to make mistakes. When the paper pushes a desk man for brighter and brighter headings, the number of mistakes increases, and it is not fair to blame the individual headline writer for what should be blamed on the paper's policy.

For years we have worshipped the action headline, but trying to put an action headline on a passive story is an almost impossible undertaking. I think that it is time we revised our whole approach to headings. It is definitely not enough to see that the point of the heading is covered in the story. Sometimes I have seen desk men write into the story an extra phrase to support the exaggeration they had dreamed up. I do not think it is too much to ask that the headline should be a fair interpretation of what the story is about and, if this cannot be done in one style of heading, the heading style sheet should be flexible enough to provide type in which it can be done.

There is nothing wrong with the label heading, and many times it tells the readers a great deal more about the story than the use of words full of sound, which so often signify nothing. In our search for action we often come up with a silly vagueness.[8]

The problem involved in stating complex matters in a few words is clear enough. How *does* one say in five words that the predictions of Free World leaders that the new year would bring peace have been refuted because the United States and the Viet Cong are continuing to fight for complex reasons that baffle almost everyone? It is to be hoped that most headline writers came closer to the goal than did the one who, for the *Wisconsin State Journal,* wrote, "WAR DIMS HOPES FOR PEACE." But it is not really possible to write a strikingly better headline, given the space and time limitations that afflict every headline writer. What *can* be achieved despite the limitations is a devotion to the facts of a story rather than to the headline writer's prejudices. Too often, on a few newspapers, a story that is as objective as a reporter can make it is twisted by its headline. Consider a wire service report on a fiery speech by Ambassador Ellis O. Briggs. The top-of-the-front-page headline published in the Nashville *Banner* read: "AMBASSADOR BRIGGS DISEMBOWELS UNCLE SAM'S NITWITS." (Had Briggs himself referred to those he attacked as "nitwits," the headline would have been justified—provided the word was placed in quotation marks.)

There are similar problems, of course, in the magazine world and on radio and television, all of which have adapted the newspaper headline system to the demands of their own presentations. But radio and television have created a problem that does not exist in newspapers or magazines. By starting most of their news programs with headline items followed by commercials and only then supplying the detail that fleshes out the story hinted at by the headlines, newscasters often create a cliff-hanging strain that the news may not deserve. And news that *is* pointed up by such treatment sometimes casts advertising in an ugly role. Allen R. Dodd Jr., has said, "We are more than a bit disturbed at what seems to be a growing tendency to use urgent headlines as teasers. This could kick up trouble for the advertiser if it continues and viewers have to sweat through commercials to find out, say, if there were any survivors in an air crash."

However the media solve these problems, the overriding problem with headlines remains. It is that too many headlines in all the media are strident, strained, and absorbed in their own immediacy. In trying to attract attention, the headline promises much more than the story delivers. The inevitable consequence of such urgency is that the reader-listener-viewer is let down. His reaction is like that of the New Yorker who was asked why he stopped buying the *Journal-American.* "The trouble was," the man said, "that paper gave me too much for my nickel."

Hoaxes, Jokes, Publicity Stunts

Some of the great circulation-building stories in the history of American journalism grew from science fiction. More than a century ago, for example, a New York newspaper drew thousands of new readers by describing, serially, a trip to the moon. There are few such elaborate hoaxes today, first because of the growing responsibility of mass communication, second because the reality of space travel and other scientific explorations makes fact more flavorful than fiction.

The hoaxes that find their way into the media today are usually small, often innocuous, and nearly always the result of trying to make a good story even better. "Stringers"—part-time employees who are paid by the amount of their material that is printed or broadcast—are often too eager to succeed. Some of them, especially in foreign countries where there is little tradition of truth to guide them, are not to be trusted.

A correspondent in Italy admitted that most of his sparkling feature writing may have been based on doubtful material. He pointed out that most of the hard news from Italy is reported by wire service correspondents and the representatives of a few large newspapers. He and other correspondents handle mostly features. He has come to suspect that most of the feature events his stringers send to him probably never happened. They *could* have happened, for they are in the true spirit of the country. And they are entertaining. The question is whether it is ethical for him to rewrite and send in some of these stories even though he cannot be sure they are authentic.

Editors and publishers who considered this case were unanimously negative. They emphasized that the correspondent and his stringers should simply report the true stories. This seems to us to be the only possible attitude.

Some jokes and funny stories are not quite in the same category with the elaborate hoaxes of another day. The Associated Press once carried a brief feature about a motorist who was stalled on Connecticut's Merritt Parkway and tried to instruct a woman motorist in helping to start his car. He told her that it would be necessary to be moving at thirty miles an hour before his automatic transmission would be activated. The woman backed up a hundred yards and rammed his car while going thirty miles an hour. The story received splashy front-page play all over the country, but on second thought some editors were unhappy. While many admitted that this story "would be remembered when a lot of significant stuff is forgotten," others urged that the editor who let the story go out on the wire should have his knuckles rapped. One AP member was "mildly concerned over the casual manner in which the AP apparently picked up a piece of gossip in a barroom or newspaper column and serviced it as a feature story which later required a corrective item." The proper approach seems to us to be outlined in the Associated Press internal publication, the *AP Log:*

> Well, no blood seems to us to have been spilled on this one, but we don't want the staff or the members filing direct on the wire to get the idea we want to compete with Joe Miller's Joke Book, or to think we enjoy handling correctives. Far from it. However, if we have any more, we hope: (1) the story is as funny and as universally appreciated; (2) it has as plain a warning in the intro: "A motorist from this city sheepishly swears this story is true—but even if it isn't, a newspaper would have to be pretty selfish not to pass it along as he tells it."[9]

A slightly different problem is posed by publicity stunts. Most of them can be recognized at a glance and ignored easily. But if a newspaper or television station wants to run pictures of pretty girls—as most do—it is difficult to ignore the kind of stunt created by a New York public-relations firm. To solve the problem of introducing to the public a new kind of fire starter, the firm hired five Miss Universe contestants to participate in a fire-starting contest judged by a troop of Boy Scouts.

It is similarly difficult to ignore a really inventive publicity man like Jim Moran. It was not always clear what Moran was publicizing—he often spent his own money on various campaigns—but it was probably himself. In Washington, D.C., he taught the public exactly how long it takes to find a needle in a haystack. He dumped a haystack on a Washington street corner and had an incorruptible official of the Board of Trade hide a needle in it. Moran dug in, and proved that a needle in a haystack can be located in eighty-two hours and thirty minutes even if the searcher pauses occasionally to sell souvenir stalks to spectators.

Moran also demonstrated that "Don't fire until you see the whites of their eyes" was a questionable military command. He went to Boston, rented six colonial uniforms and six British redcoat costumes, then hired twelve men to re-enact the Battle of Bunker Hill. Moran, playing Colonel Prescott, bellowed the famous order; his soldiers—carefully chosen for a mixture of marksmen with normal eyesight, myopia, astigmatism, and various stages of decaying vision—sprayed the air at intervals and ended by falling all over each other.

How does a newspaper ignore such inventiveness? The answer is that it doesn't. Nor do we think it should. No paper, no matter how serious, should set itself up as a Society Against Fun. But the editors should be careful to present such stunts in the spirit of fun—with whimsy, with irony, with tongue in check—and ignore enough of them to indicate to space grabbers that the paper is not an easy mark.

Can fun be carried too far?

Tiring of his routine on Saturdays during the football season, a New York sports writer began writing fictitious stories about the spectacular exploits of Sammy Chang, a whirlwind halfback for Plainfield New Jersey Tech. There is no Plainfield Tech. Chang does not exist. But the writer had presented the fictitious feats so vividly that in the balloting for the Little All America team, Chang received the greatest number of votes.

On the face of it, this is reprehensible. Regardless of the fun the writer had, and regardless of the number of readers who enjoyed a long laugh when the hoax was explained, the writer planted the seed of mistrust. If the newspaper prints some fiction, what part of it is fact? Readers have a right to ask.

It is possible to imagine a set of circumstances, however, in which the writer might deserve applause. If he set out to demonstrate the absurdity of Little All America selections—most of which are decided by people who have never seen the players perform—and if it were made clear to the readers later that this was his purpose, a different judgment would be in order.

Correcting Errors

Finally, the modern concept of accuracy clearly requires that errors be corrected fully and promptly. The common rule is that the correction should be given the same prominence as the error.

This is not always easy to do. A one-sentence correction of a one-sentence error in a newspaper can be placed on the same page in the same general position as the error. But is it really as prominent without the same size of headline as the original story carried? Much the same problem is evident in magazines, radio, and television.

The real difficulty, however, is that, by the very nature of mass communication, a correction can never quite catch up with the original error. Not everyone who received the error will also receive the correction. Moreover, the original item started a train of repetitions and elaborations, and the correction is unlikely to follow the same tracks or travel as far.

Thus it becomes evident that the best corrective for an error is to avoid making it. The awesome power of error leads us to understand why one great journalism teacher held that there are three binding necessities: the first is accuracy, and the second is accuracy, and the third is accuracy.

Too often, corrections must be wrung from the media, as reporters and editors give ground in admitting errors quite slowly, and sometimes not at all. This is a human failing, of course, and it may be that the mass media are actually more ready to admit error than other institutions. It is nonetheless refreshing, and all too rare, to find someone saying publicly, "I goofed." This, in essence, was the response of Roderick Cook to criticism of his review in *Harper's* of a novel. Unlike his too defensive colleagues, most of whom lash back when their reviews are criticized, Cook wrote in response, "I would like to refer anyone who has been misled by my review to the better-informed reviews of this book that have appeared elsewhere."

Objectivity and Interpretation

For decades, the most widely understood standard of truth and fairness in journalism was that news reports must be clearly separated from commentary. In newspapers, the news columns were to be as objectively accurate as possible; the editorial columns were to be as persuasive as possible. Noting this, in 1955 President Eisenhower advised the National Association of Radio and Television Broadcasters: "I once heard an expression with respect to newspaper standards. . . . The newspaper columns belong to the public and the editorial page belongs to the paper. And I find that an easy standard to follow and apply as I examine a newspaper. I should think that some such standard could be developed among you."[10]

Unknown to President Eisenhower, radio and television news had already developed a similar standard, with a fairly clear separation of news and commentary.

Today, however, there is widespread confusion about the role of news and the role of opinion in all the media. It is not that anyone holds today that editorializing should be part of the news—that the opinions on the editorial page and the opinions of broadcasters should be mingled with news reports. Rather, the problem is to define the role of interpretative reporting, which sometimes seems to critics of the mass media to be the illegitimate child of the news story out of the editorial.

To gain perspective, let us recall that the development of a quality called objectivity was one of the meaningful accomplishments of American (and a few other) journalists. A century ago, the news was usually filtered deliberately through the biases of the newspaper that carried it. A political figure whom the paper opposed could not expect a true report of his actions; but he probably had on his side a paper which exaggerated his better qualities as much as the opposition paper exaggerated his failings. It was understood that this kind of bias existed, and newspapers were read in this light.

But the growth and strength of the wire services brought an exchange of news, and some of the dissatisfactions with the old standard were magnified. A wire service which served newspapers of differing persuasions found it prohibitive to try to prepare a story to suit the slant of each of its clients. A paper which belonged to a cooperative like the Associated Press might exchange news with a paper of another persuasion. These problems, not to mention the growing dissatisfaction with "slanted news," led to the separation of news and opinion. Thus developed the standard news story, or "straight news" story, which called for the chronicling of sheer fact: objective, factual reporting, dispassionately setting forth a series or group of facts with all authorities and sources noted.

This had become the standard form by the beginning of World War I. The coming of that war heralded a change. It was discovered that the American people had little understanding of the causes of the war, at least in part because of piecemeal reporting. Maynard Brown pointed up the general failure in his criticism of the AP:

Where the Associated Press failed most was in preventing its reporters from sending background and informative articles based on politics and trends. It smugly adopted the attitude of permitting correspondents to report only what had definitely transpired. It wanted no interpretation of events but the mere factual reporting of the obvious.[11]

During the next two decades, the techniques of interpretative reporting began to take shape through the work of such foreign correspondents as Walter Duranty of the *New York Times* and John Gunther of the Chicago *Daily News*. Lesser papers, however, depended upon the syndicated columnists to interpret; they were afraid to change the basic structure of the news story. Moreover, even the great papers restricted interpretation to correspondents in Washington and abroad.

In Washington, straight news reporting of the conventional sort seemed inadequate with the coming of the New Deal in 1933. Some correspondents say they can fix the exact time when "the old journalism" failed: the day the United States went off the gold standard. Vainly trying to report that cataclysmic and baffling change, they appealed to the White House, and a government economist was sent over to help. Then the correspondents tried to explain the new facts of economic life to the American people in the economist's idiom, almost disastrously.

The gathering complexity during the New Deal days, during World War II, and especially when the cold war began, made it increasingly difficult to confine reporting to straight news of the sort that had been developed decades earlier. Reporting what a government official said, or what Congress did, was often misleading; the facts didn't quite speak for themselves. Journalists began, somewhat hesitantly, to build a strong structure for interpretative reporting.

The structure is still developing—and so many editors and reporters are resisting interpretation so fiercely that some of its proponents gingerly avoid the term, preferring to call it "depth reporting" or "backgrounding." For a time, a debate split the top level of the great Louisville *Courier-Journal*. Executive Editor James Pope attacked the interpreters, maintaining that, "by definition, interpretation is subjective and means 'to translate, elucidate, construe . . . in the light of individual belief or interest. . . .' Interpretation is the bright dream of the saintly seers who expound and construe in the midst of the news." At the same time, Editor Barry Bingham was arguing, "The need for interpretation becomes more insistent week by week."[12]

Eric Sevareid wrote:

Our rigid formula of so-called objectivity, beginning with the wire agency bulletins and reports—the warp and woof of what the papers print and the broadcasters voice—our flat, one-dimensional handling of the news, have given the lie the same prominence and impact that truth is given; they have elevated the influence of fools to that of wise men; the ignorant to the level of the learned; the evil to the level of the good.[13]

If it is becoming increasingly obvious that the leading newspaper reporters and broadcasters today favor interpretation, it is not always clear what each means by his use of the term. Perhaps the best explanation was offered by Lester Markel of the *New York Times* in the early 1960s, when he was the most insistent advocate of interpretation:

There are, as I see it, three approaches to dealing with the news; first, the basic facts; second, the interpretation of these facts; third, the comment on them. Thus:

What Mr. Khrushchev says about Mr. Kennedy is spot news.

Why Mr. Khrushchev says these things is interpretation.

Whether Mr. Khrushchev should have said these things and what we should do about him is opinion.

It is crucial that the difference between interpretation and opinion be fully recognized. Interpretation is an *objective* appraisal, based on background, knowledge of a situation, and analysis of primary and related facts. Editorial opinion, on the other hand, is a subjective judgment; it is a definite taking of sides; it is likely to be exhortation.[14]

Markel is arguing here, of course, that the interpretative reporter explains, while those who produce opinion pieces, the editorial writers and the columnists, advocate. Perhaps we can clarify further by setting down a rule of thumb: If the reader (or listener or viewer) cannot discern from the report where the journalist stands with respect to the issue or personality he is presenting, the interpretation is objective.

Thus it would seem that the rise of interpretation does not *necessarily* threaten the separation of news and opinion in the media. It should be obvious, though, that the reporter who is given license to interpret the news—and a great many reporters are not—must be more careful than the reporter who is armed only with the prerogatives of straight news. In *But We Were Born Free,* Elmer Davis stated the problem well:

> The good newspaper, the good news broadcaster must walk a tight rope between two great gulfs—on one side, the false objectivity that takes everything at face value and lets the public be imposed on by the charlatan with the most brazen front; on the other, the "interpretive" reporting which fails to draw the line between objective and subjective, between a reasonably well-established fact and what the reporter or the editor wishes were the fact.[15]

What can be done? Even the small newspaper or broadcasting station without a corps of experts can realize that the bare facts may not be the truth, that a factual news story may be distorted news. It can therefore permit—urge—its reporters to dig into the meaning and background of the news. It can even hold up news occasionally until more can be learned that will put the facts in perspective. Certainly it can demand of its wire services or networks that they provide a full service. And at the same time it can maintain the most rigorous safeguards against editorializing in the name of news.

One reporter gave us a practical problem:

> It is so easy to say, "Let's background that story." But what is background, and what is a knife? For instance: A big man in the shipping business made a statement last week that the United States should have the greatest merchant marine fleet in the world. It was a routine story until I checked the morgue. Just the month before, this man's firm had sold a number of ships to a Greek firm. I mentioned the fact in the paragraph after his quote. He telephoned the editor and charged that I had "knifed" him.

Was the reporter justified? Circumstances alter cases. If the United States merchant marine is not the greatest in the world because men in the shipping business sell their ships to foreigners, the reporter was justified. If, on the other hand, the merchant marine is small because it has so little cargo to carry, or for another reason not necessarily related to the sale of ships, the reporter was dismayingly subjective. The most obvious truth about this case is that finding a clipping in the morgue is not background-ing in the best sense. What we have here is a case of inadequate reporting.

As for sports news:

As sports editor, I am constantly expected to ballyhoo the coming games and fights. Coaches and managers regard it as the paper's obli-gation to furnish that kind of service. Fans seem to expect the editor to take the side of the home team, and to support it in every way. I am treated very well until I criticize the team. Then people get hurt and angry. They complain to the publisher. They say that I have no sense of loyalty, no sense of civic pride. I am hurting the sports program. Take the game this weekend. It is probably going to be a stinker, but if I don't beat the drum a little, I'll be blamed for being disloyal to the program and helping to ruin athletics here. I'm expected to be a kind of unpaid promoter.

This problem is almost exactly like that reported by a society editor:

I sometimes wonder how right we are in giving with the adjectives. For instance, we always write of socially prominent people as the *charming* Mrs. Smith, or President Jones and his *lovely* wife. The adjectives are just part of the protocol.

The adjectives in *both* cases are part of the protocol—a very old protocol that is dying too slowly. Dying it is, though, and anyone who hopes to improve journalism will help to kill it. The color, flavor, and excitement of sports need not depend upon a false loyalty. And the color and flavor of social news need not lean so heavily upon false adjectives. It is true that these habits are dying all too slowly in small towns, but many metropolitan newspapers are now informed by sports writing which is independent, and the old society pages have given way to family sections which bear only a faint resemblance to yesterday's chronicles of the Four Hundred and their friends.

Perhaps the changes in reporting sports and society news are the heralds of an era when the tenets of objectivity permeate journalism.

Balance

Consider a television classic:

The late Edward R. Murrow devoted one program of his *See It Now* series to Senator Joseph R. McCarthy. He began by offering the Senator free and equal time to answer. Then, with a skillful combination of film clips, tape recording, and his own commentary, Murrow put together a devastating attack on the Senator and his methods. In effect, the Senator was used as a witness against himself. In a closing editorial, Murrow summarized his indictment and called for a "reaffirmation of basic concepts of fair play and particularly the elementary right of dissent."

Vigorous objections were made to this program, despite the fact that Senator McCarthy took the free time for an answer. It was charged that Murrow's partisanship was contrary to the kind of balance expected of television. It was charged that television had the power to destroy, and that this power was too dangerous for television to be permitted to use it against an individual. On the other side, Jack Gould wrote that "for once television was a leader, not a passive camp follower, in the realm of public opinion."[16]

Television, like newspapers, may editorialize, although television must give equal time for rebuttal. There is no requirement that each editorial program be balanced pro and con within itself: only that an equal opportunity be furnished for the other side. We are, of course, talking about *editorial* broadcasts, not news broadcasts. We expect news items to be full, fair, and balanced. It is clear that Murrow, by offering his target free and equal time to reply, was fulfilling his obligation.

But is this a misuse of power? Is it fair for the great weight, the overpowering authority, of television to fall on one man? This is indeed a disturbing question, whatever one thinks of the merits of Murrow's program on Senator McCarthy. For if television has the power to destroy, in the hands of unscrupulous men who might have as much skill as Murrow but none of his social conscience, television might become a bridge to demagogy and dictatorship.

It is here that a keen sense of responsibility becomes essential. Television must be able to take stands on issues—and McCarthyism was one of the gravest issues of mid-century America—and it must grant an equal opportunity for rebuttal. Such a system moves important issues into the public arena. On the other hand, as Jack Gould noted, "If Mr. Murrow with his smooth and measured presentation can overnight stir up strong public reaction, what could the hypnotic, reckless, and charming firebrand achieve in like time?"[17]

Thoughtful viewers seem increasingly concerned that television documentaries be fair. When CBS broadcast a four-part series on the controversy surrounding the Warren Report in 1967, a Stanford graduate student named Charlyn Awenius wrote this letter to CBS News President Richard Salant:

I am writing to express my reaction to the third installment of your Inquiry into the Warren Report. The first two installments were interesting, although quite shallow. The sustenance of all the "conspiracy theories" rampant these days lies in minutiae—conflicting details, bizarre associations which foster innuendo. Your inquiry, understandably, dealt only in broad points and, to be fair, I must say that I was impressed by your case against Oswald and by your re-examination of the assassination.

I take particular exception to your treatment of District Attorney Garrison. To be sure, he is a controversial figure, and deliberately so. His case, to date, rests on his supremely confident claims, but little else. As your broadcast rightly pointed out, we must wait for the trial of Clay Shaw to evaluate his procedures and his claims.

CBS News, however, for one reason or another, could not wait for the trial of Clay Shaw to begin its evaluation. In regard to the treatment of Garrison I cite three major objections:

1. The initial tape of Garrison at a news conference. Ethically, the use of this footage is in the fine tradition of Murrow vs. McCarthy: "Let the man hang himself on film." He presented himself as a blustering, egotistical man (which he may very well be—in anger). But in the final phrase of his news conference, Garrison said, ". . . and I thought I had explained all this a few days ago," indicating that he had been angered at the necessity of this second and, to his mind, unneces-

sary news conference. Why did CBS News choose this press conference—Garrison in anger—as opposed to the earlier one?

2. The interview of Garrison by Mike Wallace. Wallace's technique was frankly badgering. I was surprised to see Garrison (whose "mean temperament" had already been established) remain as cool as he did. Although I cannot recapture the Wallace-Garrison interchange, I include it as my initial observation.

3. The testimony of the former Garrison aide. I congratulate CBS News on this interview; the man was powerfully articulate and highly damning. I only wish you had indicated an examination of his credentials beyond the obvious fact that until a few days ago he had worked with Garrison. However, I strongly object to the inclusion of his statement that "only a psychiatrist" could explain Garrison's motivations. Such a statement is grossly irresponsible (although not legally libelous) whether in fact true or false.

Your treatment of Garrison verged on character assassination—a seemingly deliberate attempt to discredit the most potent (in terms of public opinion) critic of the Warren Report. It would seem that, the case and the procedures closed until the Shaw trial, you chose to discredit the man behind them. In sum, I regard this third broadcast as deliberately prejudicial to the outcome of the forthcoming trial. I can but wonder why CBS News, which so many times has withheld commentary for fear of adversely affecting future news events, saw fit to "crusade" at this time.

I must confess a measure of ignorance of the whole affair; I am not an "Assassination buff." I am one of millions of Americans who, for varying psychological reasons, cannot fully accept the Commission's exclusion of conspiracy. It might be said that I know only what I have seen on television, and for this reason I felt this letter was necessary.

It may very well be that Garrison is a double-dealing opportunist, that your broadcast was an attempt to tarnish his glory, to protect Clay Shaw's rights. I cannot know your intention; I can only criticize your means.

It is always more difficult to administer a fair and balanced policy than to administer an unbalanced one. This is true whether one works in the dramatic current of national politics or on the more modest level represented by this:

A hot controversy over fluoridation is raging here, and the newspaper is receiving many letters to the editor about it. The only trouble is that the paper is receiving about three times as many letters on one side as on the other. The question is whether to publish three times as many on one side, or to give equal space in the letters column to both sides of the controversy.

A group of editors and publishers who considered this case voted overwhelmingly to print all the letters, regardless of ratio, if space was available. If the number exceeded the space available, some editors said they would run only those that raised new points, restated old points most effectively, and answered opposition arguments best. Some said they would also run a box score on the numbers favoring each side. Whatever the device, the objective of these responsible news executives was to present both sides of the controversy fairly and accurately.

The responsibility of the mass media, however, is to bring us not merely a true and balanced report of *political* controversy, but a true and balanced report of *all* noteworthy aspects of our environment. Are we able to learn enough through the media to understand foreign relations? Are we able to learn enough through mass communication to derive a balanced judgment of the implications and requirements of the nuclear age? Are we getting an adequate picture of the national government, the educational system, labor-management relations?

When you tell a journalist that the average local newspaper devotes less than a tenth of its stories to all the world outside the United States and our relations with the rest of the world; that only by reading one of half a dozen metropolitan newspapers can one get anything like an adequate picture of what happens at the President's press conferences; or that the media have succeeded in confusing rather than clarifying education—he answers that the news channels carry what will interest the public.

He is right. One of the first things a reporter learns is a list of the items the public is supposed to enjoy: sex, conflict, children, animals, etc. But the real nub of the problem is whether the portrait of man that is held before our journalists is adequate for us in the present stage of civilization.

For it is this concept of man—reading, listening, viewing man—that is chiefly responsible for the flood of trivial features which crowd out the news in our media; for the casting of every possible kind of behavior in terms of conflict, so that we invariably read of diplomatic conferences as a sort of international athletics in which there is a clear victor for every race, and of international athletics in terms of warfare between countries; for the glorification of sex that enables us to know the minutest details of the private lives of Hollywood showgirls while the public lives of public servants are far too often unreported. Is this a fair picture of the nature of man and a fair estimate of what he needs for a picture of his environment?

The most worrisome aspect of the "true and balanced picture" is the sin of omission. Our concept of news interest is based on a doctrine of massness—that the more people who can be brought to read an item, the better public service it is. This reduces news choices to a search for a common denominator. The items that will be universally noticed will indeed be a sexy story (with picture), a sensational murder trial, a cute picture of a child, a bitter conflict over almost anything. But what of minority readership?

The news media recognize some minorities, carrying sports news for the largely male minority of sports fans, home feature news (and soap operas on radio and television) for the largely female minority which has such interests. There are comics and children's programs for youth, business news for the business minority, agricultural information for the farmer.

But what of the minorities interested in news that will make them better citizens? There are, after all, minorities which would like more than the seven or eight foreign news stories they get in an average day from their hometown newspaper. There are those who would like to know more about developments in nucleonics, automation, or education. It is the responsibility of the mass media, then, to serve the minority which has had more than the ninth-grade average assumed for the mass, which has more sophistication than is represented by the eighth-grade vocabulary level which many of our more successful media try to reach.

In recent years, newspapers have been faced with the special responsibility that springs from the one-newspaper city. The energy and imagination which in a multiple situation the newspaperman might devote to beating the competition must be given to creating a market place of ideas. He must seek out opinions and present them in an equitable balance.

In a certain one-newspaper city, the paper vigorously opposes a candidate for national political office. One of its regularly syndicated columnists writes vigorously in favor of the candidate the paper opposes. Should the paper print that column? Since it is part of the editorial offering, the editor reasons, he has every right to omit it because it disagrees with editorial policy. On the other hand, he asks, does not the paper have an obligation to represent the other side on its editorial page as well as in its news columns?

The editors and publishers to whom this case was presented voted ten to one that the paper did indeed have an obligation to publish the column.

A paper is offered an advertisement which follows a line the paper opposes and advocates public action which the paper feels would be detrimental to the community. The paper can (1) reject the ad, (2) accept it and say nothing about it, or (3) accept the ad and comment on it on the editorial page. The publisher gets conflicting advice. His advertising department doesn't want an editorial written in opposition to the ad. Some members of the editorial staff believe that the ad should be rejected outright, others that it should be accepted and commented upon.

By about the same ten-to-one margin, editors and publishers believe the ad should be accepted. The newspaper offers its space for private messages, whether or not it agrees with them; a single-ownership newspaper would be on doubly dangerous ground if it refused an ad. But the newspaper is not obligated to remain silent. It should welcome the chance to state its own view and thus stimulate the functioning of the market place of ideas.

Another case: A wealthy group has been buying advertising attacking G., a school official. G. bought one advertisement to reply but apparently cannot afford to buy more. What obligation, if any, has a newspaper in a single-ownership city to represent G.'s case?

The obligation, it seems to us, is to see that G.'s side is fairly represented. This can be accomplished through publishing letters to the editor, through writing editorials, through interviews with G. It is not necessary to edit with a ruler so that G. gets as many column inches as the opposing group buys. But the management of a paper in a one-newspaper city has a responsibility not unlike the responsibility of a broadcast operation to give one who is attacked a chance to reply. Although a newspaper is not legally responsible, it has a moral responsibility to see to it that G.'s side of the story is adequately told.

Fairness and Privacy

Is it the responsibility of the mass media to mete out justice? Of course it is. For every case tried in court, a hundred are tried in print, on the air, or on film. These are not usually cases at law. More often they are cases involving what society will think of one of its members—whether he has written a good book, whether he is a conscientious and efficient public official, whether his speech made sense, whether he is at least ordinarily good-looking or is ludicrous, whether he is someone to look up to or someone who deserves sneers. The mass media have the power to try these kinds of cases, and they try them every day with the news and comment they carry and with the pictures they show.

Many of the most savage complaints the mass media receive are in response to their reviews and criticisms. Here the main principles are fairly clear; they have been set up by a long tradition of book, theater, film, and music reviewing. The reviewer should be an expert. He should have no axes to grind. He should tell enough about the work of art—and tell it accurately—so the reader can decide whether the criticism is justified. And he should review the work of art, not the artist—except as one must know the artist to understand the art. It is unfortunately true that the mass media as a whole have seldom given proper attention to the arts. Some instruments of mass communication seem more concerned that reviewers be sprightly than that they be sound. To the degree that this is true the mass media are unfair.

It seems obvious, too, that mass communication must be more careful in reporting the actions of those who cannot hit back. An editor reports:

Sometimes the little man gets it in the neck. Just yesterday a motorman operating a streetcar hit a pedestrian who was jaywalking between Twelfth and Thirteenth Avenues.

The story carelessly reported the accident at Twelfth and Broadway, giving the impression that the victim had been in a pedestrian crosswalk zone. There was no libel because the reporter mentioned that the motorman had not been cited.

But the motorman's neighbors got an impression of the accident that was all wrong. The story had emphasized the sob angles. The victim was an elderly lady with a bouquet of flowers in her hand. All the drippings.

Let's say that instead of the motorman one of our socialites had driven into the old lady under the same circumstances. Instead of just stating the driver was not cited, the reporter would have explained exactly how the accident happened. And he would have been accurate in reporting the facts.

The indictment of the newspaper is clear from this, leaving us little room for comment. Obviously, the reporter had let the emotionalism that grows from a story of an injured elderly lady distort the facts. He was obviously unfair to the motorman, who, unlike the socialite, would not be able to hit back.

One of the most difficult tasks in news gathering is promoting fair play for those we dislike. A reporter says: "I can't stand the school superintendent. Frankly. He is superior and scornful and fakes culture. I suspect he's a phony. But he's news—two or three times a week. The problem is how to keep that feeling out of the stories I write about him." This reporter will probably be able to keep his bias from showing precisely because he recognizes his problem. He is under no obligation, of course, to withhold any news which may demonstrate inefficiency or malpractice on the part of the superintendent. But he must be doubly careful, both with his sources and with his evidence, and he must give the superintendent the right to state his side of the case.

In recent years, court decisions have given the media such wide latitude in reporting and commenting on the actions of public men that journalists must be especially careful not to misuse their rights. The rule laid down by the Supreme Court in *New York Times v. Sullivan* was that comment on the actions of public officials is permissible unless malice or knowing falsity is proved. In later cases, the Court extended the rule to public figures—men and women who by virtue of their activities have become public personages. The result has been an extraordinary freedom to criticize and to invade privacy. It is a freedom that responsible journalists must use with care lest the whole structure of the developing doctrine of privacy come crashing down. The right of an individual to his private life, his own thoughts, his own beliefs, has long been valued in Western culture, and it has been given increasing attention in law since a famous article by Samuel Warren and Louis D.

Brandeis was published in 1890. It may be that no other issue of responsible performance is more important than this one.

Public Officials

In general, a public officeholder or candidate for public office puts his career up for public scrutiny. The kind of political philosophy he expresses, his honesty or dishonesty, his skill or lack of skill with human relations, even his morality, are all questions of legitimate public interest, for they help the public decide whether he is a fit person to entrust with official responsibility. But the key question which helps to determine whether or not a particular fact is publishable is: Does it reflect on that person's ability to do the job he holds or is seeking? If so, it is the reporter's responsibility to the public to publish it. If not, it is the reporter's responsibility not to invade that person's privacy by publishing it, unless, of course, there is some other good reason.

A newspaper learned that the mother of a candidate for public office had been involved in a rather messy lawsuit in a neighboring state. This would doubtless be interesting to many readers of the paper, inasmuch as the election was getting hot. Should it be published?

This case is relatively easy. It is hard to believe that a lawsuit involving a candidate's mother some years previously in a neighboring state would really affect the candidate's ability to discharge the duties of a public office. To spread these facts on the public record would be no more than indulging in malicious gossip, and the newspaper so decided.

A newspaper learned that a candidate for public office had been tried for manslaughter some years previously. The man was acquitted. Many voters doubtless remembered the case. Should this be published with the rest of the candidate's record?

This case is a little harder. If the candidate had been *convicted* of manslaughter, that would probably be a fact of importance to the voters. But he was *acquitted*. His record was therefore clear of the charge, and the newspaper should do nothing to retry the case in print. But this particular newspaper was hung up on another aspect of the question. Some people in the town would remember the case, and others would doubtless hear that the candidate had been "involved in manslaughter," without further details. Would it, therefore, be more merciful to the candidate to respect his privacy by ignoring the old case altogether or to respond to the public's right to know the facts by stating that he had been *acquitted of manslaughter?* The newspaper which faced this problem searched its conscience long and hard on this case, and finally decided to quiet the rumors by printing the truth matter-of-factly.

In general, a public figure in a public place is also fair game for photographers and reporters. But there are exceptions.

A news photographer brought in amusing candid shots of a candidate eating at a public picnic. The candidate was obviously enjoying himself, obviously relaxed and unaware of photographers. The table manners he was exhibiting would cause him great embarrassment and might affect his political fortunes. Incidentally, the paper opposed this particular candidate. The photographer argued that the candidate was in public life, and the picnic in a public place; therefore, what the candidate did there was public property. He said the public had a right to know how one of its candidates acted. Question: Would publishing the pictures unduly invade the candidate's right of privacy?

We presented this case to a number of newspaper editors. They split almost evenly on the question whether to publish the pictures, but their comments revealed some important reservations. For example:

We would publish it. A candidate for public office, especially when he displays himself at a large gathering, is exposed to the view of a large percentage of the electorate. There is no reason why the rest of the public shouldn't see him. However, if the "relaxed pose" is sought because the paper is opposing him for office, the picture then becomes as slanted as a news story would be were the reporter to write just the facts the paper wants published.

In other words, this editor is introducing the test of truth and fairness. The candidate probably gives up his right to privacy by appearing at the picnic, but the newspaper is still responsible for seeing that an unslanted picture gets to its readers. They have a right to know, but, in the noncompetitive newspaper world of most towns, the newspaper has a new responsibility for seeing that they have a chance to get a true and balanced picture. As another editor said: "Pictures should not do something we refuse to do in print:

hold someone up to ridicule needlessly. We would be particularly careful in our treatment of a political figure we opposed on the editorial page."

Another kind of problem sometimes comes up because of the *way* a story is obtained.

A reporter got a story by having a drink in a bar with a newly elected public official. The reporter hid the fact that he represented a newspaper, and the official opened up and talked quite freely about his plans for the office—a matter which he had so far refused to discuss with the press. When the reporter revealed his identity at the end, the official was restrained with difficulty from attacking the reporter physically. The reporter admitted that he might have used dubious professional ethics, but argued that any such story which the official was willing to tell a chance acquaintance in a bar should hardly be kept out of the public press.

The official in this case was indeed most indiscreet, and by his very indiscretion robbed himself of much of his right to privacy. Yet it cannot be denied that the story was obtained under false pretenses—by methods more acceptable to spies than to professional newsmen. It is not quite sufficient to say that the official talked freely to an unknown person; anyone is more likely to think twice before making a statement which he knows is destined for the public press, and to grant him the chance to think twice is only doing unto others what any newsman would have done unto him. Therefore, the situation is clouded. When we presented it to editors, we got answers which ran the gamut. Here was one extreme: "Print it. Public official should have discussed his plans freely with press. His plans are public matters. Any means of learning them is ethical, for it is to public benefit."

This is libertarianism speaking, out of three centuries of battling for access to news about government. Yet the logic in this reply is specious, for it states that the end ("public benefit") makes "any means" ethical. Another editor gave this answer:

We would not print the sneaked story as such. We wouldn't think very highly of the loose-tongued official in question, but we grant him the right to know the identity of his audience. I would handle it this way: I would build interview questions around the material the official disclosed, then send the reporter back to conduct the interview. I doubt if the official would refuse to discuss the matter this time, knowing that "no comment" answer would leave him in a peculiar position.

There is little doubt that newspapers and other news-gathering organizations are moving toward this latter position.

Prominent Figures in the News

Another group of newsworthy figures have come into the public eye in a quite different way. These persons have *done* something newsworthy. They have invented something, or created something, or run a mile faster than anyone else. There is no doubt, of course, that the *performance* should be covered fully by all the news media. The problem comes in deciding how far the public's right to know *extends* into the private life of the performer.

Here the media have a somewhat uncertain responsibility. On the one hand, they represent—in this country—the boundless curiosity of the American people. Americans like people; they are interested in how they live, what they do, even how they think; and mass communication has helped to extend this natural gregariousness and curiosity outside the neighborhood by making many distant parts of the country seem almost like next door. Hollywood, for example, is next door to many Americans. Some Broadway columnists and writers have succeeded in making New York seem like next door. Many sports fans feel very close to the great figures and centers of athletics; consider the phenomenal extent of Notre Dame's "synthetic alumni." Now the news media are responsible as representatives of this extended curiosity, which they themselves have helped create. But they are also responsible for the protection of an individual's right to privacy. This results in an uncertain border line.

Let us admit that a majority of such public figures welcome a certain degree of prying into their private lives. Publicity is helpful to them. Favorable mention, of course, is to be preferred, but even unfavorable publicity is usually to be preferred to no publicity at all. For example, actors and actresses thrive on publicity and are usually not too unwilling to have their love entanglements, their tiffs, their home lives described in detail for their fans. Professional athletes, too, usually consider that publicity will help their "box office," and hence their salaries. But the difficulty comes in the case of a newsworthy figure who sincerely wants to avoid the public eye.

A notorious incident involving the right of privacy took place at one of Toscanini's concerts. Photographs had been forbidden, and news photographers were not admitted. One reason for this was that Toscanini's eyes were extremely sensitive to light. A photographer paid his way into the concert and took a flashbulb picture of Toscanini while he was bowing at the end of a selection. The conductor was temporarily blinded and groped his way off the stage. The photographer defended his act by arguing that the concert was news, and the public wanted to see it.

In this case, there was a clear reason why the right to privacy would take precedence over the public's right to know. Isn't the dignity of the press above that kind of trick? Let us ask why the photographer went to such lengths. To protect the people against a dangerous act of government? To reveal a great opportunity or a great threat? No; the suspicion is that he was doing a stunt—showing that he could beat the restriction.

An editor reported this instance: "Like other papers, we sent reporters and photographers to cover the honeymoon of Mr. and Mrs. X, whose marriage had been exciting news. The honeymooners tried hard to give the press the slip, and were naturally quite irritated at being followed. It seemed to me that famous people have to get used to little privacy, but the idea of following them on their honeymoon bothered me a little."

Here, again, the media are under the same kinds of pressure we have been talking about—the entrepreneurs who want publicity for their stars, and the public which has an avid appetite for the vicarious kind of sex experience one gets in such stories. Yet there is clearly a limit on the right of the public to know such things when the individuals concerned do not want them known. Some of the coverage of honeymoons has been nauseating. There was at least one famous example when a press motorboat cruised most of the night around the yacht in which two well-known persons were spending their marriage night. This is hardly worthy of a great and dignified press. On the other hand, some honeymoon coverage is clearly within bounds. For example, when Grace Kelly, an internationally known film star, and Prince Rainier, the head of a sovereign principality, went on their honeymoon, it was only proper that the Prince's subjects and Miss Kelly's fans should be told where they were going, and that the people of Monaco might be permitted to see some pictures of their new and lovely princess taken during the course of the honeymoon trip. This does not mean that Monaco and the United States need know the color of the sheets on the nuptial couch.

Figures in the Backwash of the News

Another group of individuals whose privacy is challenged by the news gatherers are those who come into the stream of the news not of their volition, or because of something they have done, but because of their relationship to some other newsworthy figure. A few examples will illustrate the nature of the problem.

Some years ago, the son of a Senator came to New York intoxicated and was arrested. The Senator was a rabid prohibitionist. Some newspapers played up the story, using the angle of the father's views versus the son's conduct.

There is no doubt in this case that the story is news, and the name of the father, and his position on prohibition, are part of the news. The question is merely how much should be made of the ironic contrast between the father's views and the son's conduct. Many a father has had an erring son or daughter. Many a school teacher has had a child expelled from school or flunked out. Many a minister has had a child who has committed a moral crime. Many a merchant has had a child who stole.

In none of these cases has the child's action necessarily discredited the father, and yet each one has caused bitter grief and disappointment to the father concerned. In each case, the friends of the father have rallied around to try to soften the blow. Only the enemies, and the jealous, have gloated. The suspicion is aroused that a newspaper which played up strongly the contrast between father's views and son's conduct was in the position of gloating over the failure of the father's ideas. In other words, the paper's own attitude toward prohibition or toward the father may have had more to do with how the story was played than did the story's news value.

Another kind of situation is illustrated by the following: A photographer took, and his newspaper published, a picture of a grieving widow at the funeral of her husband. Friends of hers later told him it was a low-down trick: that she obviously wouldn't want that grieving mask preserved in public.

It is worth pointing out that grief is no disgrace, and that the face of a widow grieving at the funeral of her husband is not ordinarily something that should embarrass her in later years. The question is simply: How far does the right to know extend when it represents the morbid curiosity of the public, and how far can the news gatherers conscientiously intrude into personal privacies in order to represent that interest? Certain pictures of funerals—for example, the funeral procession of a President, a President himself entering the church for the funeral of a distinguished man, pall-bearers carrying the casket of a distinguished man—are clearly within the public domain. They are parts of history. But it is worth asking whether a responsible press should not consider itself justified in failing to represent some of the lesser curiosities of its readers, and in leaving individuals alone without benefit of flash-bulbs in moments of grief and intimacy when privacy is most valued.

A reporter, posing as a coroner's assistant, questioned relatives of a man who had died under mysterious circumstances. He got the story, the details of which definitely suggested foul play. He defended his action by saying that all other sources of news were closed to him on this particular case, inasmuch as it was under investigation, and the public was entitled to know the truth. The relatives were angry, and accused the paper of bad faith.

There are two noteworthy elements in this case. One is the fact that officials apparently would give out no news. This is doubtless sometimes justified by the nature of the case, but often does more harm than good. Actually, reporters, when not faced with a blanket of secrecy, have turned up material which has helped solve many important crimes. The reporter in this case, therefore, may have had some justification for impatience. But was he justified in posing as a coroner's assistant? We presented this problem to a number of editors and publishers, and they voted two to one that it was a wrong action.

Except under the rarest of circumstances, a responsible reporter is not justified in posing as anything but a reporter if he is collecting facts for publication. The reporter is not justified, again except under the rarest of circumstances, in obtaining facts or materials.

by trickery. This is true for both ethical and pragmatic reasons. Not only is a news source entitled to know to whom he is talking, but so also is the reporter obliged to think beyond the particular story he is covering to the kind of reputation he is building for his newspaper in the community. Getting one fact by trickery, he may lose a dozen that distrusting people will withhold.

Another kind of trickery, and another aspect of the conflict of the right to know with other rights, is illustrated by this incident:

A newspaper had no photos of a murdered man. The family had no pictures except one, which the wife, for sentimental reasons, refused to lend to the paper. The reporter slipped the picture under his coat while no one was looking. After copying it, and keeping it a day so the competing paper would have no access to it, he returned it. The wife's relatives said that the overwrought woman had been hysterical over the loss of the picture. The photographer said that her attitude was very unreasonable.

True, she was unreasonable. But what the reporter did was stealing. He would never be arrested or tried for it, but he was still outside both the pale of the law and the limits of consideration to a shocked woman. The point that this illustrates is what has been happening to our news-gathering media in the last century.

Our news systems grew up under the severest restrictions imposed by authoritarian governments. They were part of the great revolutionary movements which overthrew this authoritarianism in much of the Western world. In the democratic governments they were set up as the people's representatives to check on government, to see that authoritarianism did not return, that dishonesty or incompetence did not creep in. The news-gathering agencies therefore learned their business under compelling demands of revolution and of a basic responsibility to represent the people's right to know what was being hidden from them. Under these conditions, they learned to get the news by whatever means they could. In general, the right to know and the need to know overrode all the other considerations. They carried this same spirit over to the broader coverage of human events when the fight for governmental coverage was pretty well won.

But in the last hundred years they have learned that human curiosity is boundless and that if the right to know is not somehow bounded it will ride roughshod over all other human rights. That is what has been happening and will doubtless continue as mass communications define their responsibility in a community. The news gatherers have been re-examining their methods and re-drawing the limits of their legitimate interest. We have been trying to suggest the nature of these emerging boundaries.

Reliability

Two aspects of reliability especially trouble the mass media today, and there is evidence that both are becoming more important.

Relations with Sources

One of the most important services a news medium can provide is to state frankly and fully the sources of its information. But this principle must be violated when news comes, as it often does, off-the-record or without clear attribution. Consider these two cases:

About once every two weeks we get a story which we know to be a trial balloon. It has an indefinite source and has to do with a policy which the state government will or will not adopt, probably on the basis of public reaction. Are we justified in playing our part in this little game? That is, ought we to tell the people what the situation is, or just go on printing the stories?

We can't help getting a lot of good material without permission to quote. That is, we can use the material but not the name. We usually publish the story, crediting it to "usually reliable sources" or "an official spokesman" or "a member of the Administration who declined to be quoted." But I wonder whether we are justified in printing something whose spokesman won't stand up and be counted.

There is no simple answer to either of these questions. We believe that the tendency on the part of most journalists to try to cite sources precisely when they can is valuable. We encourage the policy, adopted by many journalists, of reporting that this story or that one is known to be a trial balloon designed to test public reaction. We applaud those reporters who refuse to hear material on a "not-for-attribution" basis when it turns out to be news whose source *should* be willing to stand up and be counted—an attack, for example. But the complexity of modern government sometimes requires a hidden source. This is true not only of stories involving national security. How, for example, is a reporter to determine the truth about a secretive President's actions except by interviewing government officials who cannot be identified if they are to hold their jobs?

The responsible reporter fights to put everything on the record with sources clearly and specifically identified, but he recognizes that this is not always possible. He is justified in cloaking his source if he can answer this question affirmatively: Is it better in this case to inform the public even though the source must be hidden?

Similarly, the responsible editor will require that letters from readers be signed. Most newspapers refuse to print unsigned letters—on the ground that otherwise they would be flooded with crackpot missives. But many responsible papers will publish letters and withhold the signature at the request of the writer. As Flint pointed out: "Sometimes persons not without courage, and actuated by the best motives, may write unsigned letters. Circumstances may render such a proceeding their only avenue of attack upon evil. Of course, in so doing they are asking the newspaper to shoulder all the responsibility. This may or may not be a fair request. But the editor may be expected to decide the question without assuming the easy attitude of contemptuous indifference toward all such publications."[18]

Here is a somewhat different kind of case: An advertiser buys space for editorial advertising but does not want to include his name as the source. In other words, he wants to publish an anonymous editorial in advertising space. The publication rules that he must publish his name as the source of the advertising.

Clearly, the source of editorial advertising should be made known to the public.

Variations on this theme might be spun out indefinitely, but the pattern should be obvious by now. The ideal is a full and frank statement of sources. In a few cases, responsible news handling will dictate that the principle be violated. But responsible media will keep these exceptions as infrequent as possible.

The Problem of Advice

Giving advice might seem to be far from the central concerns of journalism, and yet all the media are increasingly being asked for it. How-to-do-it articles are increasingly popular in magazines. Hardly a newspaper is without one or more advice columns, especially since Abigail (Abby) Van Buren and Ann Landers, Abby's sister, have perfected a formula that draws readers of all ages. "Talk programs," many of which are devoted to advice of one kind or another, proved to be highly successful on radio and are now consuming hours on television. The success of "Action Line" in newspapers has led the other media to develop their own adaptations.

It is important to recognize the chief reason for the success of the mass media in an advisory role: The person-to-person channels that were used when our communities were smaller have been hampered by the massiveness of urban living. It is essential, however, that the media hire the best experts they can find and limit their advice to topics which can be properly treated. No *individual* case of medical or dental illness can properly be diagnosed or treated through the mass media; that is a matter for consultation between the patient and his physician or dentist. There is grave doubt, also, whether problems of an individual's family relationships, of child-rearing, or of love affairs can often be adequately handled by advice columns; these, too, require too much knowledge and are too personal to be well treated by letter and print or broadcast. There is a curve of danger rising from advice about how to cultivate gardens and how to repair furniture and build homes, through advice on how to make out an income tax return and how to interpret the law, up to how to prevent and cure illnesses and maladjustments. The media are on safer ground at the lower end of the curve. They are on safer ground, at whatever point on the curve, if they stick to generalized materials as opposed to individual problems. For example, how to keep food sanitary on a picnic is a safer subject than how to explain or cure a pain in the stomach; and what to expect, in general, of a child between four and six is a safer subject than what to do about a particular five-year-old's particular problem.

This much is certain: When a publication or a broadcasting station tries to take over the duties of a physician, or a dentist or a marriage counselor, or a lawyer, or a psychiatrist, it is in danger of acting irresponsibly.

6 The Negro and the News: A Case Study

> The ability to present news objectively and to interpret it realistically is not a native instinct in the human species; it is a product of culture which comes only with the knowledge of the past and acute awareness of how deceptive is our normal observation and how wishful is our thinking.
> —WALTER LIPPMANN

After the human explosion in Los Angeles that has come to be called the "Watts Riots," the State of California began to look for causes and cures. John McCone, a no-nonsense businessman and former government official who had once headed the Central Intelligence Agency, was asked to investigate the conditions that had led to the riots. The work was well under way when staff executives of the McCone Commission became convinced that their wide-ranging investigation (which eventually employed more than forty staff workers and twenty-six consultants) must probe into the involvement of the mass media. They invited a social researcher to plan a study. The staff endorsed the plan and then, with the researcher, went to McCone himself for final approval.

McCone was instantly and emphatically negative. The researcher had hardly begun to speak when McCone broke in with a long diatribe against journalists, especially their instinct for attack and their sensitivity. It was clear, he said, that any criticism of media performance would be "counter-productive." Not only would journalists react against the section of the Commission Report which dealt with their own derelictions, but their vengeful spirit would jeopardize the entire Report.

To understand the full implications of McCone's fears, one must recognize his stature and be aware of his temperament. He is at the very center of the American Establishment, which is made up largely of those quiet movers and shakers who, regardless of political affiliation, serve and advise the leaders of both parties at the highest levels. (Significantly, Republican McCone has served both Democratic and Republican Presidents. In California, he was invited by Democratic Governor Pat Brown to investigate the Watts riots—and by Republican Governor Ronald Reagan to investigate the student uprisings at Berkeley.) Moreover, McCone is a man of stern, authoritarian temper. One reporter who has interviewed him and was told of his timidity in this case whistled and exclaimed: "But McCone's such a *crusty* old man!" The clear question is: If *he* backs away from the threat of combat with the mass media, how deep are the secret fears of less abrasive public men?

All this helps to explain why nearly every large-scale investigation of race riots has gingerly avoided exploring the role of the mass media. The 101-page McCone Commission Report is typical. In three short, carefully worded paragraphs, it does little more than urge that journalists "meet and consider whether there might be wisdom in the establishment of guide lines, completely voluntary on their part, for reporting of such disasters."[1]

If investigators of race riots had chosen to analyze the role of the media rather than tiptoe around it, they would have traced one of the deepest roots of racial turmoil. And they could have done it almost as easily in Los Angeles and Detroit as in New Orleans and Jackson, Mississippi.

Gradually, officialdom is becoming convinced that the role of the media should be analyzed. In 1967, President Johnson appointed a Commission on Civil Disorders. The fourteenth in its list of charges was to determine what effects the mass media have on riots. The Commission's report, which was issued in 1968, held that "elements of the news media failed to portray accurately the scale and character of the violence that occurred last summer. The overall effect was, we believe, an exaggeration of both mood and content." The President's Commission paid tribute to the balanced factual accounts carried by most of the media, but it charged that important segments of the press "have not communicated to the majority of their audience—which is white—a sense of the degradation, misery and hopelessness of life in the ghetto." Television is especially guilty of flaunting before the ghetto the affluence of most of the white society, the Commission held.

Senator Hugh Scott (R-Pennsylvania) and Representative Durward Hall (R-Missouri) became especially vocal about television after the riots during the summer of 1967. Senator Scott said: "The communications media must meet their responsibility to report the news, but to help dampen the fires burning in our cities they must avoid inciting to further violence by the very manner in which the news is carried." He suggested that the inflammatory speeches of H. Rap Brown and Stokely Carmichael be balanced with the voices of such responsible Negro leaders as Roy Wilkins, Whitney Young, and the late Martin Luther King. And, of course, television spokesmen were able to show that the voices of riot leaders were more than balanced by the voices of responsibility. CBS President Frank Stanton pointed out, for example, that during the three-week period of most intense rioting, Brown had appeared on CBS four times, Carmichael not at all, and Wilkins, Young, and King a total of ten times.

All this is in danger of missing the chief point.

The involvement of the mass media in the cruelest trouble of our time begins long before a riot threatens. The subtlety of this involvement can be drawn from a judgment made by Paul Lazarsfeld and Robert Merton: "Recognition by the press or radio or magazines or newsreels testifies that one has arrived. . . . The audiences of the mass media apparently subscribe to the circular belief: If you really matter, you will be at the focus of mass attention, and if you are at the focus of mass attention, then surely you must really matter."[2]

It is paradoxical but true that at a time when "civil rights" is front-page language, the Negro has not arrived. Only the superstars in entertainment, athletics, and civil rights—like Sammy Davis Jr., Willie Mays, and Martin Luther King—really matter. The everyday world of the Negro and the continuing substance of Negro life in the United States seem to matter not at all. Radio, television, films, magazines, and books occasionally focus on the Negro *plight,* which is only the most newsworthy aspect of his life. Only a few of the most enlightened newspapers give space to the three landmarks of Negro existence: birth, marriage, and death. The sensational papers have their own curious version of Jim

Crow journalism: White men must be involved in murders—as slayers, as slain, or as both—to warrant the biggest headlines and the blackest type. (It is an ironic commentary on law enforcement publicity that "Public Enemy No. 1" is a label usually reserved for whites.)

The white world created by mass communication is more pervasive than any white can know. The late Judge Loren Miller of Los Angeles, who published the *California Eagle* in Watts before he became a municipal court judge, makes the point sharply in describing the effect of white culture on the Negro child: "His concept of beauty is inevitably a picture of the white bathing beauty on the billboards, the white girls who find Coca-Cola so exhilarating on the television, and the beautiful white debs on the society pages. Subconsciously, he knows that his group is set aside and left out. That knowledge builds up the self-hate and self-contempt which is so prevalent in Negro life."

Judge Miller had always been outspoken, but it is usually difficult for outsiders to learn from other Negroes how bitterly they resent a mass culture which is so pervasively white. After the Watts riots, however, Negro intellectuals were eager to make outsiders aware. One who was interviewed, a psychiatrist, veered angrily from picturing the plight of the Negro child who reads comic strips in which "every Superman is white" to denouncing the media because "Negroes are portrayed in ninety per cent of the stories about them as problems." The same kind of point was made in a broadcast interview with a youth leader who works in the Hunters Point District of San Francisco, which was the scene of bitter riots in 1966. Asked why the Negroes of the district smashed television cameras, he replied: "Look, we're trying a lot of good things out here—drama groups, poetry readings, touch football games—and we always ask you reporters to come out and cover them. You never do. We only see you guys when you can show us at our worst."

Some newspapers are apparently aware that their Negro news *is* primarily problem-oriented. A few have tried to make Negro news an integral part of their continuing coverage of community life. Most have merely made it clear that they are luring additional readers. Even if the Los Angeles *Herald-Examiner* was motivated by the most praiseworthy goals when it began issuing a special weekly section on Negro life (a syndicated section not produced in Los Angeles), many Negroes both suspected that the motive was only monetary and resented the segregated attention. Curt Moody of the Community Relations Conference said, "I'm sure that by doing this the *Herald-Examiner* is trying to build up Negro circulation. The question that I ask is: Why can't these same feature articles be included day after day to be read by all rather than featured as something apart from the mainstream of community life?" This is a question neither newspapers nor the other media seem to have thought through.

The result of such estrangement is predictable. Although the Negro has a full opportunity to observe the white world through the mass media—indeed, he can hardly avoid it—communication flows only from white to Negro, hardly ever the other way. The one aspect of the Negro world that most whites are able to experience vicariously through the mass media is riotous and torn from its context. Few whites see Negroes except when the Negro community is inflamed.

It is not necessary to point the case by analyzing a sensationalist newspaper or television station in the bigotry belt. Some of the Negro's firmest friends in the mass media quite unconsciously distort the public view of his life. Consider *Life* magazine, which is editorially so devoted to integration that legions of segregationists have canceled their subscriptions. A study of all the integration-crisis photographs which appeared in *Life* during 1962 and 1963 —a period when most integration protests were characterized by passive resistance—revealed that more than half showed violence rather than passive resistance. In sharp contrast, only 20 per cent of the integration-crisis photographs published during the same period in *Ebony,* a *Life*-like magazine for Negroes, pictured violence, 80 per cent showing passive resistance. Moreover, nearly 10 per cent of all the photographs of Negroes which appeared in *Life* during this period were of Black Muslims, the most fearsome of the organized Negro groups. Only 1 per cent of the photographs in *Ebony* were of Black Muslims.[3]

When reporters talk to Negroes, they often pick the wrong ones. It is easy to suspect that the journalistic habit of interviewing leaders—including Negro leaders like Detroit's two Congressmen —contributed to the shocked surprise when Detroit erupted in

1967. Negroes make the point over and over in interviews that reporters only *think* they know who the Negro leaders are. As in the white world, a Negro who leads one kind of opinion may not lead another. Relying upon the judgment of an NAACP leader or a Congressman about the temper of the Negro community is dangerous. That may be the chief lesson of the Detroit riot.

Cut off from the general world of the Negro, whites are often out of touch with basic Negro attitudes. "Black power" has become to them a fearsome phrase because the most militant and frustrated Negroes have made it seem a threat. In future riots, "black power" is likely to become a battle cry. But this threat obscures the fact that the phrase symbolizes an important and growing change in the American Negro. As one of them points out, there was a recent time when the appellation "black" was offensive. A Negro boy who called another Negro boy "black" either smiled disarmingly or prepared to defend himself. A Negro man considered "black" synonymous with "nigger." Now, however, "black man" is becoming a proud term. One cannot be certain whether this springs from pride in the spirited emergence of so many African nations, from pride in the American Negro's own struggle for civil rights and equal opportunity, or from a combination of these and other reasons. It is clear, however, that the increasing pride in being black which can be observed today among some Negroes may one day submerge the self-contempt that afflicts so many. More than a few Negro leaders and intellectuals who were long suspected of holding themselves above their fellows refer proudly to the black race and speak of "Negritude" in a way that gives it an almost mystical significance. Several intellectuals who were interviewed about Negro publications are quick to say that the newspapers and magazines aimed at the Negro community must be maintained to help preserve the Negro identity. Such are the positive, and largely unrecognized, aspects of "black power."

When whites attempt to bridge this gulf of misunderstanding, they usually communicate ineptly. Those with the best will may use the most wounding words, largely because they know so little of the context of Negro life that they do not know which words wound. Consider the McCone Commission Report, which is so carefully worded and so obviously the product of well-intentioned white men that other white men cannot really analyze it. One of the first sentences reads, "Many Negroes moved to the city in the last generation and are totally unprepared to meet the conditions of city life." This seemed to the editorialists of the mass media who commented on the Commission Report to be so demonstrably true that it hardly deserved attention. Only a thoughtful Negro, Bayard Rustin, could see that the words were written from the point of view of the white man:

The burden of responsibility has already been placed on these hapless migrants to the cities. There is not one word about the conditions, economic as well as social, that have pushed the Negroes out of the rural areas; nor is there one word about whether the cities have been willing and able to meet the demand for jobs, adequate housing, proper schools. After all, one could as well say that it is the *cities* which have been totally unprepared to meet the conditions of Negro life, but the moralistic bias of the McCone Report, involving as it does an emphasis on the decisions of men rather than the pressures of social forces, continually operates in the other direction.[4]

In another section, the McCone Commission Report referred to the repeal in 1964 of the Rumford Act—the California fair-housing law—with: "In addition, many Negroes here felt and were encouraged to feel that they had been affronted by the passage of Proposition 14." Again the editorial writers seemed to nod in agreement with demonstrable fact. And again Rustin made it clear that the words have a bitter flavor for Negroes: "Affronted, indeed! The largest state in the Union, by a three-to-one majority, abolishes one of its own laws against discrimination, and Negroes are described as regarding this as they might the failure of a friend to keep an engagement."[5]

Shortly after the San Francisco riots of 1966, KQED, one of the best educational television stations, invited two Negro spokesmen to an on-the-air discussion of job opportunities with labor leaders and employment officials. Sensing an unusual chance to be heard, the Negroes invited some of their friends. When the program began, more than twenty Negroes and whites were crowded into camera focus, but not for long. The discussion became a shouting match. Just before most of the Negroes walked out—which was well before the scheduled end of the program—one declared angrily that the moderator had allowed the white participants to make their points in full but had interrupted nearly every Negro. For at least a few white viewers, and perhaps for all, it was a startling truth that they had not been able to discern for themselves. One of the Negroes emphasized it by responding to the charge that *he* had interrupted the moderator with "Man, you been interruptin' me all my life!"

If the news media are all but oblivious to the Negro during those long periods when his life is a network of quiet indignities, the contrast is sharp when racial crisis erupts. So attentive have newsmen been to the civil-rights struggle that George Hunt of *Life* has called the time since the 1954 Supreme Court decision which upset the separate-but-equal principle in education "a brilliant virtuoso period in the history of the American press."

Indeed, many journalists not only have made front-page news of racial crisis but have sometimes risked their lives to report it. First in the Southern cities and towns, where many rednecks look on visiting journalists as tools of integration and treat them harshly, then in the troubled cities of the North, the Midwest, and the West, where the black-power elite considers journalism a tool of the white power structure, reporters and photographers have needed courage, and many have shown it. During the long days and nights in Watts when the Negro war cry was "Get Whitey!" and men and women were dragged from their cars and beaten unconscious, white journalists roamed areas that were shunned by armed police. Snipers fired at those on foot and at others in a hovering helicopter. A *Life* photographer was so open and fearless in his lonely forays to photograph scenes of violence that one leader of a Negro mob stared at him in disbelief, laughed aloud at his audacity—and left him unharmed. Many reporters and photographers were hit by stones and bottles, several were beaten, and one was nearly killed by two savage mob beatings in the space of half an hour.

By the standards of professional journalism, it all seemed worth while, for never has a riot been publicized so starkly and in such extravagant detail. During long periods, the police were informed of their own operations in danger zones chiefly through the news media. So intense was the reportage that millions of television viewers could have identified in a police line-up two looters who were followed by the camera as they trudged out of a burning store and down the street carrying a huge couch, and stopped occasionally to sprawl on it and rest.

One may applaud the courage, skill, and enterprise of such journalism and yet wonder: Does intense riot coverage fan more flames than it describes?

We can begin to answer the question by quoting the sardonic observation of a television critic: When the managing editor of *American Opinion,* the John Birch Society magazine, said in a public speech that he hoped to make his first million dollars by cornering the spear concession in Watts, and radio and television stations did *not* race onto the air with the remark, "It was the first instance of electronic restraint on the question of the Los Angeles riots."

Considering some of the provocative statements that *were* put on the air, the critic's judgment is hardly too severe. Hour after hour was given over to broadcasting such a confusing mélange that rumor was institutionalized. "There's a report that one or two policemen are surrounded, so we're going over that way for a look," announced a newsman aboard the KTLA helicopter. The report was wrong, but as with so many other unfounded statements—the Shrine Auditorium is on fire, the Communists are now directing the riots, the Minute Men are invading Watts—the qualifying words ("There's a report," "police believe," and the like) got lost. In the continuing holocaust, rumor merged with vivid fact, and the qualifying words of careful reporters became entangled both in the reality and in the wild comments flowing from those call-in programs which cater to the subliterate. To the unknowing audience, it was all "news."

Even if one considers only the unvarnished facts of the Watts riots, the effects of news are awesome. As Judge Miller made clear, television was a "remarkable organizing force" for the rioters: "All you had to do was sit at the TV and look and you could say, 'Well, the police officers are there and the firemen are there, so we can do something over here.' Now this, of course, was not intentional on the part of TV; it was an inevitable part of the reporting system."

One need not condemn the system to question some of its methods. Los Angeles City Councilman Thomas Bradley pointed out, for example:

In the competition to secure exciting material for radio, television and newspaper, some went beyond the bounds of good judgment. As an example, there was a meeting called on the second day of the riot. This meeting occurred at Athens Park and was attended by several hundred community leaders. With one exception, the speakers were offering constructive ways of dealing with the outbreak of violence and were making suggestions as to how it could be controlled and the participants dissuaded.

The one exception was a 16-year-old boy who made threats that the burning would spread to the white community and made several irresponsible statements. The other people in the audience shouted him down, but this was the one and only phase of the entire meeting which was carried by the communications media.

Bradley is not alone in questioning this incident. Eight days after it occurred, Paul Udell of KNXT-TV in Los Angeles displayed on the air a film clip which showed the youth disrupting the meeting with a shout that he was "going to do the white man in tonight." Udell stated that KNXT had not shown the scene at the time "because we considered it inflammatory in the circumstances. Some stations disagreed."

Some of the other media disagreed as well. So many journalists were so shrill in their selectivity that readers, listeners, and viewers must have imagined that the entirety of Negro Los Angeles was in eruption. It was startling to learn when the Watts riots were over that Police Chief William Parker, a stern and feared critic of troubled minorities, estimated that no more than 1 per cent of Los Angeles' Negroes were involved.

If all this suggests that the news media are not concerned about their treatment of racial minorities, it is misleading. Those who complain that broadcasters and publishers are unaware of their responsibilities are themselves unaware of significant changes. The critics who say that the Southern media remain unreconstructed can cite the case of WLBT, a television station in Jackson, Mississippi, which slanted news of the civil-rights movement so obviously that in 1965 its management was rebuked and ordered to reform by the Federal Communications Commission. Few other broadcast stations or newspapers are as virulent, and none conforms to the stereotype established a century ago, when the Natchez *Courier* reacted to the Emancipation Proclamation in an editorial holding,

"A monkey with his tail off is a monkey still," and the Jackson *Daily News* advised its readers: "We must keep the ex-slave in a position of inferiority. We must pass such laws as will make him *feel* his inferiority."

Today, few Southern broadcasters and publishers are guilty of more than an unconscious bias that will not allow them to see that they view facts from a distorted perspective (a malady not limited by geography). A North Carolina publisher, for example, complained to United Press International: "As a new subscriber to U.P.I., I am beginning to realize why newspapers are so loaded with nothing but racial news centered around such people as Martin Luther King. In trying to get some items worthy of reading last night, I found long and constant harangues coming over the wire about this questionable person during his visit with an even more questionable organization in North Carolina." Checking up, a U.P.I. executive discovered that only one story on Martin Luther King had been dispatched that night, that it reported that King was entering a retreat of the Southern Christian Leadership Council, and that the story was only 150 words long.

Most Southern broadcasters and publishers must stand up to pressure from local communities whose perspectives are far more distorted. Southern media disseminate impartial news of the civil-rights movement from United Press International, the Associated Press, and the national networks and syndicates on a scale that many Southerners consider scandalous. And at least three Southern editors—Hodding Carter and Hazel Brannon Smith in Mississippi and Ralph McGill in Georgia—gave evidence in editorials of such clear understanding of Negro life and aspirations that many of their white readers consider them traitors.

A majority of the news media, North and South, long ago gave up the practice of identifying people in the news by race, except when racial identification is unavoidable. Northern as well as Southern media have been focusing for years on the fact that there are ghettos everywhere, some of the worst in the great cities of the North. Negro faces have been turning up more and more often in advertisements, in news pictures, and in television dramas.

There has also been progress in reporting civil disorder. Shaken by charges that their reporting of riots often has the effect of pouring gasoline on a fire, journalists have been reappraising their own practices. New guidelines were developed in Chicago in the 1950s and spread swiftly to other cities. After the Watts riots, Dr. Theodore Kruglak and Dr. Kenneth Harwood of the University of Southern California conferred with reporters, then drew up more extensive guidelines that have been widely praised:

1. Avoid emphasizing stories on public tensions while the tensions of a particular incident are developing. Ask the law enforcement agency involved whether the developing incident is designated as a disturbance of the peace or otherwise. Report the official designation of the incident.

2. Public reports should not state the exact location, intersection, street name or number until authorities have sufficient personnel on hand to maintain control.

3. Immediate or direct reporting should minimize interpretation, eliminate airing of rumors, and avoid using unverified statements.

4. Avoid reporting trivial incidents.

5. Because inexpert use of cameras, bright lights, or microphones may stir exhibitionism, great care should be exercised by crews at scenes of public disorders. Because, too, of the danger of injury or even death to news personnel, their presence should be as unobtrusive as possible. Unmarked vehicles should be used for initial evaluation of events of this nature.

6. Cruising in an area of potential crisis may invite trouble. Reporters should make full use of the law enforcement headquarters nearest such an area until a newsworthy event occurs.

7. Reporters who are at the scene of an explosive or potentially explosive situation should avoid reporting of interviews with obvious "inciters."

8. Reporters should inform in advance any person who is interviewed that the interview may be made public.

9. Scare headlines, scare bulletins, and sensationalism of other kinds should be avoided in magazines, newspapers, radio, and television.

10. All news media should make every effort to assure that only seasoned reporters are sent to the scene of a disaster.

11. No report should use superlatives or adjectives which might incite or enlarge a conflict, or cause renewal of trouble in areas where disturbances have quieted.

12. Advisory data for discretionary use by newsmen should be written in calm, matter-of-fact sentences. This is to avoid inflammatory results from unintended public report of discretionary information. Honest and dispassionate reporting is the best reporting.

13. Reporters should not detail how any weapon is obtained, made, or used.

14. Reporters should not identify precise locations of command posts of public officials, police, fire units, or military units.

15. Every reporter and technician should be governed by the rules of good taste and common sense. The potential for inciting public disorders demands that competition be secondary to the cause of public safety.

The changes we have noted and the guidelines for reporting civil disorder are certainly valuable, but they do not prescribe the most compelling necessity: to report violence in its full context. That is, the news media must make it clear that the savage threat of the sixteen-year-old at the Athens Park meeting was shouted down by peaceful voices and was not at all indicative of the majority sentiment. They must make it clear that many Negroes, some of them teen-agers, worked tirelessly to persuade the rioters to "cool it." They must make it clear that violence is not total merely because there are episodes of violence. Above all, the news media must focus on *why* there is unrest, and well before rioting breaks out.

The need for reporting inflammatory statements and acts of violence in their full context becomes most apparent when one examines those cities where a quite different practice is in operation—suppressing news of civil disorder. The two newspapers in Dallas, the *News* and the *Times-Herald,* initiated just such a policy in 1960, immediately before a visit to the city by Roy Wilkins of the National Association for the Advancement of Colored People. Felix McKnight of the *Times-Herald* recounts that many of Dallas's civic leaders and news media executives were brought together in the *Times-Herald's* offices. "Out of this, we selected a standing committee of fourteen, seven white and seven black. We set up some standards, some ground rules for both sides—and both papers. It has paid tremendous dividends to the *News* and us, and to the city."

A businessman who is chairman of a similar biracial commission in another city was candid (although anonymous) in describing its operations for *Columbia Journalism Review:*

In my city, we have made progress in eliminating racial friction and in establishing just racial relations because our newspapers and our broadcasting stations have joined in what journalists would call a conspiracy to suppress the news. . . . Local businessmen, drawn largely from the Chamber of Commerce, took the initiative in forming a commission. As ultimately constituted, the commission was made up of businessmen and professionals of both races, representatives of all the newspapers, white and colored, and the broadcasting stations.

. . . There was a public announcement of the original formation of the commission. Thereafter, by agreement, news coverage of its actions ceased. There has not been a single news item published about its meetings, about the particular issues it has discussed, or about the steps it has taken to bring about the desegregation of publicly used facilities.

Here is one example of how the commission has worked: Leaders of the Negro community were especially eager last year to establish the *right* of Negro citizens to eat at downtown lunch counters, where the sit-ins had failed. After long negotiations, the proprietors agreed to serve Negroes starting on an agreed date. In their turn, the Negro members of the commission agreed to select representatives of their race to go to the lunch counters on that date in small numbers. There was no incident, no demonstration. Since that beginning, Negroes have continued to patronize the counters in small numbers, scarcely noticed —because there have been no news stories on the subject.

. . . I am convinced that if these matters had received normal news treatment, the alarm would have sounded among the Ku Klux Klan and the redneck types, and that they would have been there with their baseball bats and ax handles; extremists among the Negroes would have responded in kind.[6]

These arguments are superficially persuasive. It is probably true that agreements to suppress the news prevented violence. And there may be occasions when journalists should fail to report pivotal events—but it is unlikely that these can be foreseen, and unimaginable that responsible journalists should help plan them. It is dismaying to contemplate journalists, who should be committed to breaking through walls of secrecy, helping to build them—especially in the company of civic leaders, many of whom are eager to promote the kind of friendship that leads to country club journalism. Journalists who march beside the First People of a community can neither see nor report the broad sweep of community life. Without a persistent and questioning journalism, civic leaders and public officials are unlikely to push the police into upholding the law when the Ku Klux Klan and the redneck types appear with their baseball bats and ax handles. If they are not held to account, the First People are all too likely to consider the Negro response to bats and ax handles the deplorable actions of "extremists."

The chief objection to these comfortable conspiracies is that news suppression of another kind has helped to create crisis situations. For surely the ingrained habit of gathering news and opinion from civic leaders and officials has long prevented journalists from assessing Negro poverty and inequality. Here the necessity for full context is all-important. We might not now be experiencing such a cataclysmic period had the news media alerted us to the pitiful conditions of Negro life decades ago. The context of history has long been absent. At the very least, journalistic explorations of ghetto existence would have enabled us to understand the violence that accompanies the modern demand for civil rights. Such reportage might have helped make the Negro American an integral part of his society rather than an unhappy graft upon it. Or, as one reader of a penetrating series on Watts by Jack Jones of the Los Angeles *Times* said: "Maybe if these stories had been published *before* the riots, there wouldn't have been any."

The reader was not suggesting, of course, that there is a magic preventive in a series of newspaper articles. He meant that the series would have helped to create a climate of concern about Negro life that might have prodded the community, especially community leaders, into correcting economic and social injustice. Although this is more than a single newspaper can accomplish—it is a national problem—one can imagine a concert of all the mass media awakening the nation to its responsibility. The question now is whether it is too late, whether the hour for understanding has passed. In some cities where the news media are now attempting to report fully on the conditions of Negro life, there is little evidence that they are helping to reverse the tide of violence.

No one can doubt that mistakes have been made in covering riots. But it is also clear that not even the most public-spirited newspaperman or broadcaster could have turned for guidance to any code of ethics; none could embrace all the decisions that had to be made. Nor could the best-informed newspaperman or broadcaster have predicted the full effect of the decisions he made. Responsible performance in a democratic society is a standard that evolves out of a cumulative series of decisions, reflecting a way of life and the needs of a society.

7 Popular Art

> The xenophilic critics who discuss American culture as if they
> were holding a dead vermin in their hands seem to imply that
> in some other, better age the bulk of the people were fair copies
> of Leonardo da Vinci.
>
> —DAVID MANNING WHITE

Even if one can imagine a system of mass communication that is
ultimately free, ultimately truthful, ultimately fair, there remains a
vital question: What is the effect of the mass media on American
culture?

If Alexis de Tocqueville's gloomy analysis was accurate, there is
little reason to speculate about culture in the United States; a
democracy cannot develop a culture of high quality and unques-
tioned merit. In a closely argued section of *Democracy in America,* which was published in 1835, De Tocqueville began by discussing artisanship. Aristocratic nations, he pointed out, gradually
segregate workmen until each craft forms a distinct class. Within
each class, the workers are known to each other and reputations
are built on quality of workmanship. The aim of the artisan is to
stand high among his colleagues, only secondarily to create rapidly
at a high profit, and the aristocrats prize the lasting and the well
made.

In democracies, De Tocqueville argued, no such pride of workmanship is possible. The classes and professions are ever shifting.
Every craft is open to everyone, the artisans are not necessarily
known to one another; the artisan stands in relationship to his
customer rather than to his craft. The customer, unlike the privileged classes in aristocratic nations, is himself a creature of

mobility. If he is rising on the social scale, his desires are likely to grow faster than his fortune, and he tries to acquire the objects of wealth before he can afford them, usually by short cuts that create a demand for objects of synthetic value. The customer who is sinking on the scale retains the desires that were nurtured in the days of his affluence, and he, too, satisfies himself surreptitiously. Together, the mobile publics subvert the artisan. He, too, wishes to rise on the scale, and he perceives that wealth derives from selling many items at relatively low cost. And whether he achieves his goal by developing a faster method of producing his art or by an ingenious scheme for producing more objects, the result is the same: quality deteriorates.

De Tocqueville believed that the effect of democracy runs still deeper:

Something analogous to what I have already pointed out in the useful arts then takes place in the fine arts; the productions of artists are more numerous, but the merit of each production is diminished. No longer able to soar to what is great, they cultivate what is pretty and elegant, and appearance is more attended to than reality.

In aristocracies a few great pictures are produced; in democratic countries a vast number of insignificant ones. In the former, statues are raised of bronze: in the latter, they are modeled in plaster.[1]

Dwight Macdonald, who has seldom been accused of aristocratic leanings—indeed, he is far to the left politically—evaluated American culture in somewhat the same terms. "The conservative proposal to save culture by restoring the old class lines," he has written, "has a more solid historical base than the Marxian hope for a new democratic, classless culture, for, with the possible (and important) exception of Periclean Athens, all the great cultures of the past were elite cultures." But Macdonald adds that the conservative solution "is without meaning in a world dominated by the two great mass nations, U.S.A. and U.S.S.R., and becoming more industrialized, massified all the time."[2]

Macdonald sees three different cultures in America: High Culture, Mass Culture, and Folk Art (which are roughly analogous to the division of Americans into high-brows, middle-brows, and low-brows). High Culture is the sort that De Tocqueville praised: the painstaking work of rich talent and genius carried to the ultimate degree for the sake of art. Mass Culture is De Tocqueville's art of the market place—appealing and not quite genuine because it aims at mass consumption rather than at perfection. Folk Art is the natural talent (usually of one who would be classified as a lowbrow on an intellectual scale) expressed in folk songs, spirituals, primitive drawings, and the like.

Although Macdonald's categories seem to leave little to complain about—there is, after all, room for all tastes in one or another of the divisions—he is actually as gloomy about American culture as De Tocqueville was. For the appeal and the rewards of Mass Culture (which the Germans derisively term *Kitsch*) have been gradually affecting High Culture and Folk Art:

> If there were a clearly defined cultural elite, then the masses could have their *kitsch* and the elite could have its High Culture, with everybody happy. But, the boundary line is blurred. A statistically significant part of the population, I venture to guess, is chronically confronted with the choice of going to the movies or going to a concert, between reading Tolstoy or a detective story, between looking at old masters or at a TV show: i.e., the pattern of their cultural lives is "open" to the point of being porous. Good art competes with *kitsch,* serious ideas compete with commercialized formulas—and the advantage lies all on one side. There seems to be a Gresham's Law in cultural as well as monetary circulation: bad stuff drives out the good, since it is more easily understood and enjoyed. It is this facility of access which at once sells *kitsch* on a wide market and also prevents it from achieving quality.[3]

Macdonald thus argues that Mass Culture is not just bad in and of itself: it homogenizes all culture and debases the entire spectrum. Clement Greenberg agrees, holding that *Kitsch* "predigests art for the spectator and spares him effort, provides him with a shortcut to the pleasures of art that detours what is necessarily difficult in genuine art."[4]

It is a curious commentary on the validity of these criticisms that Dwight Macdonald's own career seems to bear out his chief contention. In "A Theory of Popular Culture," which he wrote for his own little High Culture magazine, *Politics,* in 1944, Macdonald began developing the notion that the apostle of High Culture must be staunch to resist the blandishments of *Kitsch*. In "A Theory of Mass Culture," which was the article in *Politics* further developed for publication in *Diogenes* in 1953, Macdonald listed *The New Yorker* among the magazines that debase High Culture. Its short stories, he wrote, are "smooth, minor-key, casual, suggesting drama and sentiment without ever being crude enough to create it"; *New Yorker* editors developed the style by skillfully selecting in the same way a gardener develops a new kind of rose. Then, a few years later, almost as though he were proving his point that High Culture is gradually enveloped in Mass Culture, Macdonald became a writer for *The New Yorker*. The final irony came when he began writing film criticism for *Esquire,* which, more than any other magazine, resembles Macdonald's own description of the publication that borrows from and subverts High Culture.[5]

If one accepts the premises of these critics, it is extraordinarily difficult to avoid their conclusions. But there is, of course, another side of the coin, which is not likely to be seen without looking at the conditions that obtained in the last century. As they were presented by Walt Whitman, the conditions set forth entirely different premises.[6]

Much of the acclaim for Whitman springs from his poetry celebrating The People—the great, ill-defined masses that were beginning to loom on every side after the middle of the nineteenth century. But Whitman's lasting contribution may have come with the writing of *Democratic Vistas* in 1871. In it he argued for a clean break with the art of aristocratic nations. The United States was different in scope and way of life from Europe. Why should not the culture be different as well? Whitman wrote:

I should demand a program of culture, drawn out, not for a single class alone, or for the parlors or lecture rooms, but with an eye to the practical life, the west, the workingman, the facts of farms and jackplanes and engineers. . . . I should demand of this program or theory a scope generous enough to include the widest human area. It must have for its spinal meaning the formation of a typical personality of character, eligible to the uses of the high average of men . . . and not restricted by conditions ineligible to the masses. The best culture will always be that of the manly courageous instincts, and loving perceptions, and of self-respect—aiming to form, over this continent, an ideocrasy of universalism.[7]

The rapid development of urban life in the twentieth century has, of course, dictated quite different conditions from any Whitman could have imagined. His appeal for a democratic culture to reflect the pioneer spirit seems quaint in these times. But some modern observers have provided modern echoes of the original call for a democratic culture. James T. Farrell has asked his fellow writers to "recreate and thus communicate how the mass of the people live, how they feel about working, loving, enjoying, suffering, and dying." In *The Great Audience,* Gilbert Seldes laments that the artist in America has often gone abroad to seek recognition:

. . . From the time of James Fenimore Cooper to the day of Sinclair Lewis, writers have found some way to attack the average American, not in loving correction but in contempt. In all that time perhaps two dozen men and women have been artists so great that they were misunderstood; the rest were good, but not good enough to separate themselves from their fellow men; they made little effort to understand what was happening in America, were incapable of helping or guiding or comforting. The theory that the artist was respected by Americans because he disclosed the emptiness of their lives is only half true; the other half is that the artist had little to give Americans, little that was relevant to their time and situation in the world. "The American intelligentsia," says Eric Bentley, "consists of people isolated from their communities." The isolation is partly self-exile.

Perspective on this long separation between the artist and the people is helpful in understanding the present relation between them. The "misunderstood" artist of the past has given way to the one who no longer cares whether he is understood or not, since he is not trying to communicate anything in the traditional sense of the word.[8]

Although there are stark differences between the critics who argue that only an aristocratically oriented culture is viable and those who contend that there is a deep need for democratic culture, they are united in criticism of the mass media. This is entirely understandable: aspects of art—some drawings and music, for example—exist quite apart from the modern instruments of communication, but the great bulk of Mass Culture is carried by the mass media. In fact, the most severe criticisms of American culture from both factions center on the world of newspapers, magazines, radio, television, books, and films. Were they not so pervasive, the critics argue, Mass Culture would not be so overwhelming. And were the rewards of the mass media not so alluring, Mass Culture would not find it so easy to subvert High Culture and Folk Art.

It must be obvious, however, that those who argue for an aristocratic culture are the more caustic critics of the mass media: The very existence of instruments that can reach everyone is antithetical to the notion of a cultural elite. Ernest van den Haag dismisses them contemptuously:

> The circumstances which permit the experience of art are rare in our society anyway and they cannot be expected in the audience of mass media. That audience is dispersed and heterogeneous, and though it listens often, it does so intermittently and poised to leave if not immediately enthralled and kept amused. . . . And the conditions and conditioning of the audience demand a mad mixture of important and trivial matters, atom bombs, hit tunes, symphonies, B.O., sob stories, hotcha girls, round tables and jokes.[9]

The philosophers of a democratic culture are not so caustic— the exceptional products of the mass media, Gilbert Seldes has written, "are prophetic of greatness"—but neither do they applaud the chief substance of mass communications. Seldes has also written: "The tendency is to approach the lower end of the scale of values, to exclude the exceptional."[10]

It is difficult to argue with the central thesis of either faction: The real thrust of the mass media is certainly not aimed at providing culture of the sort intellectuals approve. Many of the more thoughtful spokesmen for the mass media tend to take pride only in the presentation of news and are often apologetic about the attention they must give to entertainment. It is, they say, an economic necessity, and the record tends to bear them out.

What can be claimed, clearly, is that the level of Mass Culture has risen perceptibly even as the mass media have become more powerful. Dwight Macdonald admits this, saying that Stephen Vincent Benét has replaced Edgar Guest (whose best-known line is probably "It takes a heap o' livin' in a house t' make it home"), Walter Lippmann has replaced Arthur Brisbane, and "There are no widely influential critics so completely terrible as, say, the late William Lyon Phelps." Typically, Macdonald holds that the seeming improvement is simply a corruption of High Culture: "There is nothing more vulgar than sophisticated *kitsch.*"[11] But it must be obvious that one who does not approve the advance from Guest to Benét and from Brisbane to Lippmann is simply dedicated to negativism.

Should the Public Be Given What It Wants?

As the British Royal Commission said, the standard of the responsible press is "compounded partly of what it thinks its public wants to read about, and partly of what it thinks the public ought to read about."[12] Or, as William Allen White used to say, the editor tries to give his readers a "little better paper than they know they want." This is the general attitude one can observe among responsible newspaper and magazine editors, broadcasting executives, and film makers. And there are many cases showing how these men have taken courageous steps to rise above the ceiling of public taste.

Let us analyze the question a little more closely.

It isn't a sharp question, for a number of reasons. For one thing, our knowledge of what the public "wants" inevitably looks backward. A motion picture producer discovers by a survey or by other means that his potential audience is interested in pictures of refugees' escapes from the Communist-dominated countries of eastern Europe. He orders a story written, a picture made. It is probably a year before the picture can circulate in the theaters. Meanwhile, public interest may have shifted to another subject. What the producer would really like to know is what the public *will* want one year from now, and there is no sample-survey technique for determining that. That is what Ben Hibbs, editor of the *Saturday Evening Post,* was talking about when he entitled a speech "You Can't Edit a Magazine by Arithmetic."[13]

Furthermore, there is a very real question whether the public can know what it wants. It knows what it prefers among alternatives it has already experienced; it can decide, that is, whether it prefers the concert it heard Tuesday or the concert it heard Thursday. But the very essence of art is newness. And the public can't know whether it wants what it hasn't experienced. Did the public "want" Shakespeare before it saw any of his plays? Did the public "want" Bach before he became known, or Brahms before the First

Symphony? The evidence is rather on the other side. Very often, the artists who come to be most popular have the hardest time establishing their popularity. For example, Edgar Dale recalls that during the lifetime of Brahms a sign in a Boston auditorium read, "Exit, in case of Brahms."

And what is this public we are talking about? Isn't it really many publics? When we make a costly film, we expect it to reach large audiences in many parts of the world. Does that mean that its public is the three billion people in the world, or, in this country, the 200 million people now resident in the United States? Certainly not. There are many publics within those great masses of people. There is a public for a soap opera and a public for a symphony. There are few "majority" publics. Even the farthest-reaching of our mass entertainment productions usually reaches only a small minority of the total "public." It is no paradox, therefore, to say that any piece of mass programing is really minority programing. Therefore, when we talk about what the public wants, we are usually talking about what *some segment* of the public *will* want or, rather, *would* want if it had experienced the kinds of choice it will have sometime in the future.

Then why is this question so often asked and argued today? For one thing, because of the new demands on the media for responsibility, and also because of the tremendous economic pressure which bigness and fewness of units exert on the makers of popular art. Consider the enormous capital resources and investments usually required of the popular-art media: ability to take an initial $5-million loss in order to start a popular magazine; ability to bet millions on a fairly ordinary Class A picture; ability to cover recurring costs up to $200,000 for thirty minutes of national television. These figures indicate the incredible cost of making a bad decision in popular art. A bad decision, of course, means misjudging what the public will buy. The pressure of corporate ownership is an additional weight on the artist and the manager, and the very ponderousness of the system tends to substitute corporate or managerial decision for what, in a smaller medium, would be the artist's decision.

Therefore a certain amount of anxiety has been generated. The critics who look from the outside wonder whether the media are going to prostitute themselves by pandering to the very lowest denominator of public taste. The media men who look from the inside out wonder whether the critics and the commissions are going to force them to ignore public taste and go broke. Some of the critics have still another angle of approach: They fear that some of the media are actually molding public taste into the form which is most advantageous commercially, the easiest and simplest to service.

Here are some examples of how the relationship between public taste and standards is decided by the mass media.

From newspapers:

Today we played big a murder, two accidents, and a society divorce. The UN and the new bond issues got secondary play. We say, "But that is the stuff people are interested in. That's what sells the paper." But is it right? (Reported by a Midwestern editor.)

Some people say our comics are cheap, and I'm not very fond of them myself. But the devil! Every readership survey has them right up at or near the top readership. They're what the people seem to want. Who am I to censor the public will? (Another editor.)

All of us wrote about the Olympic games as an international conflict—U.S. vs. Russia. Now we hear that it's false to the spirit of the Olympics to do that. It's not sporting. I say, that makes the stories more interesting. That's the way people want it, and they ought to be able to get it. (A sports editor.)

From magazines:

A magazine could obtain an article by one of the world's greatest historians, discussing eruditely the philosophic choices which are before the human race as a result of developments during the last century. The article was expensive, it was difficult, and it was unquestionably important. In an editorial conference, the editors estimated that perhaps only 5 per cent of their readers would really understand it. Yet it would start discussion, and the ideas ultimately would permeate much more than 5 per cent. After considerable thought, the magazine bought and published the article.

From broadcasting:

A network had to choose a new master of ceremonies for a forum program. It had the choice between a man who was known for his ability to conduct a clear, orderly, and penetrating discussion, and a man who was known for his ability to generate heated controversy. It chose the latter because, it said frankly, that is what the people want. Perhaps clear and temperate discussion might teach them more about the subject, but they really want entertainment out of their forum programs—or so the network said. They want the participants to lose their heads and shout at each other. As Frederick C. Gruber says, that's the kind of forum they call "terrific."

From comics:

Some members of the comics industry have given thought to the possible effects of a number of comics like *Superman, Steve Roper*, and some of the crime strips which feature a hero doing superhuman deeds to right wrongs and bring criminals to justice without often calling on the forces of organized law enforcement or showing any of the ordinary weaknesses of human beings. But, on the other hand, they say, if we changed the nature of these strips, the public would have a fit. They want the heroes as they are, the more superhuman the better.

From motion pictures:

A studio bought rights to a novel which had received high critical acclaim and hired the author to come out and prepare a movie script. When the author arrived, he was somewhat surprised to be told gently and over the space of some weeks that the public would not accept a film which carried the very frank message of his novel. What the producers really wanted out of his novel was the romance and the well-advertised title. Even the romance would have to be cooled down, he discovered. Not that the public wouldn't want it, but the Motion Picture Production Code said they shouldn't have it.

Apparently, he told friends later, what goes into a film is compounded of what the original author thinks the public should have and wants, plus what the studio thinks the public wants, minus what the studio thinks the public doesn't want, minus what the Code says it can't have. Ultimately it was discovered that the original author couldn't write a satisfactory script for shooting, and other writers were brought in. At the end, the story was so different from the novel that it seemed to demand a new title; so even the title was dropped.

These cases are all built on the theme that the media could give the public better stuff if something would only let them—if public taste itself would permit—or the economic situation—or the Code.

A hundred years ago, this matter would not have been so important as it is today. There was a little better balance then between serious art for the "high hats," folk art for the little people and the separate groups, and popular art for anybody. A medium could be a great success, by the standards of those times, in serious as well as in popular art. There were no national voice-and-picture media to make people dissatisfied with their own storytellers, their own dancers, their own ballad singers. But the great wave of popular art, the coming of mass circulations and mass audiences, have tended to obscure these distinctions. In a very real sense, every medium has tended to become an entertainment medium. Few communication services have been able to continue to exist solely for an enlightened minority. Folk art and artists have been outshone by the popular artists on television, radio, and film.

The question many critics raise is really one of dynamics: Has the sweeping trend toward popular art come about because public taste has shaped the media in its own image or because the media have manipulated public taste into a pattern which they can most easily and profitably serve? There must be some of both: the media are the way they are partly because of what the public wants and will buy, and partly because of what the media want and feel they can produce. But the question, nevertheless, has some weight because of its implications concerning responsibility.

For example, if the media are really manipulating public taste to fit their commercial purposes, as a certain group of critics contend, we could expect a vastly greater change if the media were to behave more responsibly, but we should have a harder time persuading them to behave responsibly. On the other hand, if the media are merely following the demands of public taste—if the public itself is the motivating factor—we can expect less change as a result of more responsible behavior by the media, but there will be less difficulty in bringing about that change.

These authors stand rather on the side of the people who think that taste shapes the media—not wholly, however, for it is obvious that people can choose only from the alternatives they have at hand. They cannot be sure that they would or would not like what they have not seen or read. Therefore, there is unquestionably a certain amount of conditioning of the public taste by the media.

What governs what the media offer? First, a careful effort to anticipate the demands of public taste, illustrated by audience research, media research, and attention to mail and telephone calls. Second, the economics of the industry, which force it to try to meet the taste of a very large number of people and to engage in all this audience-studying activity to determine what those tastes are. And, finally, the standards of the media executives, which unquestionably result in a better product than a mere parroting of taste would make possible.

It seems obvious that the leaders of the popular-art media who are trying to raise standards of public taste outnumber by far the leaders who are trying to manipulate public taste for cynically commercial ends. Why has CBS maintained such a superlative news service? Why do *Life* and *Look* publish the courageous and thoughtful articles which do not seem to be aimed at the common-denominator audiences that many of the picture stories in the same magazines are aimed at? Why does Hollywood take a real pride in a picture which wins acclaim for its artistic validity?

We can count on a certain amount of free will and of willingness, on the part of media executives, to raise the level of popular art if they are convinced that it can be raised. True, their freedom is seriously restricted both by public taste and by the economic ponderousness of the industry. But we can realistically ask the media to face the hard questions which the emerging age of responsibility is posing.

When Is Popular Art a Success?

By what criteria do the makers of popular art propose to judge whether their work is having a desirable effect on their audiences? When is popular art a success?

Let us begin with the latter question: when is popular art a success? The answer of the media, their basic rule, is: when it is a *commercial* success. Such a test is not always necessary for fine or high art. Many a fine artist has not been appreciated in his own time. For fine art to be a success it is merely necessary (1) that it please the artist or (2) that at some time in human history it be approved by the critical elite. But popular art cannot afford to have approval withheld until the next generation or the next century. It must earn money for its makers.

That is the basic economic reality. Popular art will be judged first according to the number of people who will pay money (in the case of films, magazines, and books) or time (in the case of television and radio) to experience it. Behind the makers of popular art are always the cost accountants, the owners, and the stockholders, reminding them of the tremendous costs, the tie-up of talent and equipment and time, and the frightening cost of making a mistake.

The effect of all this is, obviously, to restrict what can be done. The maker will depend on the tried and proved patterns—Boy Meets Girl, Loses Girl, Wins Girl (or vice versa); the attractions of sex; the excitement of conflict; the themes of love, hate, loyalty, sacrifice, etc. He will fill his medium with fiction; even factual articles and biographies must be told like stories. He will be exceedingly cautious about trying something new. Faced with a medium which demands unbelievable amounts of new material, surrounded by owners and executives who warn him against misjudging public taste, he lives in a sort of occupational schizophrenia. In practice, he seeks gadgets, gimmicks, tricks that will make the old seem superficially new. When a maker discovers a new slant that proves successful, all his competitors jump in to copy it—always adding a gimmick to make it "new." Thus the same joke makes the rounds of broadcast comedians, the same situations repeat themselves in different comic strips, several movies of the same kind tend to come out at the same time.

But the maker of popular art must also avoid what will antagonize potential audiences. This is an enormous universe of material. Especially in the case of the movies, which are international in scope, the complaints are constant, and the resultant restrictions are almost as broad as human experience.

Probably the most articulate and effective pressure group in the United States, so far as its influence on movies is concerned, is the Roman Catholic Church, which operates by rating films, by protest, and by boycott. The makers of popular art have to consider constantly not only the need to *please* but also the need *not* to *teach* anything which would offend effective segments of the audience and thus make for failure of the program, the picture, or the publication.

The objections are usually moral. That is, they are objections to what people may be taught by popular art—the opinions and kinds of behavior they might learn. And the more one thinks about this, the more evident it becomes that Lyman Bryson was thoroughly right in beginning his essay "Popular Art" (which makes as much sense as any writing on the subject) with Plato and Aristotle, whose ghosts, he says, stand constantly at the elbows of the critics of popular art. Imagining Plato and Aristotle in a modern movie theater, he says:

> We can imagine them, disguised by darkness, watching a vividly photographed and competently acted modern story. It makes little difference what the story is. They would both be wondering what was happening to hundreds of men and women and boys and girls who sat together in the magic darkness seeing themselves do deeds of courage and cleverness, sweeping up rewards of honor and romance. Plato, I think, would be wondering if it was good experience. Aristotle would be wondering if it was good art. . . .
>
> So Aristotle in the movie theater would be looking for a work of fine art. He would be judging the movie by its logical consistencies; the balance of character elements. He would be seeking something to respond to emotionally, but it would not be the obvious vicissitudes of the heroine. . . . One can be reasonably sure that Aristotle would not consider the laughter and tears of his companions the kind of purgation that makes art a noble experience.
>
> Plato, being an older and sadder and quite possibly a wiser man, is unhappy for a different reason. He takes it for granted that the imaginary life that is enjoyed with tears and laughter by the people around him is precisely the purpose of the whole institution. People have come to the theater to be absorbed for a time in the affairs of imaginary persons, and they are quite properly letting themselves be swept on by the story. Plato's unhappiness would be because he would, as he listened and looked, pass judgment on all the moral implications of what was happening on the screen.[14]

These are the only two ways to judge popular art, besides the purely commercial test. That is, is it good art, and is it good teaching? The aesthetic critics blame popular art, in effect, for not being fine art. But it is exceedingly hard to lift popular art—with its enormous scale of production, its need to turn up so much new material, and its need to reach and attract vast audiences—to the level of logical balance, fresh insight, and subtlety of meaning which we expect of fine art. It is much easier to make popular art fit moral standards. And certainly this is a key to the understanding of what goes out under the name of popular art. For it goes out in the spirit of Plato—a timid and cautious Plato—rather than the spirit of Aristotle.

The maker of popular art is constantly forced to measure his product against moral standards: what is it going to teach its audiences? Where does he get his standards? From the pooled standards of all the societies and groups he wants to include in his audience; from the Master Plumbers, who care what picture people get of their members; from the Japanese, who don't want their youth to be corrupted by seeing a girl's elbow; from the Roman Catholic Church, which doesn't want the media to inform audiences about birth control; from all the groups which are articulate enough and potent enough, in a box-office sense, to deserve his attention.

The popular-art media have institutionalized their consciences. They have created codes of conduct, of which we shall talk at greater length later, but which all have roughly the same origin in the sensitivities and moral dislikes of audience groups. Thus the maker of popular art is restricted not only to a relatively small number of plots, forms, and character relationships which he can count on to please without fail a very large number of different people, but also, in theory, to having his characters do and say only what will not offend the codes.

The Nature of Media Man

Man, as viewed by popular art, is what we might call *generalized man* or *common-denominator man*. The major attention of the entertainment media must, naturally, be directed to the tastes and interests on which people agree, rather than to those on which they disagree. This is, of course, true to a different extent in different media.

The large popular magazine has considerable latitude. It can present one story or article which will appeal primarily to one kind of man, another story or article which will appeal to another kind. It doesn't expect that every reader will read every article. Television and radio have, perhaps, less latitude than the magazine, but they have more latitude than film, for they can afford to program for women in the afternoon, for children at 5:00 P.M., for families in the evening, for intellectuals at odd hours, and for sports fans on week ends. Motion pictures are the most restricted of the media, for a much larger proportion of their resources is tied up in one film, which must be seen over and over in as much of the world as possible.

But all these media are clearly interested in the aspects of human taste which are common throughout most of the human race and in presenting the kinds of idea and behavior which will offend as few of the human race as possible. Do 3 per cent of the potential great audience like Bach, 50 per cent like jazz, 80 per cent like Irving Berlin? Then, obviously, jazz is safer than Bach, Berlin safer than either. Is a large audience group going to be advised not to go to a picture in which an adulterer is allowed to work his way back to a happy, normal, proper life? Then, obviously, that subject is out of bounds. Popular-art man is simple, undifferentiated man, dwelling in the fenced-off territory that the stones of protesting pressure groups cannot reach, where life and its problems are kept as simple as possible.

Popular-art man is regarded as a person who comes to radio, television, and films (and to the entertainment parts of magazines and newspapers) chiefly for relaxation, excitement, escape. The movies are more purely an entertainment art than either broadcasting or magazines, for radio and television recognize a responsibility for informing their audiences through news and other treatments of public affairs, and magazines, in varying degrees, feel a responsibility for devoting part of their content to material which will stimulate rather than divert, encourage rather than discourage critical thought.

All these media look at man with the eyes of an adolescent Plato, not with the eyes of Aristotle. They think of man as coming to the movies, or sitting before the television screen, not in a mood to think about the artistic form of the product before him, but rather in a mood to suspend his critical facilities, to give himself to the story, to identify with the characters and to experience vicariously what they do, to forget for a while the problems of his daily life and the aspirations which he may hold for art or society.

And, by the same token, popular art conceives man to be rather immature in his reactions to the teaching content of entertainment, and highly susceptible to moral corruption. Now this is not to say that all films appeal only to the infantile members of society, that all broadcasts discourage rather than encourage thought, or that no popular art has the earmarks of fine art. There are films that do not hew to the line of the common denominator; there are stimulating broadcasts; there is popular art, of many kinds, that catches some of the aesthetic perfection and fresh insight that we look for in fine art. But what we have been describing is the broad central stream of popular art. And, viewing it as we have done, with emphasis on its basic economics and its basic assumptions, we can perceive some of the challenges which the emerging concept of social responsibility in mass communication presents to the makers of popular art.

Is the concept of *generalized audience* adequate? How can the media avoid the artistic strait jacket of programing for all and offending none? As we have suggested, this problem is sharpest in the motion pictures and least sharp in the large magazines. In radio, which has lost some of its mass audience, group programing is now good policy. Television can reach different segments at different times of the day and occasionally can afford to satisfy the intellectuals with a program or two.

Is the concept of *immature, susceptible man* at too low a level? It is a very serious and fundamental question whether the concept of news-reading and news-hearing man as a rational being, able to distinguish between truth and error and make up his own mind, is compatible with the concept of entertainment-receiving man as unable to distinguish between truth and error, and dangerously susceptible to whatever doctrine appears in the popular art he experiences. It is hardly necessary to say that the latter of these concepts is an authoritarian one, which puts the media in the role of caretaker of the people, whereas the former concept is a libertarian one. Yet these two exist side by side in the codes and the practice of the mass media.

But, in order really to judge whether the second concept of media man is too pessimistic, we should look in more detail at the kinds of content that man is to be protected from—that is, the kinds of content which are regarded by the custodians of popular art as corrupting to his taste and morals and dangerous to his social behavior.

What Is "Bad" Art?

Once again we are speaking the language of Plato rather than the language of Aristotle. We mean something that is *morally* bad. When we talk about a "bad" picture, program, story, or comic book, we mean one that teaches undesirable behavior, whether irreverent, indecent, in poor taste, or criminal. In other words, a bad piece of popular art, in the Platonic sense, is one that threatens or subverts the current mores and values of the society.

To understand the struggles and gyrations which popular art undergoes in order to avoid violating the mores, one has to consider the almost impossible situation in which popular art finds itself. What is "bad" in one culture is not necessarily so in another; so, the wider the audience the more cultures it will embrace, and the more kinds of behavior that must be avoided. Stories that would be all right in a traveling salesmen's or luncheon club's culture are not all right in the home culture into which television enters. The treatment of cows which is perfectly all right in American movie theaters is taboo in India, where Hollywood wants to sell the same films. A treatment of divorce which might be quite all right in an American Protestant culture is not all right in an American Catholic culture. And so the wider the audience the fewer the kinds of behavior that popular art may teach without violating the mores of some important group within the audience.

Furthermore, the larger the audience the more pressure groups feel a need to act as caretakers. Many a play that runs without complaint on Broadway could never be televised or filmed without substantial changes—moral, that is, rather than aesthetic changes. Salty language that is all right for a public speech is dangerous for radio.

Even in book circulation, the rule applies. Dan Lacy cites the case of *The Catcher in the Rye,* which sold about 40,000 copies in its original hard-cover edition, was purchased by public libraries throughout the United States, was a choice of the Book-of-the-Month Club (where it sold 115,000 more), and was widely and favorably reviewed as a "sincere, thoughtful, and sensitive treatment of adolescence"; but it had a quite different history when it became a paperback and began to circulate from magazine racks, stations, and drugstores. Its paperback edition was bitterly attacked before various state and city commissions, and was banned in a number of cities. The same thing has happened to Nobel Prize winners, Pulitzer Prize winners, National Book Award winners. As long as they stayed in hard covers and sold at five or six dollars, they were not regarded as threatening even though they had very large circulations. But, as soon as they went into paperbacks at a low price, the objectors, the caretaker groups, the police, and the censorship boards went into action.

Why? Obviously to protect the mores of society, to shield the younger and more corruptible members of society. There is an implicit assumption here that the person who can afford to pay five dollars for a book is less corruptible than one who can pay only fifty cents; that the person who can afford to go to a Broadway play is less corruptible than one who has to get his drama at the neighborhood movie house or from his television screen. It is interesting to realize that the shocked reaction of censors and objectors to *The Catcher in the Rye* in its paperback edition, as Lacy points out, was due in large measure to the book's exposure to "large masses of people previously habituated only to carefully industry-censored magazines, movies, and radio programs, and unaccustomed to the greater latitude always enjoyed by books."[15]

The large producers of popular art have institutionalized their consciences and codified their practices, so as to avoid offending the mores of the societies to which they sell. These codes, of course, are guides for the media producing for large audiences. More correctly, perhaps, they indicate what content to avoid if one also wants to avoid attack and loss of patronage from offended groups. As such, they are the industry's own definition of what constitutes good or bad popular art, and we may well begin by looking at what they recommend and what they proscribe.

The Newspaper Code

Unlike the other industry codes, the Canons of the ASNE (American Society of Newspaper Editors) have very little to say about decency, morality, and the other concerns of popular art. They are concerned with information rather than entertainment, and they assume a free, self-righting process in society, and a public able to distinguish between good and bad, truth and error. If they make any assumption about morality, it is the Socratic one that the intelligent man prefers a moral to an immoral society. The topics of the Canons, therefore, are responsibility, freedom, independence, sincerity, truthfulness, accuracy, impartiality, fair play, and decency. Only the last, decency, covers the ground which most concerns popular art. "A newspaper cannot escape conviction of insincerity if, while professing high moral purpose, it supplies incentives to base conduct, such as are to be found in details of crime and vice, publication of which is not demonstrably for the public good."

The Motion Picture Code

In contrast to the newspaper code, which is essentially a series of *positive* directions—what the newspaper *should* do—the motion picture code is essentially negative. Giving little attention to positive ideals of performance, it lays down a number of general and specific prohibitions.

Until recently, the motion picture code was almost overpoweringly negative. It called for respect for "pure love" as exemplified by marriage and the home and required that the movie maker seek to curb the passions of his audience. It called for respect for religion and national feelings. But the list of prohibitions was longer and more detailed. Designations such as "Chink," "Wop," and "Dago," depiction of nudity, sexual dances, and lustful love, profane and vulgar language (including "S.O.B.," "louse," and "broad" as applied to a woman)—all these and many other words, acts, and ideas were prohibited.

By 1966, however, the Motion Picture Association of America became convinced that its code was almost useless. Flagrant violations had become common. The code was heavily revised, the MPAA announced, "to keep in closer harmony with the mores, the culture, the moral sense and the expectations of our society."

Replacing the strongly detailed provisions for production standards were the following:

The basic dignity and value of human life shall be respected and upheld. Restraint shall be exercised in portraying the taking of life.

Evil, sin, crime and wrong-doing shall not be justified.

Special restraint shall be exercised in portraying criminal or anti-social activities in which minors participate or are involved.

Detailed and protracted acts of brutality, cruelty, physical violence, torture and abuse shall not be tolerated.

Indecent or undue exposure of the human body shall not be presented.

Illicit sex relations shall not be justified. Intimate sex scenes violating common standards of decency shall not be portrayed. Restraint and care shall be exercised in presentations dealing with sexual aberrations.

Obscene speech, gestures or movements shall not be presented. Undue profanity shall not be permitted.

Religion shall not be demeaned.

Words or symbols contemptuous of racial, religious or national groups shall not be used so as to incite bigotry or hatred.

Excessive cruelty to animals shall not be portrayed and animals shall not be treated inhumanely.

Later, in 1968, the motion picture industry all but threw up its hands. The latest productions were ignoring even the relaxed standards set by the new codes. So industry leaders formalized a series of labels designed to guide parents toward suitable movies. In effect, the code began to adapt itself to the practice of producers rather than prescribe their conduct.

The Radio Code

The radio code is both positive and negative, perhaps more the former than the latter. It does state general ideals of performance, but it also outlines proscribed content. Further, it represents a move from a pure code of ethics toward a code of ethics including a statement of trade practices.

The code considers radio a medium of both enlightenment and entertainment. Perhaps for that reason, it combines features of both the newspaper code and the motion picture code in its delineation of ethical behavior. And since, unlike the ASNE code, it recognizes the commercial aspects of broadcasting, it has an additional proviso for ethical conduct.

Ethical behavior, as defined implicitly by the code, consists of (1) promoting the democratic process by enlightening the public; (2) promoting accepted standards of public morality by presenting wholesome entertainment; and (3) maintaining a proper balance between enlightenment and entertainment on the one hand and contributions to the economic welfare on the other hand, as well as maintaining high standards of advertising. The code reflects some trust in the self-righting process. Radio can expedite the process by presenting news from reliable sources, by clearly distinguishing commentary from straight reporting, by "willingness to expose its convictions to fair rebuttal," by ensuring equality of opportunity "in allotting time for the presentation of public issues," and so forth.

Yet broadcasters seem to doubt if the process is really self-righting. Reading the code, one senses that they have reservations about man's rationality, that they do not want discussion to be *too* controversial, that they put narrower limits to it than do newspaper editors. The newspaper code positively and purposely states that the area of discussion should be large: "It is unquestionably right to discuss whatever is not explicitly forbidden by law." No such statement appears in the radio code. On the contrary, the radio code sets itself the difficult task of respecting "the rights and sensitivities of all people," which, if carried out thoroughly, would impose severe limitations on what can be discussed. Moreover, participation in the presentation of public issues should be limited to "qualified, recognized, and properly identified groups or individuals whose opinions will assist the general public in reaching conclusions."

The public good for the broadcaster also embraces a concern for public morals. In all operations, broadcasters should "observe the proprieties and customs of civilized society." In news programs, they should not present "morbid, sensational, or alarming details." In entertainment, in children's programs especially, they should maintain accepted standards. Programs for children, the code notes, "should convey the commonly accepted social and ethical characteristics of American life. They should contribute to the healthy development of personality and character."

The ethical broadcaster, as well as the ethical movie maker, will therefore respect certain moral principles and institutions. First, law and order. He will not make crime attractive, for example; will not encourage listeners to imitate the activities of criminals; and will not disparage law enforcement. Second, he will respect what the motion picture code calls "pure love"; he will, as the code stipulates, "honor the sanctity of marriage and the home." Third, he will respect all religion.

In contributing to the economic welfare, too, the ethical broadcaster shall be judged by "high standards of performance," for he has a "responsibility to the public." One measure of performance is how well he keeps advertising in proper proportion. The code specifically suggests the maximum time to be used for advertising by a single sponsor at various periods of the day. But the "quality and integration" of advertising are as important as its quantity. Therefore, the ethical broadcaster will make sure that advertising meets certain minimum standards, some of which are specifically set forth in the code.

The Television Code

The television code is as heavily negative as the now outdated motion picture code, which indeed seems to have been a model for some sections of it. More than any of the other codes, it embodies a statement of good business practices.

The TV code acknowledges the duty of television to promote the democratic process by public enlightenment. The responsible telecaster, for instance, will offer a well-balanced and adequate news presentation, which must be "factual, fair, and without bias." He will "seek out and develop with accountable individuals, groups and organizations, programs relating to controversial public issues of import to his fellow citizens; and . . . give fair representation to opposing sides of issues which materially affect . . . a substantial segment of the public."

But overriding the telecaster's duty as enlightener is his duty to make program content conform to the accepted beliefs and behavior of the majority. "Education via television," the code states, "may be taken to mean that process by which the individual is brought toward informed adjustment to his society."

The ethical telecaster, then, will keep discussion within rather narrow bounds. He will make sure that the views presented are "responsible" ones, and he should evaluate requests for discussion time "on the basis of their individual merits, and in the light of the contribution which the use requested would make to the public interest, and to a well-balanced program structure."

The code closely links promoting the public good with promoting public morals. Even news and analysis must be offered with concern for public morals. "At all times," says the code, "pictorial and verbal material for both news and comment should conform to other sections of these standards, wherever such sections are reasonably applicable."

As propagator of public morals, the ethical telecaster has obligations similar to those of the movie maker. In his programs, he must respect law and order. Although the code recognizes that crime is a part of the world at large, the ethical telecaster will not lead the young to believe that crime plays a greater part in life than it actually does. He will portray criminality as "undesirable and unsympathetic." He will uphold law enforcement and the dignity of the law. He will not inspire his viewers to engage in crime, nor will he furnish them with information on criminal techniques.

The ethical telecaster will maintain respect "for the sanctity of marriage and the value of the home." By implication, he will uphold what the movie code calls "pure love" and will not portray "impure love": he will not, for example, depict divorce with levity or as a "solution for marital problems." He will not portray illicit sex relations or sexual perversions.

The ethical telecaster will seek to hold in check the baser emotions of his viewers and to shield the viewers from temptation. "The presentation of cruelty, greed, and selfishness as worthy motivations," says the code, "is to be avoided." The ethical telecaster will transmit no scenes involving lascivious dances, indecorous costumes, excessive horror, cruelty to animals, and so forth. He will respect sobriety. "Drunkenness should never be presented as desirable," the code says. "Narcotic addiction shall not be presented except as a vicious habit." Another section forbids the advertising of hard liquor and requires that ads for beer and wine be "in the best of good taste." Gambling can be depicted only when essential to the plot and then only with discretion and moderation.

The ethical telecaster will respect religion. He will emphasize "broad religious truths" rather than "controversial or partisan views." He will respect national feelings by avoiding words, especially slang, derisive of any nationality or national derivation. He will not permit profanity of any sort.

The television code acknowledges that advertising enables telecasters to make available programs of enlightenment and entertainment. Nevertheless, the ethical telecaster must keep advertising in proper proportion and must exercise unceasing care to supervise the form it takes. Nearly half of the code deals with advertising; this part amounts to a statement of good trade practices.

In general, the ethical telecaster will try to make the advertising carried by his station conform to the standards of his programs of enlightenment and entertainment. Just as he should present news which is truthful and labeled as to source, for example, so should he carry only advertising that is free of misrepresentation. Just as discussion should be conducted by responsible persons, so should advertising be presented by firms of integrity. Just as other programs should avoid offending the majority by profanity, indelicacy, and so on, so should advertising avoid being "objectionable to a substantial and responsible segment of the community."

The Comic Book Code

Ethical conduct for the publisher of comic books, the code suggests, consists of avoiding "violations of standards of good taste, which might tend toward corruption of the comic book as an instructive and wholesome form of entertainment." The test of his ethical behavior, then, is how little he offends public morals.

The comics code, like the motion picture code, is primarily negative. It says, in effect, that certain things constitute violations of ethical behavior, but does not formulate ideals of performance.

Like the movie maker and the broadcaster, the ethical publisher of comic books must respect certain moral standards and American institutions. As the code puts it, "Respect for parents, the moral code, and for honorable behavior shall be fostered."

First, the ethical publisher must respect law and order. "In every instance," the code says, "good shall triumph over evil." Comic books should, therefore, never engender sympathy for crime and the criminal; on the contrary, crime shall be depicted as "a sordid and unpleasant activity." The books should not teach criminal methods, nor should they disparage "policemen, judges, government officials, and respected institutions."

Second, the ethical publisher must respect marriage and the home. He should never treat divorce as a subject for humor or as desirable. He should respect what the movie code calls "pure love." The comics code says: "The treatment of love-romance stories shall emphasize the value of the home and the sanctity of marriage." On the other hand, the publisher shall avoid references to "impure love": he shall not refer, explicitly or by innuendo, to "illicit sex relations," to "sexual abnormalities," or to "sex perversion." The ethical publisher will try to restrain the passions of his readers. "Passion or romantic interest," the code says, "shall never be treated in such a way as to stimulate the baser or lower emotions." Comic books will not use pictures involving nudity, suggestive postures, or "exaggeration of any physical qualities" of the female.

The ethical publisher will also respect religion. And he should keep his books free from profanity and vulgarity; indeed, he should even have them use "good grammar" whenever possible.

The standards of the advertising carried by comic books also should be a concern of the responsible publisher. "Good taste" is his guiding principle in accepting or rejecting advertising. In general, "good taste" means rejecting advertisements for products which promote crime, gambling, drinking, and sexual vice.

How well do the media live up to their codes? Thirty graduate students set out to provide a partial answer by measuring the performance of each medium against the provisions of its code. Naturally, only a few newspapers, movies, radio and television programs, and comic books could be analyzed. But so many practices were repugnant to the codes—not a single medium was found to observe every provision—that the project became as absurd as it was instructive. Perhaps such results are predictable. After all, the codes are subject to wildly different interpretations. In any case, it is much more useful to consider the codes broadly, to examine the assumptions that created them.

The Assumptions of Popular Art

Behind all these codes there is an implicit assumption that popular art has a powerful effect on its audiences. It is evident, for example, that a great many things which are widely observ-

The Media Codes*

	When and How Adopted	The Code's View of Man	View of the Medium	View of Function of Medium	Principles of Ethical Behavior
News-papers	When newspaper was almost 300 years old, and newsmen spoke of a "profession" of journalism; no pressure on papers to adopt code	Primarily a rational being, able to discover truth and separate right from wrong by power of reason	Appeals to the intellect—to the critical sense	Primarily enlightenment	Promoting democracy by enlightening the public (expediting the self-righting process); independence, accuracy, truthfulness, impartiality, fair play, decency, no invasion of privacy, no opinion in news reports, no incentive to base conduct
Movies	Fairly early in history and a few years after advent of sound—against background of organized criticism and official censorship	Much of audience will be immature and highly susceptible to corruption of morals	Capable of suspending the audience's critical faculties	Primarily entertainment, though it can contribute to "correct living," presumably by indoctrination	Promoting public morals (in general, by respecting the home and the sanctity of marriage, religion, law, and justice, national feelings; by curbing the base emotions; by avoiding violence, vulgarity, and profanity)
Radio	After about a decade and a half, amid public criticism, government regulation, and threat of further government intervention	Much of audience will be highly susceptible to corruption of morals	Capable of suspending the audience's critical faculties	Enlightenment, entertainment, service to economic system	Promoting democracy by enlightening the public (expediting the self-righting process); promoting public morals (in general, by respecting the sanctity of marriage and home, religion, law, and justice, national feelings; by avoiding vulgarity and profanity); keeping advertising in proportion and maintaining high standard for it

Television	Very early in history; no serious threat of further government intervention (but code may have helped to forestall it)	Much of audience will be highly susceptible to corruption of morals	Capable of suspending the audience's critical faculties	Enlightenment, entertainment, service to economic system	Promoting democracy by enlightening the public—but not at expense of task of promoting public morals (in general, by respecting the home and the sanctity of marriage, religion, law, and justice, national feelings; by curbing base emotions; by avoiding vulgarity and profanity); keeping advertising in proper proportion and maintaining high standards for it
Comic Books	At end of first decade—against backdrop of public criticism, official censorship, and threat of further government intervention	Immature, highly susceptible to corruption of morals	Capable of suspending readers' critical faculties, if any	Entertainment	Promoting public morals (in general, by respecting the home and the sanctity of marriage, religion, law, and justice; by curbing base emotions; by avoiding violence, vulgarity, and profanity; by teaching that good must triumph)

* Prepared by Theodore B. Peterson for this book.

able in actual life are "bad" in popular art. Likewise, many subjects that can freely be talked about in news or in print are "bad" in popular art. This extends even to advertising, for the same audience which is not permitted to see hard-liquor advertising on television can turn to large-circulation magazines and be urged to emulate "men of distinction" in drinking whisky. It is apparent that we need to examine this assumption about the dangerous power of popular art.

The Assumption of Effect

Here let us emphasize that it is very difficult to demonstrate a causal relationship between the mass media and any of the criminal or perverted behavior for which the media are sometimes blamed. On the other hand, it must be admitted that, when audiences go to popular art, they seem to have a different attitude and expectation from what they have, for example, as they turn to the evening news or observe a street scene. They are much readier, in a motion picture theater or in a comfortable chair before the television set, to suspend their critical faculties. They are more likely, someone has said, to *feel* than to *think* about what they receive. They go to popular art, not overtly to learn or be informed or even to undertake the responsibilities of a conversation or a buying-selling relationship. They go, for the most part, to be entertained. They are relaxed. And the most evident feature of their behavior as listeners or viewers or readers is that they *identify* with the characters in the story.

Everyone who has explored the psychology of the popular-art audience has noted the identification. Waugh, writing about the comics, says that "people read comics because they find themselves reflected in them."[16] Orwell, writing of boys' magazines, notes that "the characters are so carefully graded as to give almost every type of reader a character he can identify with."[17] Herta Herzog says in regard to soap operas: "In identifying themselves and their admittedly minor problems with the suffering heroes and heroines of the stories, the listeners find an opportunity to magnify their own woes. This is enjoyed if only because it expresses their 'superiority' over others who have not had these profound emotional experiences."[18]

But Miss Herzog notes further that the soap operas which are so profoundly identified with "are liked because they 'explain'" things to the inarticulate listener. Furthermore, they teach the listener appropriate patterns of behavior. 'If you listen to these programs and something turns up in your own life, you would know what to do about it' is a typical comment, expressing the readiness of women to use these programs as sources of advice."[19]

There is no doubt that people do accept some advice from the media. Consider a homely example. One of the large magazines for women came out with a reducing diet which was in fact only an infant's feeding formula, although intended in this case for adults. Within a few days, drugstore counters were full of the dextrose that went into the formula, evaporated milk and corn syrup were selling briskly, and apparently large numbers of people were on the "formula diet." In a more subtle way, too, people get "help" and advice from the soap operas and similar sources.

Likewise, there is no doubt that people imitate some behaviors from the characters with whom they identify. The way phrases and gestures from Hollywood and Broadway go around the country is more than coincidence.

Furthermore, some people are clearly more suggestible than others. And all people are more likely to accept suggestions they are looking for. If a boy is rather planning to run away from home anyway, he may be more swayed than others by Huckleberry Finn's adventures. A disturbed person, whose aggressions or criminal tendencies are already well developed, may find a crime program useful in a way that was never intended—for example, as a demonstration of how to burglarize a second story, or strangle a victim, or avoid the police.

There is no doubt (1) that audiences approach popular art less critically than they approach the news and public affairs; (2) that because of the large and diverse audiences which are attracted to popular art, these audiences unquestionably contain more uncritical and suggestible persons than, say, the audiences of fine art; (3) that many people will identify strongly with the characters of popular art, and therefore become more suggestible; and (4) that some people at some time under some conditions will accept advice and imitate behavior from popular art. What is not known is the extent of this effect—how many people under what conditions will accept what kind of advice or imitate what kinds of behavior.

So it isn't proved and isn't disproved. What does popular art do about that? Gilbert Seldes expresses himself strongly. He says it would be criminal to take a chance. "As meager an ethical standard as can be imagined," he calls it, to make the standard of acceptability that "as long as no positive proof of harm is presented, the program may be transmitted." And certainly one can understand why Hollywood and New York, and all the groups and individuals who have put pressure on them to frame the codes as they have framed them, should bend over backward in order to avoid doing individual and social harm.

But this problem has a positive as well as a negative side. The codes have proscribed a number of kinds of conduct which, it is feared, might be injurious. When you eliminate these large aspects of human experience from popular art, what is left? Is this expurgation, this negative approach, injurious? Does it ensure the responsibility of popular art? To approach that question we shall have to look at some other assumptions.

The Assumption Regarding Sensation, Crime, and Violence

The codes say that violence is never justified for its own sake. With that we can hardly argue. The question is, then: How does popular art justify the enormous amount of violence, crime, and sensation it carries? And the answer seems to be that it makes a further assumption of considerable importance: that a great amount of such material may be justified if the audience is carefully informed that crime never pays, that evil-doing is punished, and that accepted social mores have a way of enforcing themselves.

This is an eat-your-cake-and-have-it-too ethic.

For example, when some newspapers—functioning more as entertainment media than as information channels—sensationalize such a case as the Sheppard trial, their theory is that nothing destroys an infection like sunlight. But one can wonder whether the result is not, rather, that everybody wallows in the filth without any sense of moral guilt.

Again, consider the way power is treated in popular art. Attention to power is nothing unusual. Folk and legendary heroes since the beginning of time have tended to be men of great power: Hercules, Roland, Robin Hood, Lancelot, and Paul Bunyan. And so in comic strips, the crime dramas, and the westerns, some of the leading characters are usually men of great power, engaged in adventures of thrilling violence and danger.

For the most part, these powerful characters take one of two forms. They may be villains. Such, for example, are many of the men James Bond pursues so relentlessly. They are men of great canniness, strength, and daring. True, they are always captured, sometimes after they have strewn their way with corpses, and they are suitably punished. But, in the meantime, one may identify with the character who is willing to dare such adventures, has so much skill, and makes fools of the cops. Orwell remarks on the tendency in American popular art to tolerate crime, "even to admire the criminal so long as he is successful." It is this attitude, he says, "that has made it possible for crime to flourish upon so huge a scale. Books have been written about Al Capone that are hardly different in tone from the books written about Henry Ford, . . . Lord Northcliffe, and all the rest of the 'log cabin to White House' brigade."[20] It is perfectly all right with the codes to write of the power and skill of this kind of criminal, so long as his ultimate fate is disposed of according to rule. But *is* it right?

Hortense Powdermaker wrote:

The MPAA gave its seal of approval to a picture in which the two leading characters committed adultery and then murder and, of course, were finally punished for all their sins. What the MPAA ignored were the implications of a sexy-looking, beautiful woman and a strong, handsome he-man, both popular stars, irresistibly drawn to each other, committing adultery, and finally murder. That they are punished at the end would not necessarily destroy the identification of the preceding sixty or eighty minutes.[21]

A second form these powerful characters take is that of great heroes who settle the problems of society without needing the help of the usual agents of justice. Such, for example, are Superman, Steve Roper, and all the successors of Robin Hood and Sherlock Holmes. These are individuals of great charm and power, all of whom fall into one general pattern. Martha Wolfenstein describes it: "The hero, the self-appointed investigator and agent of justice, is able to set things right independently. The world, which is not effectively policed, does not need to be policed at all."[22]

Miss Wolfenstein pays her respects to another kind of falsity. It is in false appearances, she writes, that

the forbidden wishes are realized which the hero and heroine so rarely carry into action. In a false appearance the heroine is promiscuous, the hero is a murderer, the young people carry on an illicit affair, two men share the favors of a woman. This device makes it possible for us to eat our cake and have it, since we can enjoy the suggested wish fulfillments without emphatic guilt; we know that the characters with whom we identify have not done anything.[23]

In fact, it may be argued that there is a basic dishonesty about the practice of popular art in this whole area. A man of great power can operate outside the accepted channels and the realistic patterns of society, provided he does it for a good cause—for example, if he does what the police should be doing. A criminal may be depicted as powerful, smart, successful, attractive, just so justice catches up with him at the end. All kinds of sexy and violent ideas may be written into popular art, provided we are told at the end that it is all a mistake; it didn't really happen.

But perhaps the most interesting of all these basic dishonesties is the way the codes enforce and the producers create a kind of popular art which is moral in the little things, but still full of crime, cruelty, and violence. In other words, although a picture may observe meticulously every rule of the code and every ruling of the Code Administrator, it does not observe the spirit of the code, and the question is whether it has the opposite of the intended result. This is what happens when you tell a maker of popular art what *not* to do. It is much harder, perhaps impossible, to tell him what to do.

The result of these restrictions, and their occasional circumvention, is to create a kind of unreality about popular art, which raises another serious question.

The Assumption Regarding Reality

It would seem that another implicit assumption of popular art is something like this: if one is exposed to popular art in which desired mores are demonstrated in a somewhat unreal and simple world, one will learn desirable behavior for a much more complicated world.

When Wolcott Gibbs resigned as motion picture reviewer for *The New Yorker,* he characterized the world of the cinema as "an astounding parody of life devoted to a society in which anything is physically and materially possible, including perfect happiness, to a race of people who operate intellectually on the level of the New York *Daily News,* morally on that of Dayton, Tennessee, and politically and economically in a total vacuum."[24]

It is a dangerously simplified world. The need of writing for the enormous, undifferentiated audience makes it difficult, if not impossible, to deal with the subtleties of life. The need of producing such a mass of new material each year makes it difficult, if not impossible, to create new characters, different from each other in the subtle ways of human beings. Instead, we have types and stereotypes. The Frenchman is likely to be excitable, to wear a beard, to gesticulate. Spaniards, Mexicans, Arabs, and Chinese are likely to be sinister and treacherous. The Swede and the Dane are usually kindhearted, usually stupid. The Negro is comic and faithful.

But even beyond this, the moral code, which is made necessary by the fact of the enormous audience, makes a mental and moral type even of a character who is not a physical type. Right must triumph. Wrong must always be punished. A character must always be good or bad; the blends and combinations that one sees in life are not very frequent in popular art. For a long time, it was impossible even to expiate sin on the screen; the wrongdoer relentlessly had to be carried to a sad end.

Hortense Powdermaker wrote:

Only rarely does a movie-goer have the experience of seeing real human beings living in a complicated world. Instead, he is treated to static characters not unlike the symbolic personifications of sin and virtue in medieval miracle plays. It is only the exceptional movie which portrays any human being, member of majority or minority group, with truthfulness or understanding. The reality of most movies usually consists only in the photography, the setting, the curve of a star's leg, the friendly or handsome looks of the hero and heroine, and other surface characteristics. Seldom is anyone concerned with the reality of emotions and with truthfulness of meaning.[25]

To get some idea of what this means in practice, consider a few instances from the popular arts:

A certain newspaper has the practice of using "disrobe" for "undress," when reporting that a woman takes off her clothes. The theory is that this is more dignified, less offensive.

Hollis Alpert has written:

In the film "From Here to Eternity" a Honolulu brothel was called the New Congress Club and was converted into a place where soldiers could dance with hostesses and could even hire an upstairs room for private conversations. Only the most naive would have assumed that soldiers use their hard-earned pay to rent a room for a chat with a strange girl. . . . The New Congress Club resembled no social or sexual institution known to man since Adam (certainly nothing an enlisted man would have found in Honolulu) and inexcusably injected one small sour note into a powerful but realistic movie.

Alpert also reported: In *Slightly Scarlet* Rhonda Fleming

is seen as an expensively dressed and groomed girl employed as secretary of a rich and prominent businessman. On her secretary's wages, and with no sign of other income, she manages to live in a $50,000 house (from the looks of it), drive a spanking new convertible, dress in clothes that might put Grace Kelly to shame, and apply all the latest California-style decorative features to her home, patio, and large-sized swimming pool. One might be pardoned, then, for assuming that she is being kept by the businessman. But just in case any of us does take such a view there is provided an illuminating scene between Miss Fleming and her employer. He tells her he loves her and pleads with her to marry him. But Miss Fleming has standards. She informs her employer that she can't marry him because she doesn't love him. Obviously she is just a girl with a fantastic ability to make ends meet.

A scene in a television play was deliberately vague about what, if anything, had happened between a young couple during the night. But the director was careful to have the girl enter the apartment in the morning, not from the bedroom, but from the balcony.

These cases all have a similarity in that they are concerned with the details rather than with the broad meaning of the art. And, to one degree or another, all result in an abortion of reality.

Miss Wolfenstein analyzed several hundred entertainment films from several countries and constructed what she feels is the typical pattern of British, French, and American films.[26]

British films, she says, evoke the feeling that "danger lies in ourselves, especially in our impulses of destructiveness. . . . The essential plot is the conflict of forbidden impulses with conscience. Either one of the contending forces may win out." In French films, "human wishes are opposed by the nature of life itself. The main issue is not one of inner or outer conflicts in which we may win or lose, be virtuous or get penalized. It is a contest in which we all lose in the end, and the problem is to learn to accept it." As for American films, the major plot configuration is like neither of the others:

> Winning is terribly important and always possible though it may be a tough fight. The conflict is not an internal one; it is not our own impulses which endanger us nor our own scruples that stand in our way. The hazards are all external, but they are not rooted in the nature of life itself. They are the hazards of particular situations with which we find ourselves confronted. The hero is typically in a strange town where there are apt to be dangerous men and women of ambiguous character and where the forces of law and order are not to be relied on. If he sizes up the situation correctly, if he does not go off half-cocked but is still able to beat the other fellow to the punch, once he is sure who the enemy is, if he relies on no one but himself, if he demands sufficient evidence of virtue from the girl, he will emerge triumphant. He will defeat the dangerous men, get the girl, and show the authorities what's what.

There is something about the cabined, restricted, mechanical, unreal pattern of much of our popular art that is deeply disappointing. It is almost as though we were unwilling to spend enough on it. We spend enough in money, for we are lavish with the cost of film, the cost of television, the cost of thick, slick magazines, and all the rest; but not with the cost of emotion and the cost of penetrating inside the human mind. William E. Hocking, in an eloquent passage, talked about this: "The most available emotion is the laugh, and the most external; it has become the habitual American sign of enjoyment, because it is cheapest in terms of sympathetic understanding. The moral emotions are most costly, the indignant response to injustice, pity toward misery, the expansion of one's being in presence of an element of human greatness. Readers are not prepared to spend lavishly in these costly terms." And the mass media, Hocking continued, "must deal with entertainment, with the 'funnies,' with a crime, catastrophe, and adventure, because these involve the common emotion of semi-physical 'reaction'; they make no heavy drafts on either thought or conscience or faith."[27]

A second respect in which popular art seems to fall disturbingly short is the range of the behavior it reports. Alpert quoted a movie script writer as asking what would happen if someone told the movies, "Try it. Don't play it safe. What have you got to lose?" Then the script writer answered his own question.

Do you know what could happen? There'd be motion pictures in which a married man would have an affair with his secretary and return to his wife with his marriage enriched; a husband and wife would quarrel, get a divorce, their friends would conspire to get them together again, and it wouldn't work, because the couple genuinely disliked each other; an unmarried woman would fall in love with a man, live with him for two years, and leave him because she'd met someone else, and the left-behind lover would go out and celebrate with his friends because he'd been tiring of her; a married man would visit a call-girl one night and nothing—but absolutely nothing, not even pangs of conscience—would happen later; a married couple would decide they didn't want children, and they wouldn't have any, and they'd be quite happy; a fortune hunter would have a choice between a lovely but poor young girl and a bitchy but rich heiress, and he would marry the heiress, fade-out the end; a doctor would give up his small-town practice to become a Park Avenue doctor, meet a rich girl, build up a lucrative practice, never go back to the home-town, and become one hell of a happy guy. The possibilities are endless!

"As endless as life," Alpert comments.[28]

The Assumption Regarding the Nature of Man

Popular Art Man is somewhat more developed than Pithecanthropus or Peking Man, but not much more. He cannot be trusted with a true and realistic picture of the way men live, the problems they face, and the way those problems are settled. He cannot be trusted to distinguish good from evil, at least when the choice is presented in popular art. The only safe thing, therefore, is to show him a world in which human beings are pretty clearly divided into a good class and a bad class (although some who are *really* good *seem* bad, and vice versa) and in which right always wins and wrong is always punished. It is unsafe to show him in popular art many of the kinds of behavior which he must see around him in life.

Especially is it unsafe to let him see or hear anything in popular art which might arouse elemental emotions. It is dangerous to expose him to anything which might test his faith in the sanctity of marriage or the home, or in his religion, or in law or justice; he might fail the test. It is dangerous also to let him hear anything profane or vulgar: he might pick it up. More important, it is useless to expect him to respond to any very deep and insightful treatment of human nature and human life; instead, he must be expected to respond only at a superficial level, only on the level of what is funny, what is scary, what is physically powerful.

In these respects, Popular Art Man is a child. In other respects he is a fool. For the media seem to assume that they can attract him by violence and sex ("Alluring! Seductive! Wicked!") and then cover up the sex and punish the violence in the show so that he won't see it, or at least won't find it in any way attractive.

Now, obviously, there are many high-minded men in the popular-art industry who do not appear to hold this view of man. Some of our large magazines, notably *Esquire* and *Playboy*, do not seem to be edited with that kind of man in mind; Mike Nichols' pictures are not made that way; *CBS Reports* is not prepared that way. But the picture we have painted is the dead-center picture: the level of the majority of the entertainment films, of the crime dramas, the serials, and most of the variety shows on radio and television, and of much of the content of entertainment magazines.

And if we now ask whether that concept of man is adequate for today, we must answer that it is not. At least it is not adequate for a very large part of our population. There are certainly children among us, adult and juvenile children. There are undoubtedly fools among us. But in programing for these more susceptible elements of our population, is not popular art selling us short?

If we ask whether a popular art which had higher aspirations would really be dangerous to the mores and values of society, then we should have to answer frankly that we don't know. But everything we have seen leads us to believe that the great majority of human beings could take that in stride, and that the danger would lie only with the more susceptible few, the children and the fools and the disturbed.

The Problems of an Adequate Service

The popular arts have a Gargantuan hunger for new material, and this makes all the other problems more difficult. Some are hungrier than others. Motion pictures have to come up with the fewest new stories per year. Magazines are somewhat hungrier, and most editors complain bitterly about the shortage of good material. But it is on television and radio that the popular arts reach their climax in demanding new material. A play that would run for a year in the theater plays itself out in a night on radio or television. A vaudeville act that would last a comedian for most of his professional lifetime expends its audience in one broadcast performance. A lecture that would take a man around the country or serve a professor for many classroom years can be heard but once on the broadcast media. And television is more demanding even than radio, for it must fill in all the sights that are imagined on radio.

Therefore, the makers of popular art are caught between millstones. Although they must be infinitely careful not to drive away any considerable part of their possible audience, and thus fail to meet the economic demands of large-media operation, they are constantly harried about material. Although desperate for new material, they are constantly warned not to make a mistake. The only possible result is to make change difficult. A producer can't afford to experiment much. He seeks innovation in the unimportant aspects of his productions, but not in their basic qualities. Audiences can't say very clearly what changes they would like if they have no chance to see the alternatives. Thus success tends to be imitated, and the same pattern of common-denominator popular art repeats itself over and over again.

It is common practice to blame the codes for the ills of the popular arts and especially of motion pictures. This is a little short of nonsense. Two things enchain us to the codes. One is what has been called the "code mentality." This is taking the codes in minutiae, as a series of tiny rules of conduct, rather than as a guide to the spirit of conduct. There is a tendency to be concerned with the trivial in the aspects of censorship, whether imposed by governments, or by industry-organized authorities (such as the Motion Picture Association of America), or by the media themselves (as, for example, by the program acceptance offices of the networks).

There is a game played with a large map, in which one player challenges the other to find within a certain number of seconds a certain name on the map. A new player as challenger will choose a name in very small type, but the experienced player will choose a name that is in very large type with the letters spread far apart. This, he finds, is less obvious than the small compact names. Censorship typically works with the small compact items. Smart writers have driven many censors crazy by giving them trivia to correct, while slipping the message through in the generalities. This is characteristic of popular-art censorship, too.

To illustrate the difference between the trivial and the significant in self-censorship, here are two cases quoted by the acceptance department of a broadcast network:

A character in a dramatic script was supposed to say, "I followed the first commandment: 'Live it up.' " This was cut out of the script on the ground that it would offend Jewish and Christian religious groups.

A network was considering a sponsored religious program to be called something like *Men in Black,* and to feature each week a different clergyman. The network liked the sample scripts and was given to understand that a sponsor was available. But the head of the network, after considerable thought and consultation, said no to the idea. He asked, "Where would you put the commercials?" He said that it would be improper and irreverent to sell goods when the audience is in the mood for looking at men of God.

These cases illustrate radically different levels of judgment. The first was on a triviality. It was not contended that the character might not say such a thing; or that such a statement would be presented as a favorable character trait; or that it would necessarily corrupt a hearer—but merely that it might offend a religious group, and result in a protest. By definition, it was therefore "irreverent." The other case is a different kind of attention to reverence and religion. Without passing on the rightness or wrongness of the decision—which one could hardly do without seeing the scripts and the commercials—it is clear that the network head was concerned with the spirit of the program, rather than the details. He was asking not whether a phrase would be picked up and protested but whether the total result of the program would be to contribute to the spirit of reverence in the audience. If the codes were always interpreted in this spirit, we would not have the contrast of sexy films with behavior on the screen that is carefully, even unreally, circumspect, or very attractive criminal behavior that is carefully punished at the end.

The second circumstance that enchains us to the codes is that we *treat* them as chains rather than as guides. The popular-art codes, for the most part, were introduced as protection and adopted out of fear. They were not so much to represent the conscience of the industry as to protect it from audience disaffection; not so much to make good programs as to make programs which would offend audiences as little as possible. As far as one can see from outside, the codes have been treated as a necessary evil, just as censorship has been treated since the beginning of time. At best, censorship is a sporting proposition to be outsmarted and circumvented wherever possible. At worst, censorship is a negative guide to conduct, a spelling-out of things one may not do; one can surrender one's conscience to it, avoid carefully what it proscribes, and then freely go about doing what one wishes except for the specified "don't." This is an inadequate concept of the kind of responsibility we expect of the mass media. And yet one sees evidence of both these kinds of attitude toward the codes on the part of some of the popular-art makers.

Many of the custodians of popular art, particularly of entertainment films and entertainment broadcasting, and particularly in the early stages of those arts, have come from the ranks of business rather than the ranks of fine arts. Whether they were financiers or entrepreneurs (spiritual descendants of Barnum, whose exploits and legends they in many cases surpassed), they tended to bring to the new arts the ethics of nineteenth-century business. Therefore, they accepted the codes—too often—as morality. They followed meticulously—and too often—the details of the codes, and neglected the spirit. In short, they used the codes as negative guides. The positive guide turned out, more often than not, to be the voice of economics: this art must be a success—that is, make money.

How the spirit of the code should be observed is represented, curiously, by one of the most violent programs to appear on television, *Combat*. If one grants that a war series deserves to be shown (and considering the stark scenes of real war which appear on the early evening news shows, why not?), *Combat* was presented with admirable restraint. Army Colonel Frank Gregg, who was a military adviser on the program, explains how the violence was restricted through built-in safeguards:

The safeguards include the actors, directors, producer, and the Continuity Office of the American Broadcasting Company. The Continuity Office is the moral guardian of all ABC programs.

Actors who have reached star status are quite image-conscious and balk at appearing in any scenes which might tarnish that image. Directors are familiar with the provisions of the code and exercise care in filming questionable scenes. However, they are generally less concerned with what is acceptable under the code than is the producer. Even after a director films a scene, the producer will delete it if *he* considers it excessively violent or morbid. Here is how this safeguard works. In one segment of "Combat," the director wanted to emphasize the difficult position in which the squad leader found himself—whether to leave one of his seriously wounded men and continue the mission or jeopardize the mission by taking the wounded man back to his lines. To give greater visual impact to the squad leader's dilemma, the director ordered a closeup of the stab wound in the man's abdomen. When the producer reviewed the film the next morning at "dailies," he directed the editor to throw out the scene.

For shows owned by the network, such as "Combat," scripts are reviewed by the Continuity Office before the segments are filmed. Passages considered in violation of the code are flagged for revision. This occurred in the segment titled "A Child's Game." A group of teen-aged German soldiers were holed up in a farmhouse. The Americans tried for some time to persuade them to surrender, but without success. Finally, one of the GIs maneuvered close enough to lob a grenade through the window. All resistance ceased. When the smoke cleared, the American sergeant rushed into the house. The bodies of the young soldiers were scattered in grotesque positions. He was so sickened by the scene that he staggered out of the house, over to a stone fence, and threw up. This was considered too morbid and violent by the Continuity Office.

Very infrequently, a violent or morbid scene is allowed to go through. In one segment, Fernando Lamas and Sal Mineo played roles as brothers in the French Resistance. They were captured and interrogated by the Germans. The actual interrogation was not shown, but the condition of the men as they emerged from the interrogation room was. They were cut and bruised, their faces were swollen, and their shirts were in shreds. Later, at the climax, one brother killed the other to prevent him from divulging information to the enemy. The Continuity Office objected to the scenes showing the condition of the men following interrogation. The producer argued that if these scenes were not included, the audience would not understand why one brother had to silence the other. In the end, the Continuity Office relented and the segment was shown as originally filmed.

If the producers of entertainment want to lift their concept of man, there is room within the codes to do it. If they want to lift their idea of Plato a bit, so as to take account of how *important* the subjects are on which their art tries to be "good teaching," there is nothing in the code to keep them from doing it. If they want to introduce a little of Aristotle's test to try to make their popular art better art as well as good teaching, there is still room within the code. There is nothing really to stop them except the voice of the producer saying, "This film must make money." And there have been superior films—in both Platonic and Aristotelian senses—which have made money. There have been superior broadcasts and superior magazines which have packed in the audiences.

The point is that, even within the existing limitations, more can be accomplished. An example from broadcasting indicates that children's programs need not necessarily be based on the low-common-denominator concept of man to which the serials, for adults and children, have accustomed us. They need not necessarily grind along on their old rusty track of violence and infantilism. This is a memorandum from network officials to the production staff of the best children's program that has appeared so far on television:

TO "CAPTAIN KANGAROO" PRODUCTION STAFF

The following are some random thoughts for your general guidance —not necessarily in order of importance.

1. The child viewer of TV can enjoy a clever game or a baby raccoon more than a pie thrown in a face.

2. No child should be called such names as "fatty," "shorty," or "string bean," by his school chums as a result of a character skit or anything appearing on this show.

3. A behavior hint can sound to a child like a common-sense idea or an irritating coy preachment from his prissiest aunt—depending on how it is handled.

4. When choosing the show's music, remember that it's to be played not for a small, tone-deaf animal, but for a young human of potentially great taste.

5. We think that our audience can enthusiastically admire a character without our providing any evidence that he can beat someone up.

6. It's possible for a child's oft cited "innate aggression" to be worked off without the aid of a villain on our show for him to hate.

7. We have heard no psychological theory stating that a child's attention span is increased by loud noise and chaos.

8. In regard to props—we would rather a child learn from us that he can use his imagination and a kitchen chair to make an airplane than that he see a real superjet on this show.

9. The widespread TV tradition, that if it's tasteful, kids won't like it, is one we reject entirely.

10. In general, the fact that children are imitators outlines our scope and our limitations. If you're writing or planning anything that can create an undesirable model for a child to imitate in action or thought —throw it out, there's a better way to entertain him.[29]

It seems obvious that this is a properly adult way of thinking about children's programing. The great trick is to find a properly adult way of thinking about adult programing.

8 Responsibilities: the Government, the Media, the Public

> Abuses of the freedom of speech ought to be repressed, but to whom dare we commit the power of doing it?
> —BENJAMIN FRANKLIN

Society has three great instruments which can encourage or prod the mass media to responsible performance: government, the mass media themselves, and the general public. If we ask which has the responsibility for promoting change, then quite clearly the answer is that they share it. And although these instruments are armed with varying degrees of power to promote change, none can accomplish it alone, and none is exempt. What we must search for is a desirable balance of responsibility and some notions as to how it can be used.

Government

The responsibility of government officials is clear, sweeping, and almost entirely negative: They must keep their hands off mass communication. Hardly anything government can do will be so important as restraining itself, and hardly anything will be so difficult. We have become accustomed to big government, to powerful government, to government that can set things right. Faced with gigantic problems, we have found that only government has the power to solve them.

Many Americans now feel that mass communication has grown

so big, so powerful, so removed from the public, that only government can control it. There is a vast difference between the way the Americans of a century ago perceived their relation to one of the tiny newspapers of that time and the way an American today perceives his relation to a giant newspaper, a network, or a motion picture studio. He feels a kind of helplessness today. And therefore, when he is dissatisfied, he automatically turns to a power center which can cope with such vast power.

This is the kind of pressure that works on Congress, on regulatory bodies such as the Federal Communications Commission, and on state and local licensing authorities. They are forever being exposed to the worries, the dissatisfactions, and the indignations of the public, and to the alleged shortcomings of the media. Religious and socially minded spokesmen among their constituents are forever pointing out instances in which the mass media may be endangering the morals of youth, or contributing to crime, or offending minority groups, or eroding religion. Political spokesmen are forever citing instances in which mass communication is presenting less than a clear lens to political realities. And public officials are moved to action by some of their own contacts with the mass media. Judges become dissatisfied with the way trials are reported. Elected officials may feel that they are being misinterpreted or misquoted or neglected in favor of their opponents. The members of regulatory bodies may look at mass communication with special sensitivities because of their own children or their neighbors' children.

All these people may sincerely believe that the mass communication system is out of hand. There is every incentive to take the direct, the obvious, the simple way to remedy the trouble: use the police power, the regulatory power, the legislative, judicial, or administrative power of government. Order a book or a magazine banned. Remove the reporters from the courtroom. Put a tight-lipped public-relations man between a public official and the reporters who want to see him. Require certain programs of a broadcasting station or deny it a license. Call a Congressional investigation. Prohibit multiple ownership or cross-media ownership. Do it simply: let government do it.

This is beguilingly simple and direct. But it should be resisted fiercely because it is dangerous.

This is the point at which we must decide what we believe. If we no longer believe in a democratic political philosophy, if we believe in some form of authoritarianism, then we can properly call upon government to correct every ill that besets mass communication. But these authors assume that we still believe fundamentally in the kind of democracy that is reflected in the Constitution, including the Bill of Rights, and that has developed over the years as new conditions required; that the changes in our attitudes toward the media and our expectations of them spring primarily from changes in the media and the generally increasing complexity of the life around us; and that what we chiefly want is a high degree of social responsibility in mass communication so that we can maintain the flow of information which is essential for a democracy. If these are fair assumptions, then we must be guarded in encouraging government to raise a strong hand.

We do not contend that government should ignore the mass media or that it bears no responsibility for their performance. It seems to us that Hocking was essentially correct when he called government a "residual legatee" of responsibility.[1] That is, government inherits such responsibility as is not adequately borne by the media themselves or by the public. But of the three instruments which can promote change—government, the media, and the public—government should be the third.

It takes real courage to let people alone, to refrain from correcting by governmental action what seem to be social abuses. But that is what we must ask government to do. And we give it a rule by which it can determine whether it should intervene in any given case. It is the rule stated first by Justice Oliver Wendell Holmes and echoed by the President's Commission on Civil Rights: "only where the danger to the well-being of society is clear and present."[2] Among the valuable amplifications of this doctrine is one cited by Chief Justice Fred M. Vinson in 1951:

Chief Justice Learned Hand, writing for the majority [in the lower court], interpreted the phrase as follows: "In each case [courts] must ask whether the gravity of the 'evil,' discounted by its improbability, justified such invasion of free speech as is necessary to avoid the danger."[3]

This is, to be sure, a difficult line to draw. Where one sees a danger, another may not. Where one sees "gravity" and "probability," another sees none. But the impressive thing is how careful the Supreme Court has been about declaring a clear and present danger to society, and how vigorous the Court has been in keeping the mass communication system free of government.

The Commission on Freedom of the Press recommended that the government "maintain competition among large units through the antitrust laws."[4] The motive for taking such action is clear and defensible: we want competition in our mass media. For the last fifty years economic forces have created fewer and larger economic units, and the development is troublesome; a true clash of ideas becomes difficult when the mass media are concentrated. As Morris Ernst said: "Nobody would favor having all of the radio stations owned by newspapers. . . . The only dispute is at what point should we be frightened, at what point should we stop—30 out of 800, or should we wait until 600, 700? There can be honest differences of opinion as to just where is the frightening point. I am telling you my prejudices. I am frightened when I see *one*."[5]

The Commission on Freedom of the Press also recommended that the government should, where necessary, supplement existing mass communication and "facilitate new ventures in the communication industry."[6] The promise and the dangers of such a policy are being explored even as this is written. Since the commercial networks seek to reach the largest audience possible to please sponsors, and since this effort forces them to aim at the lowest level of potential viewers, the demand for stronger noncommercial programing has become intense. In the fall of 1965, the Carnegie Commission on Educational Television, which was created with President Johnson's approval, began to consider a new role for educational television. In 1967, the Carnegie Commission recommended that Congress establish the Corporation for Public Television (CPTV), which would be funded by a tax on new television sets. The chief problem is that six of the corporation's twelve directors would be appointed by the President with the consent of Congress, and these six would then choose an additional six. *Broadcasting* pointed up the danger: "No presidential appointee who hoped for reappointment would vote for an electoral director who was unacceptable to the President."[7] *Television Magazine* warned that the proposal could lead to federal domination of educational television: "A CPTV that depended wholly upon federal underwriting and a CPTV directorate that owed its appointments directly to the President will hardly be totally immune to pressure from political strong points, especially if the pressures are subtly applied."[8] Whatever the dangers, it is now clear that Public Television, as it is generally known, will be a force. Whether it can overcome the danger of presidential control is still in doubt.

The point to remember is that government always tends to do the work that other units of society don't do for themselves. If the media are irresponsible and the public is ineffective, the government will step in to act. We are not saying that government *should* act. On the contrary, even a considerable degree of irresponsibility and ineffectiveness would be preferable to government interference. Our mechanism for maintaining responsibility is a delicate balance of forces. Government, for good or ill, is the residual legatee, and it is essential that the other forces restrict government action to a minimum.

The Media

The basic responsibility of mass communication is to turn out the highest-quality product it can, which requires that it develop an awareness of the depth and breadth of the public's needs and interests. There are two patterns in which the communicator organizes his sense of responsibility.

Self-regulation

The media codes were made by well-intentioned men and administered by careful and scrupulous men. Especially in the cases of motion pictures and comic books, the codes and the industry czars have contributed to cleaning up what can only be described as a mess. Radio and television have benefited from another form of self-regulation—the network acceptance offices, which exercise a benevolent censorship. We should not undervalue the machinery of self-regulation.

The danger is that we may count on the codes to accomplish more than they can. There is a tendency to rest secure in the confidence that establishing a code is the final answer. We must try to understand the limitations of codified morality.

It is important to emphasize the fundamental difference between the newspaper code—the Canons of Journalism adopted by the American Society of Newspaper Editors—and the others. The Canons are positive, eloquent, couched in generalities, and based on a concept of rational man and a libertarian philosophy. Moreover, the ASNE code was made and subscribed to by employees—editors, who work for publishers. It is a statement of objectives and standards which can be read for enlightenment and inspiration, but it has neither the force nor the mechanism of regulation.

The Canons of Journalism seem to represent what might be called the newspaperman's quest for professional status. Indeed, the formation of the American Society of Newspaper Editors was itself a sign of striving for status. The Canons were adopted at the very first meeting, in 1923. Since then, ASNE meetings have been notable for discussions of ethics and press freedom. But the code has never been formally subscribed to by the men who command policy, the publishers. Nor has there been any move to write enforcement provisions. The code is notable primarily because it was adopted without any special pressure on newspapers to reform.

The other codes are more negative, highly specific, based on a caretaker philosophy and on a concept of man as suggestible and malleable, in need of protection from moral and political ideas that might harm him. They are subscribed to by owners and provide for varying degrees of enforcement. To understand the nature and limitations of these codes it helps to emphasize that they grew out of fear and were designed for protection from public criticism and official action. As the Commission on Freedom of the Press pointed out, the standards are minimal, are not goals of ideal, or even adequate, performance. To be blunt, these codes are designed to keep the communicators out of trouble.

What have the codes accomplished? They have succeeded in eliminating many undesirable and offensive practices and materials from broadcasts, motion pictures, and comic books. They have enforced a degree of surface morality, although arbitrarily and mechanically. They have not enforced—and certainly cannot enforce—quality. They have not necessarily made for any aesthetically better programs and pictures. They have not even promoted any more truthful pictures or programs—that is, productions which emphasize the essentially honest rather than the phony, or in which the characters are real people rather than robots moving about in a rather artificially delimited world. Truthfulness is a quality of morality, and in that sense they have not even been able to legislate morality; in fact, they have accomplished the opposite by making it impossible for producers to treat certain problems and kinds of behavior which are essential to life and to understanding the variety of life.

In short, the responsibility of mass communicators is a higher horizon than can be reached through codes of conduct.

Professionalization

The slow, even painful way to promote change in mass communication requires a long process in which change takes place in people before it affects the system. This is professionalization.

When we speak of professionalizing the mass media, we do not mean to require of it all the characteristics and trappings of law and medicine. By any of the traditional definitions, mass communication (or journalism, or broadcasting, or film making, or even writing) is not a profession. A profession is an occupation which performs certain important types of public service. A large proportion of its members are self-employed. They usually maintain a confidential relationship with the members of the public they serve. In general, before they are admitted to practice of the profession, they must show mastery of a substantial body of knowledge which is unique to the profession. To acquire this knowledge, a candidate usually spends a long time in a professional school, which is a center of research and criticism as well as teaching. The profession has a conscience which is usually expressed in a code (for example, the oath of Hippocrates). The new member vows to maintain the profession's standards. If he fails, an authority, usually acting on the advice of his peers, has the power to disbar him. There is a tradition that the professional will perform needed public service regardless of the income from it. That is, the physician will treat a patient in the most ethical way and to the extent of his abilities, even though he might profit more by quackery; he will minister to a sick man even though the man cannot pay the fee.

The branches of mass communication obviously do not meet all these qualifications. Although no occupation has a higher public service to perform than to serve man's need to know, and although there is a trace of the confidential relationship between news gatherer and the source of news, the parallel recedes beyond that point. Except in a few cases, the practitioners of mass communication are employees, and thus the ultimate responsibility for their work and the quality of their service rests on their employers. Many mass communicators attend quasi-professional schools of journalism and communication, but these schools have only begun to develop the substantial and unique body of knowledge that is essential. So far, they can only introduce the students to some of the skills required and prepare them to go understandingly into the occupation by exposing them to the history of the craft and discussing its social responsibilities, its relationships to other social activities, and the way it works.

But the really substantial body of knowledge which the mass communicator needs is not so channeled or specialized; it is a complex of whatever helps him to understand the world around him. As Roy Lewis and Angus Maude say in *Professional People,* "Journalists are employed in reporting, writing up, interviewing, sub-editing, and though these are not jobs which anyone can do without a considerable amount of experience, no specialized intellectual training is an indispensable preliminary."[9] Moreover, the very nature of our system makes it unlikely that entrance to mass communication would ever be restricted by examinations of the sort that determine which candidates become physicians or lawyers. Even if the subject matter could be decided upon, an examination would almost certainly be interpreted as a restriction on free expression. There might be some advantages in a system of examinations and licenses, and in several other countries journalists are licensed. Here, however, the dangers would overbalance the advantages. To give either the government or a nongovernmental organization the right to determine who enters the profession is tantamount to allowing that authority the right to say who can use the mass communication system. By the same token, the possibility of expelling a communicator for malpractice would have to be approached carefully, if at all.

Having made all these technical points, let us argue that we can expect professional standards, attitudes, and behavior from mass communication. And let us suggest that a profession develops, not by asking how another profession is organized, but by asking what kind of behavior is necessary to public-service obligations. If that question is seriously asked, thoughtfully answered, and acted upon, communication will be on the road to professional status. As Lewis and Maude say, "There is, nevertheless, in the aspirations of the journalists toward a strict guardianship of the truth . . . an indication that journalism seeks (and often achieves) a responsible professional attitude, even comparable with that in medicine and law."[10]

What more can be done to professionalize mass communication?

The longest step that can be taken is perhaps to emphasize the *individual* sense of responsibility rather than the corporate sense—that is, the responsibility of the communicator as a public servant and as a professional, quite apart from his obligations to the business that employs him. Although legal and administrative responsibility for a communicator's actions rests with his employers, the mass media—and especially the journalists within mass communication—do not really operate like other businesses. We have cited instance after instance in which employees have acted according to a code quite apart from instructions issued above. More freely than employees in any other business do journalists respond to questions about their practices with "I would do this" or "I wouldn't do it that way." Enhancing this sense of a personal ethic is vital.

We would encourage the building of such attitudes throughout the mass communication structure. We include the owners, whom we expect to distinguish between good business practices and public responsibility, and we include the cub reporter, whom we expect to be accurate and fair and free of corrupting influences even on his first assignment. We include the advertising men and the management personnel, the writers and the "talent." If they cannot perform at the level of the angels, we expect them to operate somewhat above the level of the pitchmen.

The employers can help professionalize by upgrading their staffs. We seem to hope that journalists will be prepared for their work by obtaining a world view in breadth and depth such as few college graduates ever get; yet their salaries are considerably below those paid by businesses hiring graduates with scientific or business training. This is one reason why so many reporters are only technicians, smart but not informed. This is not to say that all the ills of mass communication can be cured by raising the pay scale. The communication industry is no longer notably low-paid, and other kinds of rewards are almost as important: professional recognition for jobs well done, initiative and freedom and responsibility.

Fortunately, one of the deepest needs of journalists for many years is now being met. For too long a time, the Nieman Program at Harvard was almost alone in providing a full opportunity for journalists in mid-career to return to the campus to study what they needed to study. Now, especially because of Ford Foundation grants to Harvard, Columbia, Northwestern, Stanford, and the Southern Regional Education Board, almost any journalist can study his specialty in depth. Programs ranging from three-day seminars to a full academic year are operating successfully.

Unfortunately, very few broadcast journalists even apply for these programs. There are more than enough applicants from newspapers, and sizable numbers from magazines. Many broadcast journalists, on the other hand, seem to feel that leaving for even short periods may jeopardize their jobs, even though the most evident need throughout the mass media is for greater depth, which advanced study may help to encourage.

If mass communicators gave more attention to informing themselves, some of the anti-intellectual snideness that pervades so many news reports and commentaries might be reduced significantly. Perhaps the media would develop new attitudes toward research.

Not long ago, the Chicago *Sun-Times* echoed some members of Congress by publishing a jeering little piece on the fact that the U.S. government, in the midst of its agony over the balance of payments, is paying foreign scientists to investigate death rates among Italian railroad employees. A total of $17,400 was being spent to discover the incidence of coronary heart disease among railroad conductors in Italy.

On the face of it, the jeers seemed deserved. Yet if the reporter had looked beneath the surface facts, he would have discovered that this was a very small outlay on a very important project. Coronary heart disease is by far the leading cause of death in the United States. It accounts for nearly a third of all deaths of men and nearly a fourth of all deaths of women in this country. Medical researchers believe that premature coronary heart disease can be prevented. And they have found that men in Italy, for reasons that they do not yet understand, are seldom victims. Medical researchers have also discovered that the U.S. Railroad Retirement Board keeps excellent records on U.S. railroad employees. Since many jobs in the railroad industry are the same the world over, comparing the diets of railroad employees in the United States and in Italy may yield important information about coronary heart disease in this country.

In short, jeering at those spendthrift bureaucrats—briefcase-toters every one—is simple. Understanding their reasons sometimes asks for analysis.

First, the news media need to develop a sense of respect for research and researchers. Not blind respect. It is not anti-intellectual to question research. It is anti-intellectual simply to jeer at it.

The other attitude toward research that the news media should develop involves doing some of it. This does not mean that newspaper, magazine, and broadcast journalists should set up their own survey research organizations. It means that they should research the researchers.

Consider the reports on polls. It is one of the major ironies of journalism that in an era when reporters pride themselves on analysis and interpretation—probing and questioning every act of public men—they accept the findings of polls (almost *any* polls) and report them with hardly a murmur. It sometimes seems that journalists consider one poll exactly as valuable as another.

Consider a front-page story in the august *New York Times* headed 54 PER CENT IN OHIO POLL ASSERT U.S. ROLE IN WAR IS MISTAKE. The story under that headline ran fourteen column inches on the front page and another thirteen inches on an inside page. To the unknowing reader, Gallup, or Louis Harris, or some other practitioner of the mystic science had surveyed Ohio on the Vietnam war. What had actually happened was that Congressman Charles Mosher had mailed out a questionnaire to constituents in his 13th Ohio District—one of those questionnaires designed to enhance his election chances—and had received returns from 3.5 per cent. That was the basis for a prominently displayed 27-inch story in the *Times*.

It was, of course, crushingly misleading. It must have been mystifying as well to readers who saw, a short while later in the

Times, a Gallup Poll showing quite different attitudes toward the war.

Researching the researchers should begin with eight items established as standards by the American Association of Public Opinion Research:

1. Who sponsored the survey? Obviously, if a Congressman with a stake in the answers asked the questions, the public should be made aware of that fact.

2. How, exactly, were the questions worded? In *News Research for Better Newspapers,* Chilton Bush cites one Congressman's question to his constituents: "In 1958, I publicly proposed an extra tax credit for parents of college students. Are you in favor of such a tax credit exemption as presently gaining bipartisan support in Congress?"

3. What was the population sampled? Only a tortured version of the English language could translate the 13th District of Ohio into "an Ohio poll."

4. What was the size of the sample? If it was a mail survey, how many answers were received?

5. What is the allowance for sampling error?

6. Are any of your findings based on only part of the total sample?

7. How was the interview made—by phone, by mail, on street corners?

8. What was the timing of the interview in relation to related events? For example, immediately before the 1968 Republican Convention, one national poll reported Rockefeller leading Nixon, another reported Nixon leading Rockefeller. Was the latter poll affected by the strong endorsement given Nixon by former President Eisenhower immediately before the interviewing began? We cannot be certain, but the public should be made aware of the fact.

Finally, we can hope for the beginnings of self-criticism. There is the seed of a self-critical spirit in the incisive judgments of a few journalists, notably Ben Bagdikian, Walter Lippmann, James Reston, Eric Sevareid, and Howard K. Smith. There are glimmerings of a new spirit, too, in the fact that the mass media are now quoting other critics as never before—a change that some of the old-timers cannot understand. Shortly before his retirement as Vice President and Editor of United Press International, Earl Johnson wondered in print why newspapers were publishing letters to the editor and editorials critical of the Associated Press and his own UPI. "It is odd," he wrote, "that newspapers would pass such views along to their readers about their own two main sources of campaign news." It is odd, but encouraging.

Judged in terms of the need, however, self-criticism is a languid thing: the news magazines snipe occasionally at newspapers; a few newspapers shoot back; both make scatter-shot surveys of the failings of prime-time television. Only the organs of politics and opinion—*The Nation, The New Republic, Harper's, The Atlantic, Saturday Review, National Review, Human Events* (fugitive publications by the standards of mass journalism)—seem to be consistently concerned. Only *Columbia Journalism Review* and *Nieman Reports* are consistently acute.

What is needed is a critical apparatus. As Walter Lippmann has pointed out, "There are . . . only the first beginnings of the equivalent of bar associations and medical societies which set intellectual and ethical standards for the practice of the profession. Journalism, we might say, is still an under-developed profession."

A model, of sorts, for a critical apparatus that would encourage professionalism exists in the British Press Council. It receives complaints, calls on the responsible editors for explanations, then pronounces judgments. And although it has no ultimate authority —no means of imposing penalties—the Council has succeeded because it has used wisely a weapon the press has reason to respect: publicity.

A narrower concept is now operating in a few cities in the United States: local press councils. The Mellett Fund for a Free and Responsible Press, which was established by a bequest of Lowell Mellett, is funding several press council experiments. Although it is much too early to judge whether the press council idea will catch on, observers are encouraged by the eagerness of many newspapers to take part in the experiments, which subject their performance to the critical review of their readers.

Two highly successful local councils are now operating in the West, one in Littleton, Colorado, the other in Bend, Oregon. In both cases, the editors considered the degree of their community responsibility and decided that they could improve their papers by meeting regularly with representative groups of readers. The Bend Council, which was one of those established originally by a one-year grant from the Mellett Fund, began its second year in

October, 1968, without outside funding. Editor Bob Chandler, one of the most respected journalists in the Northwest, named as moderator a local lawyer of the opposite political persuasion to give his council full range to express their opinions.

The plan is useful for newspapers, nearly all of which are locally oriented, but the existence of the far-flung wire services and the nation-spanning networks and magazines suggests that local councils will not solve the larger problem. It would be solved by a proposal offered by Harold Lasswell of Yale for a national Committee on Public Communication, which would operate much as the British Council does. Lasswell proposes that the Committee be composed entirely of representatives of the mass media—those, he said, who are "suspected of integrity."

It is hardly heretical to suggest that a profession seek to purify itself, and most journalists today consider themselves professionals whatever the explicit definition. Medicine and law have long tried to purify their ranks. Even the much-maligned public-relations practitioners have expelled from the Public Relations Society of America those who have not subscribed to the PRSA code.

A somewhat different commission has been suggested by former Senator William Benton (who made a fortune running an advertising agency). Elaborating on this proposal, Frank Kelly, Vice President of the Center for the Study of Democratic Institutions, told the FCC:

Whether the commission be created by presidential appointment or other official act, as Mr. Benton has proposed, or be created and supported by purely private means, it should be made up of interested, informed, and concerned citizens completely independent of the industry. Having no regulatory or coercive powers, such a commission would encounter no conflict with the First Amendment. It could perform a critical function in regard to program content properly denied to the FCC but clearly needed by a developing industry which has demonstrated that it cannot sustain its own declared standards of responsibility and taste in the face of commercial pressures which dominate it.

Such a commission might cause pain to some of those who now control broadcasting. But if it succeeded in mobilizing public opinion it would also free the medium of the tyranny which forces it to base most programming on the advertiser's estimate of the common denominator.

With its great financial resources, and its still exciting if largely unrealized potential, television commands the greatest pool of creative talent our country has ever known. Yet this talent has no effective command over the medium, with the result that the creative urge is frustrated and often perverted. At the least this is a tragic waste of a great natural resource; it may also be a positive threat to the national interest in a time when there is general agreement that we need a new spiritual awakening.

The performance of the broadcasters is a proper matter of public concern, as is the performance of the proprietors of the printed media. The role of the government in determining what that perform-ance shall be is, of necessity, essentially negative; the government may define certain outer limits of free speech on grounds of obscenity and libel, and it may set general standards that must be met in return for governmental bounty in the form of monopoly broadcast licenses or mail subsidies.

The government has an obligation to see to it that there is a fair field for broadcasting. Private citizens—educators, philanthropists, and ordinary viewers and listeners—have an obligation to see to it that the field is occupied by the bold as well as the bland.

It is not enough to say, as some do, that standards and criti-cisms are useless because of the doctrine of press freedom. It is certainly true that no newspaper or magazine can be forced to cease publication, no radio or television program can be driven off the air by professional outrage. But the American Association of University Professors has shown that public condemnation can work remarkable changes in supposedly impregnable institutions. Many a college and university has been compelled by AAUP cen-sure to soften its authoritarian tone.

This is not to say that there should be concerted attacks from the right on those organs of the left that seem to be drifting toward "socialism" or attacks on the organs of the right that seem committed to the restoration of William McKinley. This simply asks that a reporter, an editor, a publisher, or a broadcaster who abuses the canons of responsibility at least be tested by pitiless publicity to determine whether he is incapable of chagrin.

It is easy to suspect that the time is near when the mass media will themselves feel a need for an organization that, while it may censure them for their failings and excesses, will understand their problems and explain them to the larger community. For it seems almost axiomatic that the curve of criticism will rise. Not only is there a growing dissatisfaction because disadvantaged groups feel that they do not have proper access to the media; certain tendencies toward concentration of ownership have excited thoughtful critics to question the future course of mass communication in the United States.

The most cogent single commentary on these tendencies has come from Commissioner Nicholas Johnson of the FCC. In "The Media Barons and the Public Interest," an article in *The Atlantic,* Commissioner Johnson took a long, horrified look at the mergers and conglomerates that have been formed in mass communication during recent years. He concluded that we may "have already reached the point in this country where the media, our greatest check on other accumulations of power, may themselves be beyond the reach of any other institution: Congress, the President, or the Federal Communications Commission, not to mention governors, mayors, state legislators, and city councilmen."

The Public

The listening, viewing, reading public underestimates its power. Anyone who studies mass communication as a social institution cannot fail to observe the sharp push and pull of public tastes. The program pattern of the networks vibrates like a wind harp to the breeze from the ratings. New films go out to sneak previews, sample public reaction, then go back to the cutting room. One hundred letters to a network will bring a review of policy; a few letters to a station will bring a review of a program or of a program structure. One visit of a serious committee to a newspaper editor will lead him to consider changes, even though he will probably be crusty about making promises to the committee. The motion picture industry has always feared boycotts more than censorship.

In short, the audience calls the tune.

Few listeners, viewers, or readers realize what a fundamental problem was posed by the coming of bigness and fewness to mass communication. When the media were many and their audiences were small, when only a small percentage of the population could read, and a small elite group was the audience for most newspapers, magazines, and books—then there was a quick and vigorous feedback of demands and judgments. Now a great anonymity has settled over the audiences, and they are known to the media only as program ratings or percentages of readership or circulation figures.

Is there a realistic hope that some of the intimacy of yesterday—when the readers knew the editors and the performers even knew some of their audiences—can be recaptured? CBS or MGM or *Reader's Digest* is never likely to recapture the relationship which *The Dial* maintained with its audience when that influential magazine had 200 subscribers, most of them known to the editor, Margaret Fuller. But between that situation and the far end of the scale, at which audiences are an anonymous mass, it is clearly possible for the audiences of mass communication to move far up the scale from anonymity to personality. It is possible, that is, for the great audience to become a live, responsive, discriminating audience which makes its wishes known and in its own quiet way enforces those wishes. And if it should appear that in this audience there are different levels of taste and kinds of need, it is clearly possible for the audience to insist that the media serve those different tastes and needs rather than serve up an insipid common-denominator broth which appeals a little to each and satisfies none.

The first responsibility of the public, then, is to make itself an alert, discriminating audience. This will require a somewhat different habit of mind from that commonly displayed by many who, by virtue of position or education, might be expected to be the leaders of and spokesmen for the public in its demands on mass communication. The common attitude—"Oh, I never watch television except when there's something like a political convention on; it's just trash"—is fundamentally irresponsible. It neglects the fact that television need not be all trash, if indeed it is. Television is potentially our widest window on the world, our best hope for expanding our horizons, bringing a sense of reality to faraway events, making informed judgments on public figures, sharing the lectures and demonstrations at our greatest universities, seeing the kind of opera, ballet, drama, museums, and concert artists formerly available to few, most of them in great cities. If television is not being used in this way, what a social waste! And basically it is the fault of the people who will not watch it and will do nothing to improve it.

To make ourselves a discriminating audience, we must consider what the media might be giving us. We must discuss the media with friends. We must try to see that the schools give some attention to using mass communication intelligently. After all, our children will be giving perhaps five hours a day—nearly a third of their waking time—to mass communication.

The next step is to make our views known, perhaps primarily through letters—to the editor, to the station, to the network, to the theater, or to the studio. The more individual the letter is, the better, for wastebaskets are filled with letters written in about the same words and revealing clearly that a pressure group is at work. Individual letters are read and valued, and so are individual contacts. They help to describe what a thinking member of the audience believes.

These informal and individual efforts can be supplemented by organization. We have spoken harshly at some points in this book about the work of pressure groups. They are often ineffective because they are negative—but sometimes the worst effects for the total society spring from their work to ban this or down that. Why can't pressure groups learn that positive requests would be refreshing? Certainly, requests for more and longer reports on city council action, Little Theater performances, and international news, or for a music column, will encourage the media to publish and broadcast the kinds of things that may crowd out the things the pressure group opposes.

There could be more newspapers covering public affairs somewhat as the *New York Times* does, but in other parts of the country, if publishers thought readers would buy them. The continuing development of the Los Angeles *Times* is heartening. There could be more and better community television stations, covering local public affairs and carrying the best in local entertainment and information, if audiences would give them a few dollars per viewer per year. The university radio and television stations could furnish a better—even an exciting—service if the public persuaded administrations and legislatures to support them adequately. More theaters would specialize in high-quality films, and more studios would make such films, if the public would patronize them.

Finally, the public can encourage and promote responsible communication by encouraging and promoting education. In the end, the determination of the future American culture will depend largely upon a concert of mass education and mass media. The media have always shaped their product along lines the masses could understand. When, in 1940, only one American in four had a high school education, the media were predictably at a low level. Now, well over half of every high school graduating class goes to college, and there is a slow upgrading of mass communication, but too slow.

Higher education is not itself a panacea. One of the most discouraging aspects of American life is the progression of many college students from the narrow world of the local environment to the wide world of the university—then back into a restricted environment. The task of the mass media is to offer a wider view of the world for those who are tempted to regress. This can be accomplished only if the media can attract men and women who are dedicated to the first affairs of their time, and only if the public understands that it has the power to determine the course of mass communication.

Appendix A

THE CANONS OF JOURNALISM

AMERICAN SOCIETY OF NEWSPAPER EDITORS

The primary function of newspapers is to communicate to the human race what its members do, feel, and think. Journalism, therefore, demands of its practitioners the widest range of intelligence or knowledge and of experience, as well as natural and trained powers of observation and reasoning. To its opportunities as a chronicle are indissolubly linked its obligations as teacher and interpreter.

To the end of finding some means of codifying sound practice and just aspirations of American journalism, these canons are set forth:

I

Responsibility. The right of a newspaper to attract and hold readers is restricted by nothing but considerations of public welfare. The use a newspaper makes of the share of public attention it gains serves to determine its sense of responsibility, which it shares with every member of its staff. A journalist who uses his power for any selfish or otherwise unworthy purpose is faithless to a high trust.

II

Freedom of the Press. Freedom of the press is to be guarded as a vital right of mankind. It is the unquestionable right to discuss whatever is not explicitly forbidden by law, including the wisdom of any restrictive statute.

III

Independence. Freedom from all obligations except that of fidelity to the public interest is vital.

1. Promotion of any private interest contrary to the general welfare, for whatever reason, is not compatible with honest journalism. So-called news communications from private sources should not be published without public notice of their source or else substantiation of their claims to value as news, both in form and substance.

2. Partisanship, in editorial comment which knowingly departs from the truth, does violence to the best spirit of American journalism; in the news columns it is subversive of a fundamental principle of the profession.

IV

Sincerity, Truthfulness, Accuracy. Good faith with the reader is the foundation of all journalism worthy of the name.

1. By every consideration of good faith a newspaper is constrained to be truthful. It is not to be excused for lack of thoroughness or accuracy within its control, or failure to obtain command of these essential qualities.

2. Headlines should be fully warranted by the contents of the article which they surmount.

V

Impartiality. Sound practice makes clear distinction between news reports and expressions of opinion. News reports should be free from opinion or bias of any kind.

1. This rule does not apply to so-called special articles unmistakably devoted to advocacy or characterized by a signature authorizing the writer's own conclusions and interpretation.

VI

Fair Play. A newspaper should not publish official charges affecting reputation or moral character without opportunity given to the accused to be heard; right practice demands the giving of such opportunity in all cases of serious accusation outside judicial proceedings.

1. A newspaper should not invade private rights or feelings without sure warrant of public right as distinguished from public curiosity.

2. It is the privilege, as it is the duty, of a newspaper to make prompt and complete correction of its own serious mistakes of fact or opinion, whatever their origin.

VII

Decency. A newspaper cannot escape conviction of insincerity if while professing high moral purpose it supplies incentives to base conduct, such as are to be found in details of crime and vice, publication of which is not demonstrably for the general good. Lacking authority to enforce its canons, the journalism here represented can but express the hope that deliberate panderings to vicious instincts will encounter effective public disapproval or yield to the influence of a preponderant professional condemnation.

Appendix B

THE TELEVISION CODE

PREAMBLE

Television is seen and heard in every type of American home. These homes include children and adults of all ages, embrace all races and all varieties of religious faith, and reach those of every educational background. It is the responsibility of television to bear constantly in mind that the audience is primarily a home audience, and consequently that television's relationship to the viewers is that between guest and host.

The revenues from advertising support the free, competitive American system of telecasting, and make available to the eyes and ears of the American people the finest programs of information, education, culture and entertainment. By law the television broadcaster is responsible for the programming of his station. He, however, is obligated to bring his positive responsibility for excellence and good taste in programming to bear upon all who have a hand in the production of programs, including networks, sponsors, producers of film and of live programs, advertising agencies, and talent agencies.

The American businesses which utilize television for conveying their advertising messages to the home by pictures with sound, seen free-of-charge on the home screen, are reminded that their responsibilities are not limited to the sale of goods and the creation of a favorable attitude toward the sponsor by the presentation of entertainment. They include, as well, responsibility for utilizing television to bring the best programs, regardless of kind, into American homes.

Television and all who participate in it are jointly accountable to the American public for respect for the special needs of children, for community responsibility, for the advancement of education and culture, for the acceptability of the program materials chosen, for decency and decorum in production, and for propriety in advertising. This responsibility cannot be discharged by any given group of programs, but can be discharged only through the highest standards of respect for the American home, applied to every moment of every program presented by television.

In order that television programming may best serve the public interest, viewers should be encouraged to make their criticisms and positive suggestions known to the television broadcasters. Parents in particular should be urged to see to it that out of the richness of television fare, the best programs are brought to the attention of their children.

I. *Advancement of Education and Culture*

1. Commercial television provides a valuable means of augmenting the educational and cultural influence of schools, institutions of higher learning, the home, the church, museums, foundations, and other institutions devoted to education and culture.

2. It is the responsibility of a television broadcaster to call upon such institutions for counsel and cooperation and to work with them on the best methods of presenting educational and cultural materials by television. It is further the responsibility of stations, networks, advertising agencies and sponsors consciously to seek opportunities for introducing into telecasts factual materials which will aid in the enlightenment of the American public.

3. Education via television may be taken to mean that process by which the individual is brought toward informed adjustment to his society. Television is also responsible for the presentation of overtly instructional and cultural programs, scheduled so as to reach the viewers who are naturally drawn to such programs, and produced so as to attract the largest possible audience.

4. The television broadcaster should be thoroughly conversant with the educational and cultural needs and desires of the community served.

5. He should affirmatively seek out responsible and accountable educational and cultural institutions of the community with a view toward providing opportunities for the instruction and enlightenment of the viewers.

6. He should provide for reasonable experimentation in the development of programs specifically directed to the advancement of the community's culture and education.

7. It is in the interest of television as a vital medium to encourage and promote the broadcast of programs presenting genuine artistic or literary material, valid moral and social issues, significant controversial and challenging concepts and other subject matter involving adult themes. Accordingly, none of the provisions of this code, including those relating to the responsibility toward children, should be construed to prevent or impede their broadcast. All such programs, however, should be broadcast with due regard to the composition of the

audience. The highest degree of care should be exercised to preserve the integrity of such programs and to ensure that the selection of themes, their treatment and presentation are made in good faith upon the basis of true instructional and entertainment values, and not for the purposes of sensationalism, to shock or exploit the audience or to appeal to prurient interests or morbid curiosity.

II. *Responsibility Toward Children*

1. The education of children involves giving them a sense of the world at large. It is not enough that only those programs which are intended for viewing by children shall be suitable to the young and immature. In addition, those programs which might be reasonably expected to hold the attention of children and which are broadcast during times of the day when children may be normally expected to constitute a substantial part of the audience should be presented with due regard for their effect on children.

2. Such subjects as violence and sex shall be presented without undue emphasis and only as required by plot development or character delineation. Crime should not be presented as attractive or as a solution to human problems, and the inevitable retribution should be made clear.

3. The broadcaster should afford opportunities for cultural growth as well as for wholesome entertainment.

4. He should develop programs to foster and promote the commonly accepted moral, social and ethical ideals characteristic of American life.

5. Programs should reflect respect for parents, for honorable behavior, and for the constituted authorities of the American community.

6. Exceptional care should be exercised with reference to kidnapping or threats of kidnapping of children in order to avoid terrorizing them.

7. Material which is excessively violent or would create morbid suspense, or other undesirable reactions in children, should be avoided.

8. Particular restraint and care in crime or mystery episodes involving children or minors, should be exercised.

III. *Community Responsibility*

1. A television broadcaster and his staff occupy a position of responsibility in the community and should conscientiously endeavor to be acquainted fully with its needs and characteristics in order better to serve the welfare of its citizens.

2. Requests for time for the placement of public service announcements or programs should be carefully reviewed with respect to the character and reputation of the group, campaign or organization in-

volved, the public interest content of the message, and the manner of its presentation.

IV. *General Program Standards*

1. Program materials should enlarge the horizons of the viewer, provide him with wholesome entertainment, afford helpful stimulation, and remind him of the responsibilities which the citizen has towards his society. The intimacy and confidence placed in television demand of the broadcaster, the network and other program sources that they be vigilant in protecting the audience from deceptive program practices.

2. Profanity, obscenity, smut and vulgarity are forbidden, even when likely to be understood only by part of the audience. From time to time, words which have been acceptable, acquire undesirable meanings, and telecasters should be alert to eliminate such words.

3. Words (especially slang) derisive of any race, color, creed, nationality or national derivation, except wherein such usage would be for the specific purpose of effective dramatization such as combating prejudice, are forbidden, even when likely to be understood only by part of the audience. From time to time, words which have been acceptable, acquire undesirable meanings, and telecasters should be alert to eliminate such words.

4. Racial or nationality types shall not be shown on television in such a manner as to ridicule the race or nationality.

5. Attacks on religion and religious faiths are not allowed. Reverence is to mark any mention of the name of God, His attributes and powers. When religious rites are included in other than religious programs the rites shall be accurately presented. The office of minister, priest or rabbi shall not be presented in such a manner as to ridicule or impair its dignity.

6. Respect is maintained for the sanctity of marriage and the value of the home. Divorce is not treated casually as a solution for marital problems.

7. In reference to physical or mental afflictions and deformities, special precautions must be taken to avoid ridiculing sufferers from similar ailments and offending them or members of their families.

8. Excessive or unfair exploitation of others or of their physical or mental afflictions shall not be presented as praiseworthy.

The presentation of cruelty, greed and selfishness as worthy motivations is to be avoided.

9. Law enforcement shall be upheld and, except where essential to the program plot, officers of the law portrayed with respect and dignity.

10. Legal, medical and other professional advice, diagnosis and treatment will be permitted only in conformity with law and recognized ethical and professional standards.

11. The use of animals both in the production of television pro-

grams and as part of television program content, shall at all times, be in conformity with accepted standards of humane treatment.

12. Care should be exercised so that cigarette smoking will not be depicted in a manner to impress the youth of our country as a desirable habit worthy of imitation.

13. Criminality shall be presented as undesirable and unsympathetic. The condoning of crime and the treatment of the commission of crime in a frivolous, cynical or callous manner is unacceptable.

The presentation of techniques of crime in such detail as to invite imitation shall be avoided.

14. The presentation of murder or revenge as a motive for murder shall not be presented as justifiable.

15. Suicide as an acceptable solution for human problems is prohibited.

16. Illicit sex relations are not treated as commendable.

Sex crimes and abnormalities are generally unacceptable as program material.

The use of locations closely associated with sexual life or with sexual sin must be governed by good taste and delicacy.

17. Drunkenness should never be presented as desirable or prevalent. The use of liquor in program content shall be de-emphasized. The consumption of liquor in American life, when not required by the plot or for proper characterization, shall not be shown.

18. Narcotic addiction shall not be presented except as a vicious habit. The administration of illegal drugs will not be displayed.

19. The use of gambling devices or scenes necessary to the development of plot or as appropriate background is acceptable only when presented with discretion and in moderation, and in a manner which would not excite interest in, or foster, betting nor be instructional in nature.

20. Telecasts of actual sport programs at which on-the-scene betting is permitted by law should be presented in a manner in keeping with Federal, state and local laws, and should concentrate on the subject as a public sporting event.

21. Program material pertaining to fortune-telling, occultism, astrology, phrenology, palm-reading, numerology, mind-reading, or character-reading is unacceptable when presented for the purpose of fostering belief in these subjects.

22. Quiz and similar programs that are presented as contests of knowledge, information, skill or luck must, in fact, be genuine contests and the results must not be controlled by collusion with or between contestants, or any other action which will favor one contestant against any other.

23. No program shall be presented in a manner which through artifice or simulation would mislead the audience as to any material fact. Each broadcaster must exercise reasonable judgment to determine

whether a particular method of presentation would constitute a material deception, or would be accepted by the audience as normal theatrical illusion.

24. The appearances or dramatization of persons featured in actual crime news will be permitted only in such light as to aid law enforcement or to report the news event.

25. The use of horror for its own sake will be eliminated; the use of visual or aural effect which would shock or alarm the viewer, and the detailed presentation of brutality or physical agony by sight or by sound are not permissible.

26. Contests may not constitute a lottery.

27. Any telecasting designed to "buy" the television audience by requiring it to listen and/or view in hope of reward rather than for the quality of the program, should be avoided.

28. The costuming of all performers shall be within the bounds of propriety and shall avoid such exposure or such emphasis on anatomical detail as would embarrass or offend home viewers.

29. The movements of dancers, actors, or other performers shall be kept within the bounds of decency, and lewdness and impropriety shall not be suggested in the positions assumed by performers.

30. Camera angles shall avoid such views of performers as to emphasize anatomical details indecently.

31. The use of the television medium to transmit information of any kind by the use of the process called "subliminal perception," or by the use of any similar technique whereby an attempt is made to convey information to the viewer by transmitting messages below the threshold of normal awareness, is not permitted.

32. The broadcaster shall be constantly alert to prevent activities that may lead to such practices as the use of scenic properties, the choice and identification of prizes, the selection of music and other creative program elements and inclusion of any identification of commercial products or services, their trade names or advertising slogans, within a program dictated by factors other than the requirements of the program itself. The acceptance of cash payments or other considerations in return for including any of the above within the program is prohibited except in accordance with Sections 317 and 508 of the Communications Act.

33. A television broadcaster should not present fictional events or other non-news material as authentic news telecasts or announcements, nor should he permit dramatizations in any program which would give the false impression that the dramatized material constitutes news. Expletives (presented aurally or pictorially) such as "flash" or "bulletin" and statements such as "we interrupt this program to bring you . . ." should be reserved specifically for news room use. However, a television broadcaster may properly exercise discretion in the use in non-news programs of words or phrases which do not necessarily imply that the material following is a news release.

34. Program content should be confined to those elements which entertain or inform the viewer and to the extent that titles, teasers and credits do not meet these criteria, they should be restricted or eliminated.

35. The creation of a state of hypnosis by act or demonstration on the air is prohibited and hypnosis as an aspect of "parlor game" antics to create humorous situations within a comedy setting cannot be used.

V. *Treatment of News and Public Events*

NEWS

1. A television station's news schedule should be adequate and well-balanced.

2. News reporting should be factual, fair and without bias.

3. A television broadcaster should exercise particular discrimination in the acceptance, placement and presentation of advertising in news programs so that such advertising should be clearly distinguishable from the news content.

4. At all times, pictorial and verbal material for both news and comment should conform to other sections of these standards, wherever such sections are reasonably applicable.

5. Good taste should prevail in the selection and handling of news: Morbid, sensational or alarming details not essential to the factual report, especially in connection with stories of crime or sex, should be avoided. News should be telecast in such a manner as to avoid panic and unnecessary alarm.

6. Commentary and analysis should be clearly identified as such.

7. Pictorial material should be chosen with care and not presented in a misleading manner.

8. All news interview programs should be governed by accepted standards of ethical journalism, under which the interviewer selects the questions to be asked. Where there is advance agreement materially restricting an important or newsworthy area of questioning, the interviewer will state on the program that such limitation has been agreed upon. Such disclosure should be made if the person being interviewed requires that questions be submitted in advance or if he participates in editing a recording of the interview prior to its use on the air.

9. A television broadcaster should exercise due care in his supervision of content, format, and presentation of newscasts originated by his station, and in his selection of newscasters, commentators, and analysts.

PUBLIC EVENTS

1. A television broadcaster has an affirmative responsibility at all times to be informed of public events, and to provide coverage consonant with the ends of an informed and enlightened citizenry.

2. The treatment of such events by a television broadcaster should provide adequate and informed coverage.

VI. *Controversial Public Issues*

1. Television provides a valuable forum for the expression of responsible views on public issues of a controversial nature. The television broadcaster should seek out and develop with accountable individuals, groups and organizations, programs relating to controversial public issues of import to his fellow citizens; and to give fair representation to opposing sides of issues which materially affect the life or welfare of a substantial segment of the public.

2. Requests by individuals, groups or organizations for time to discuss their views on controversial public issues, should be considered on the basis of their individual merits, and in the light of the contribution which the use requested would make to the public interest, and to a well-balanced program structure.

3. Programs devoted to the discussion of controversial public issues should be identified as such. They should not be presented in a manner which would mislead listeners or viewers to believe that the program is purely of an entertainment, news, or other character.

4. Broadcasts in which stations express their own opinions about issues of general public interest should be clearly identified as editorials. They should be unmistakably identified as statements of station opinion and should be appropriately distinguished from news and other program material.

VII. *Political Telecasts*

1. Political telecasts should be clearly identified as such. They should not be presented by a television broadcaster in a manner which would mislead listeners or viewers to believe that the program is of any other character.

VIII. *Religious Programs*

1. It is the responsibility of a television broadcaster to make available to the community appropriate opportunity for religious presentations.

2. Telecasting which reaches men of all creeds simultaneously should avoid attacks upon religion.

3. Religious programs should be presented respectfully and accurately and without prejudice or ridicule.

4. Religious programs should be presented by responsible individuals, groups and organizations.

5. Religious programs should place emphasis on broad religious truths, excluding the presentation of controversial or partisan views not directly or necessarily related to religion or morality.

6. In the allocation of time for telecasts of religious programs the television station should use its best efforts to apportion such time fairly among the representative faith groups of its community.

IX. *General Advertising Standards*

1. This Code establishes basic standards for all television broadcasting. The principles of acceptability and good taste within the Program Standards section govern the presentation of advertising where applicable. In addition, the Code establishes in this section special standards which apply to television advertising.

2. A commercial television broadcaster makes his facilities available for the advertising of products and services and accepts commercial presentations for such advertising. However, a television broadcaster should, in recognition of his responsibility to the public, refuse the facilities of his station to an advertiser where he has good reason to doubt the integrity of the advertiser, the truth of the advertising representations, or the compliance of the advertiser with the spirit and purpose of all applicable legal requirements.

3. Identification of sponsorship must be made in all sponsored programs in accordance with the requirements of the Communications Act of 1934, as amended, and the Rules and Regulations of the Federal Communications Commission.

4. In consideration of the customs and attitudes of the communities served, each television broadcaster should refuse his facilities to the advertisement of products and services, or the use of advertising scripts, which the station has good reason to believe would be objectionable to a substantial and responsible segment of the community. These standards should be applied with judgment and flexibility, taking into consideration the characteristics of the medium, its home and family audience, and the form and content of the particular presentation.

5. The advertising of hard liquor (distilled spirits) is not acceptable.

6. The advertising of beer and wines is acceptable only when presented in the best of good taste and discretion, and is acceptable only subject to Federal and local laws.

7. The advertising of cigarettes should not be presented in a manner to convey the impression that cigarette smoking promotes health or is important to personal development of the youth in our country.

8. Advertising by institutions or enterprises which in their offers of instruction imply promises of employment or make exaggerated claims for the opportunities awaiting those who enroll for courses is generally unacceptable.

9. The advertising of firearms and fireworks is acceptable only subject to Federal and local laws.

10. The advertising of fortune-telling, occultism, astrology, phrenology, palm-reading, numerology, mind-reading, character reading or subjects of a like nature is not permitted.

11. Because all products of a personal nature create special problems, such products, when accepted, should be treated with especial emphasis on ethics and the canons of good taste. Such advertising of personal products as is accepted must be presented in a restrained and obviously inoffensive manner. The advertising of particularly intimate products which ordinarily are not freely mentioned or discussed is not acceptable.

12. The advertising of tip sheets, race track publications, or organizations seeking to advertise for the purpose of giving odds or promoting betting or lotteries is unacceptable.

13. An advertiser who markets more than one product should not be permitted to use advertising copy devoted to an acceptable product for purposes of publicizing the brand name or other identification of a product which is not acceptable.

14. "Bait-switch" advertising, whereby goods or services which the advertiser has no intention of selling are offered merely to lure the customer into purchasing higher-priced substitutes, is not acceptable.

15. Personal endorsements (testimonials) shall be genuine and reflect personal experience. They shall contain no statement that cannot be supported if presented in the advertiser's own words.

X. *Presentation of Advertising*

1. Advertising messages should be presented with courtesy and good taste; disturbing or annoying material should be avoided; every effort should be made to keep the advertising message in harmony with the content and general tone of the program in which it appears.

2. The role and capability of television to market sponsors' products are well recognized. In turn, this fact dictates that great care be exercised by the broadcaster to prevent the presentation of false, misleading or deceptive advertising. While it is entirely appropriate to present a product in a favorable light and atmosphere, the presentation must not, by copy or demonstration, involve a material deception as to the characteristics, performance or appearance of the product.

3. The broadcaster and the advertiser should exercise special caution with the content and presentation of television commercials placed in or near programs designed for children. Exploitation of children should be avoided. Commercials directed to children should in no way mislead as to the product's performance and usefulness.

Appeals involving matters of health which should be determined by physicians should not be directed primarily to children.

4. Appeals to help fictitious characters in television programs by purchasing the advertiser's product or service or sending for a premium should not be permitted, and such fictitious characters should not be introduced into the advertising message for such purposes.

5. Commercials for services or over-the-counter products involving health considerations are of intimate and far-reaching importance to

the consumer. The following principles should apply to such advertising:

(a) Physicians, dentists or nurses, or actors representing physicians, dentists or nurses shall not be employed directly or by implication. These restrictions also apply to persons professionally engaged in medical services (e.g., physical therapists, pharmacists, dental assistants, nurses' aides).

(b) Visual representations of laboratory settings may be employed, provided they bear a direct relationship to bona fide research which has been conducted for the product or service. In such cases, laboratory technicians shall be identified as such and shall not be employed as spokesmen or in any other way speak on behalf of the product.

(c) Institutional announcements not intended to sell a specific product or service to the consumer and public service announcements by non-profit organizations may be presented by accredited physicians, dentists or nurses, subject to approval by the broadcaster. An accredited professional is one who has met required qualifications and has been licensed in his resident state.

6. Advertising should offer a product or service on its positive merits and refrain by identification or other means from discrediting, disparaging or unfairly attacking competitors, competing products, other industries, professions or institutions.

7. A sponsor's advertising messages should be confined within the framework of the sponsor's program structure. A television broadcaster should avoid the use of commercial announcements which are divorced from the program either by preceding the introduction of the program (as in the case of so-called "cow catcher" announcements) or by following the apparent sign-off of the program (as in the case of so-called trailer or "hitch-hike" announcements). To this end, the program itself should be announced and clearly identified, both audio and video, before the sponsor's advertising material is first used, and should be signed off, both audio and video, after the sponsor's advertising material is last used.

8. Since advertising by television is a dynamic technique, a television broadcaster should keep under surveillance new advertising devices so that the spirit and purpose of these standards are fulfilled.

9. A charge for television time to churches and religious bodies is not recommended.

10. Reference to the results of bona fide research, surveys or test relating to the product to be advertised shall not be presented in a manner so as to create an impression of fact beyond that established by the work that has been conducted.

XI. *Advertising of Medical Products*

1. The advertising of medical products presents considerations of intimate and far-reaching importance to the consumer because of the direct bearing on his health.

2. Because of the personal nature of the advertising of medical products, claims that a product will effect a cure and the indiscriminate use of such words as "safe," "without risk," "harmless," or terms of similar meaning should not be accepted in the advertising of medical products on television stations.

3. A television broadcaster should not accept advertising material which in his opinion offensively describes or dramatizes distress or morbid situations involving ailments, by spoken word, sound or visual effects.

XII. *Contests*

1. Contests shall be conducted with fairness to all entrants, and shall comply with all pertinent laws and regulations. Care should be taken to avoid the concurrent use of the three elements which together constitute a lottery—prize, chance and consideration.

2. All contest details, including rules, eligibility requirements, opening and termination dates should be clearly and completely announced and/or shown, or easily accessible to the viewing public, and the winners' names should be released and prizes awarded as soon as possible after the close of the contest.

3. When advertising is accepted which requests contestants to submit items of product identification or other evidence of purchase of products, reasonable facsimiles thereof should be made acceptable unless the award is based upon skill and not upon chance.

4. All copy pertaining to any contest (except that which is required by law) associated with the exploitation or sale of the sponsor's product or service, and all references to prizes or gifts offered in such connection should be considered a part of and included in the total time allowances as herein provided.

XIII. *Premiums and Offers*

1. Full details of proposed offers should be required by the television broadcaster for investigation and approved before the first announcement of the offer is made to the public.

2. A final date for the termination of an offer should be announced as far in advance as possible.

3. Before accepting for telecast offers involving a monetary consideration, a television broadcaster should satisfy himself as to the integrity of the advertiser and the advertiser's willingness to honor complaints indicating dissatisfaction with the premium by returning the monetary consideration.

4. There should be no misleading descriptions or visual representations of any premiums or gifts which would distort or enlarge their value in the minds of the viewers.

5. Assurances should be obtained from the advertiser that premiums offered are not harmful to person or property.

6. Premiums should not be approved which appeal to superstition on the basis of "luck-bearing" powers or otherwise.

XIV. *Time Standards for Advertising*

In accordance with good telecast advertising practice, the time standards for commercial material are as follows:

1. Prime Time (Programs)

Definition: A continuous period of not less than three evening hours per broadcast day as designated by the station between the hours of 6:00 P.M. and midnight.

Commercial material, including total station break time, in prime time shall not exceed 17.2% (10 minutes and 20 seconds) in any 60-minute period. Not more than three announcements shall be scheduled consecutively. Commercial material in prime time includes billboards, public service announcements, promotional announcements (except those for the same program) and below-the-line credits as well as commercial copy.

2. All Other Time (Programs)

Definition: All time other than prime time.

Commercial material, including total station break time, within any 60-minute period may not exceed 27.2% (16 minutes and 20 seconds). Individual programs of 5 minutes duration may include commercial material not in excess of 1 minute and 15 seconds and individual programs of 10 minutes duration may include commercial material not in excess of 2 minutes and 10 seconds.

Not more than three announcements shall be scheduled consecutively. Commercial material in *all other times* includes billboards, promotional announcements (except those for the same program), below-the-line credits and commercial copy. Public service announcements are excluded from this definition.

3. Station Breaks

Definition: Station breaks are those periods of time between programs, or within a program as designated by the program originator, which are set aside for local station identification and spot announcements. In prime time a station break shall consist of not more than two commercial announcements plus non-commercial copy such as station identification, public service or promotional announcements. Total station break time in any 30-minute period may not exceed 1 minute and 10 seconds. In other than prime time individual station breaks shall consist of not more than two commercial announcements plus the conventional sponsored 10-second ID, *or three commercial announcements*, and shall not exceed 2 minutes and 10 seconds.

Station break announcements shall not adversely affect a preceding or following program.

4. Multiple Product Announcements

A multiple product announcement is one in which two or more products or services are presented within the framework of a single announcement.

(1) Only those multiple product announcements which meet the following criteria shall be counted under the Code as a single announcement:

(a) The products or services are related in character, purpose or use; and

(b) The products or services are so treated in audio and video throughout the announcement as to appear to the viewer as a single announcement; and

(c) The announcement is so constructed that it cannot be divided into two or more separate announcements.

(2) Multiple product announcements not meeting the criteria of 4(1) above (commonly referred to as "piggybacks") shall be counted as two or more announcements under this section of the Code.

(3) Multiple product announcements of retail or service establishments are exempted from the provisions of (1)(a) above.

5. Prize Identification

Reasonable and limited identification of prize and statement of the donor's name within formats wherein the presentation of contest awards or prizes is a necessary and integral part of program content shall not be included as commercial time within the meaning of paragraphs 1 and 2, above; however, any aural or visual presentation concerning the product or its donor, over and beyond such identification and statement, shall be included as commercial time within the meaning of paragraph 1, above.

6. Care should be exercised in the selection, placement and integration of non-program material in order to avoid adversely affecting the program content or diminishing audience interest.

7. Programs presenting women's services, features, shopping guides, fashion shows, demonstrations and similar material with genuine audience interest provide a special service to the viewing public in which what ordinarily might be considered advertising material is an informative and necessary part of the program content. Because of this, the Time Standards may be waived to a reasonable extent and limited frequency.

The Code Authority will evaluate each such program on its own merits.

8. Except for normal guest identifications, any casual reference by talent in a program to another's product or service under any trade name or language sufficient to identify it should be condemned and discouraged.

9. Stationary backdrops or properties in television presentations showing the sponsor's name or product, the name of his product, his trade-mark or slogan may be used only incidentally. They should not obtrude on program interest or entertainment. "On camera" shots of such materials should be fleeting, not too frequent, and mindful of the need of maintaining a proper program balance.

10. Each opening and closing billboard, regardless of the number of sponsors, shall not exceed 10 seconds in program periods of one half-hour or less, or in the ratio of 10 seconds of opening and closing billboard per 30 minutes of program time in periods exceeding 30 minutes, provided that a billboard for any one sponsor at no time shall exceed 20 seconds in programs exceeding 30 minutes.

11. Billboard language may not include a commercial message and should be confined to the sponsor's name, product and established claim or slogan. Billboards should not mention contests, premiums, offers or special sales.

INTERPRETATIONS OF THE TELEVISION CODE

Interpretation No. 1
June 7, 1956, Revised June 9, 1958
"Pitch" Programs
The "pitchman" technique of advertising on television is inconsistent with good broadcast practice and generally damages the reputation of the industry and the advertising profession.

Sponsored program-length segments consisting substantially of continuous demonstrations or sales presentation, violate not only the time standards established in the Code but the broad philosophy of improvement implicit in the voluntary Code operation and are not acceptable.

*　　　　　*　　　　　*

Interpretation No. 2
June 7, 1956
Hollywood Film Promotion
The presentation of commentary or film excerpts from current theatrical releases in some instances may constitute commercial material under the Time Standards for Advertising. Specifically, for example, when such presentation, directly or by inference, urges viewers to attend, it shall be counted against the commercial allowance for the program of which it is a part.

*　　　　　*　　　　　*

Interpretation No. 3
June 7, 1956
Non-Acceptability of Particularly Intimate Products
Paragraph 11 of the General Advertising Standards reads in part, "The advertising of particularly intimate products which ordinarily are not freely mentioned or discussed is not acceptable."

Products for the treatment of hemorrhoids and for use in connection with feminine hygiene are not acceptable under the above stated language.

*   *   *

Interpretation No. 4
January 23, 1959
Prize Identification
Aural and/or visual prize identification of up to ten seconds duration may be deemed "reasonable and limited" under the language of Paragraph 5 of the Time Standards for Advertising. Where such identification is longer than ten seconds, the entire announcement or visual presentation will be charged against the total commercial time for the program period.

*   *   *

Interpretation No. 5
February 25, 1965
Below-the-Line Credits
"Below-the-line" credits are deemed to mean those for technical and physical services and facilities as distinct from generally recognized artistic and creative services such as those performed by cast, writers, directors, producers and the like.

*   *   *

Interpretation No. 6
March 4, 1965
Drinking on Camera
Paragraph 6, Section IX, General Advertising Standards, states that the "advertising of beer and wine is acceptable only when presented in the best of good taste and discretion." This requires that commercials involving beer and wine avoid any representation of on-camera drinking.

Appendix C

THE RADIO CODE

Preamble

The radio broadcasters of the United States first adopted industry-wide standards of practice in 1937. The purpose of such standards, in this as in other professions, is to establish guideposts and to set forth minimum tenets for performance.

Standards for broadcasting can never be final or complete. Broadcasting is a creative art and it must always seek new ways to achieve greater advances. Therefore, many standards must be subject to change. In 1945, after two years devoted to reviewing and revising the 1937 document, new standards were promulgated. Further revisions were made in 1948, 1954, 1955, 1958, 1960, 1961, 1962, 1964 and 1965 and now there follows a new and revised Twelfth Edition of the Radio Code of the National Association of Broadcasters.

Through this process of self-examination broadcasters acknowledge their obligation to the American family.

The growth of broadcasting as a medium of entertainment, education and information has been made possible by its force as an instrument of commerce.

This philosophy of commercial broadcasting as it is known in the United States has enabled the industry to develop as a free medium in the tradition of American enterprise.

The extent of this freedom is implicit in the fact that no one censors broadcasting in the United States.

Those who own the nation's radio broadcasting stations operate them—pursuant to this self-adopted Radio Code—in recognition of the interest of the American people.

THE RADIO BROADCASTER'S CREED

We Believe:

That Radio Broadcasting in the United States of America is a living symbol of democracy; a significant and necessary instrument for maintaining freedom of expression, as established by the First Amendment to the Constitution of the United States;

That its influence in the arts, in science, in education, in commerce, and upon the public welfare is of such magnitude that the only proper measure of its responsibility is the common good of the whole people;

That it is our obligation to serve the people in such a manner as to reflect credit upon our profession and to encourage aspiration toward a better estate for all mankind; by making available to every person in America such programs as will perpetuate the traditional leadership of the United States in all phases of the broadcasting art;

That we should make full and ingenious use of man's store of knowledge, his talents, and his skills and exercise critical and discerning judgment concerning all broadcasting operations to the end that we may, intelligently and sympathetically:

Observe the proprieties and customs of civilized society;

Respect the rights and sensitivities of all people;

Honor the sanctity of marriage and the home;

Protect and uphold the dignity and brotherhood of all mankind;

Enrich the daily life of the people through the factual reporting and analysis of news, and through programs of education, entertainment, and information;

Provide for the fair discussion of matters of general public concern; engage in works directed toward the common good; and volunteer our aid and comfort in times of stress and emergency;

Contribute to the economic welfare of all by expanding the channels of trade, by encouraging the development and conservation of natural resources, and by bringing together the buyer and seller through the broadcasting of information pertaining to goods and services.

Toward the achievement of these purposes we agree to observe the following:

I. PROGRAM STANDARDS

A. *News*

Radio is unique in its capacity to reach the largest number of people first with reports on current events. This competitive advantage bespeaks caution—being first is not as important as being right. The following Standards are predicated upon that viewpoint.

1. *News Sources.* Those responsible for news on radio should exercise constant professional care in the selection of sources—for the integrity of the news and the consequent good reputation of radio as a dominant news medium depend largely upon the reliability of such sources.

2. *News Reporting.* News reporting shall be factual and objective. Good taste shall prevail in the selection and handling of news. Morbid, sensational, or alarming details not essential to factual reporting should be avoided. News should be broadcast in such a manner as to avoid creation of panic and unnecessary alarm. Broadcasters shall be diligent in their supervision of content, format, and presentation of news broadcasts. Equal diligence should be exercised in selection of editors and reporters who direct news gathering and dissemination, since the station's performance in this vital informational field depends largely upon them.

3. *Commentaries and Analyses.* Special obligations devolve upon those who analyze and/or comment upon news developments, and management should be satisfied completely that the task is to be performed in the best interest of the listening public. Programs of news analysis and commentary shall be clearly identified as such, distinguishing them from straight news reporting.

4. *Editorializing.* Broadcasts in which stations express their own opinions about issues of general public interest should be clearly identified as editorials and should be clearly distinguished from news and other program material.

5. *Coverage of News and Public Events.* In the coverage of news and public events the broadcaster has the right to exercise his judgment consonant with the accepted standards of ethical journalism and especially the requirements for decency and decorum in the broadcast of public and court proceedings.

6. *Placement of Advertising.* A broadcaster should exercise particular discrimination in the acceptance, placement and presentation of advertising in news programs so that such advertising should be clearly distinguishable from the news content.

B. *Controversial Public Issues*

1. Radio provides a valuable forum for the expression of responsible views on public issues of a controversial nature. The broadcaster should develop programs relating to controversial public issues of importance to his fellow citizens; and give fair representation to opposing sides of issues which materially affect the life or welfare of a substantial segment of the public.

2. Requests by individuals, groups or organizations for time to discuss their views on controversial public issues should be considered on the basis of their individual merits, and in the light of the contributions which the use requested would make to the public interest.

3. Programs devoted to the discussion of controversial public issues should be identified as such. They should not be presented in a manner

which would create the impression that the program is other than one dealing with a public issue.

C. *Community Responsibility*

1. A broadcaster and his staff occupy a position of responsibility in the community and should conscientiously endeavor to be acquainted with its needs and characteristics in order to serve the welfare of its citizens.

2. Requests for time for the placement of public service announcements or programs should be carefully reviewed with respect to the character and reputation of the group, campaign or organization involved, the public interest content of the message, and the manner of its presentation.

D. *Political Broadcasts*

1. Political broadcasts, or the dramatization of political issues designed to influence an election, shall be properly identified as such.

2. They should be presented in a manner which would properly identify the nature and character of the broadcast.

3. Because of the unique character of political broadcasts and the necessity to retain broad freedoms of policy void of restrictive interference, it is incumbent upon all political candidates and all political parties to observe the canons of good taste and political ethics, keeping in mind the intimacy of broadcasting in the American home.

E. *Advancement of Education and Culture*

1. Because radio is an integral part of American life, there is inherent in radio broadcasting a continuing opportunity to enrich the experience of living through the advancement of education and culture.

2. The radio broadcaster, in augmenting the educational and cultural influences of the home, the church, schools, institutions of higher learning, and other entities devoted to education and culture:

(a) Should be thoroughly conversant with the educational and cultural needs and aspirations of the community served;

(b) Should cooperate with the responsible and accountable educational and cultural entities of the community to provide enlightenment of listeners;

(c) Should engage in experimental efforts designed to advance the community's cultural and educational interests.

F. *Religion and Religious Programs*

1. Religious programs shall be presented by responsible individuals, groups or organizations.

2. Radio broadcasting, which reaches men of all creeds simultaneously, shall avoid attacks upon religious faiths.

3. Religious programs shall be presented respectfully and without prejudice or ridicule.

4. Religious programs shall place emphasis on religious doctrines of faith and worship.

G. *Dramatic Programs*

1. In determining the acceptability of any dramatic program containing any element of crime, mystery, or horror, proper consideration should be given to the possible effect on all members of the family.

2. Radio should reflect realistically the experience of living, in both its pleasant and tragic aspects, if it is to serve the listener honestly. Nevertheless, it holds a concurrent obligation to provide programs which will encourage better adjustments to life.

3. This obligation is apparent in the area of dramatic programs particularly. Without sacrificing integrity of presentation, dramatic programs on radio shall avoid:

(a) Techniques and methods of crime presented in such manner as to encourage imitation, or to make the commission of crime attractive, or to suggest that criminals can escape punishment;

(b) Detailed presentation of brutal killings, torture, or physical agony, horror, the use of supernatural or climactic incidents likely to terrify or excite unduly;

(c) Sound effects calculated to mislead, shock, or unduly alarm the listener;

(d) Disrespectful portrayal of law enforcement;

(e) The portrayal of suicide as a satisfactory solution to any problem.

H. *Responsibility Toward Children*

The education of children involves giving them a sense of the world at large. It is not enough that programs broadcast for children shall be suitable for the young and immature. In addition, programs which might reasonably be expected to hold the attention of children and which are broadcast during times when children may be normally expected to constitute a substantial part of the audience should be presented with due regard for their effect on children.

1. Programs specifically designed for listening by children shall be based upon sound social concepts and shall reflect respect for parents, law and order, clean living, high morals, fair play, and honorable behavior.

2. They shall convey the commonly accepted moral, social and ethical ideals characteristic of American life.

3. They should contribute to the healthy development of personality and character.

4. They should afford opportunities for cultural growth as well as for wholesome entertainment.

5. They should be consistent with integrity of realistic production, but they should avoid material of extreme nature which might create undesirable emotional reaction in children.

6. They shall avoid appeals urging children to purchase the product specifically for the purpose of keeping the program on the air or which, for any reason, encourage children to enter inappropriate places.

7. They should present such subjects as violence and sex without undue emphasis and only as required by plot development or character delineation. Crime should not be presented as attractive or as a solution to human problems, and the inevitable retribution should be made clear.

8. They should avoid reference to kidnapping or threats of kidnapping of children.

I. *General*

1. The intimacy and confidence placed in Radio demand of the broadcaster, the networks and other program sources that they be vigilant in protecting the audience from deceptive program practices.

2. Sound effects and expressions characteristically associated with news broadcasts (such as "bulletin," "flash," "we interrupt this program to bring you," etc.) shall be reserved for announcement of news, and the use of any deceptive techniques in connection with fictional events and non-news programs shall not be employed.

3. The acceptance of cash payments or other considerations for including identification of commercial products or services, trade names or advertising slogans, including the identification of prizes, etc., must be disclosed in accordance with provisions of the Communications Act.

4. When plot development requires the use of material which depends upon physical or mental handicaps, care should be taken to spare the sensibilities of sufferers from similar defects.

5. Stations should avoid broadcasting program material which would tend to encourage illegal gambling or other violations of Federal, State and local laws, ordinances, and regulations.

6. Simulation of court atmosphere or use of the term "Court" in a program title should be done only in such manner as to eliminate the possibility of creating the false impression that the proceedings broadcast are vested with judicial or official authority.

7. Quiz and similar programs that are presented as contests of knowledge, information, skill or luck must in fact, be genuine contests and the results must not be controlled by collusion with or between contestants, or any other action which will favor one contestant against any other.

8. No program shall be presented in a manner which through artifice or simulation would mislead the audience as to any material fact. Each broadcaster must exercise reasonable judgment to determine whether a particular method of presentation would constitute a material deception, or would be accepted by the audience as normal theatrical illusion.

9. Legal, medical and other professional advice will be permitted only in conformity with law and recognized ethical and professional standards.

10. Program material pertaining to fortune-telling, occultism, astrology, phrenology, palm-reading, numerology, mind-reading, character-reading, or subjects of a like nature, is unacceptable when presented for the purpose of fostering belief in these subjects.

11. The use of cigarettes shall not be presented in a manner to impress the youth of our country that it is a desirable habit worthy of imitation in that it contributes to health, individual achievement or social acceptance.

12. Profanity, obscenity, smut and vulgarity are forbidden. From time to time, words which have been acceptable, acquire undesirable meanings, and broadcasters should be alert to eliminate such words.

13. Words (especially slang) derisive of any race, color, creed, nationality or national derivation, except wherein such usage would be for the specific purpose of effective dramatization, such as combating prejudice, are forbidden.

14. Respect is maintained for the sanctity of marriage and the value of the home. Divorce is not treated casually as a solution for marital problems.

15. Broadcasts of actual sporting events at which on-the-scene betting is permitted should concentrate on the subject as a public sporting event and not on the aspects of gambling.

II. ADVERTISING STANDARDS

Advertising is the principal source of revenue of the free, competitive American system of radio broadcasting. It makes possible the presentation to all American people of the finest programs of entertainment, education, and information.

Since the great strength of American radio broadcasting derives from the public respect for and the public approval of its programs, it must be the purpose of each broadcaster to establish and maintain high standards of performance, not only in the selection and production of all programs, but also in the presentation of advertising.

This Code establishes basic standards for all radio broadcasting. The principles of acceptability and good taste within the Program Standards section govern the presentation of advertising where applicable. In addition, the Code establishes in this section special standards which apply to radio advertising.

A. *General Advertising Standards*

1. A commercial radio broadcaster makes his facilities available for the advertising of products and services and accepts commercial presentations for such advertising. However, he shall, in recognition of his responsibility to the public, refuse the facilities of his station to an

advertiser where he has good reason to doubt the integrity of the advertiser, the truth of the advertising representations, or the compliance of the advertiser with the spirit and purpose of all applicable legal requirements.

2. In consideration of the customs and attitudes of the communities served, each radio broadcaster should refuse his facilities to the advertisement of products and services, or the use of advertising scripts, which the station has good reason to believe would be objectionable to a substantial and responsible segment of the community. These standards should be applied with judgment and flexibility, taking into consideration the characteristics of the medium, its home and family audience, and the form and content of the particular presentation.

B. *Presentation of Advertising*

1. The advancing techniques of the broadcast art have shown that the quality and proper integration of advertising copy are just as important as measurement in time. The measure of a station's service to its audience is determined by its overall performance.

2. The final measurement of any commercial broadcast service is quality. To this, every broadcaster shall dedicate his best effort.

3. Great care shall be exercised by the broadcaster to prevent the presentation of false, misleading or deceptive advertising. While it is entirely appropriate to present a product in a favorable light and atmosphere, the presentation must not, by copy or demonstration, involve a material deception as to the characteristics or performance of a product.

4. The broadcaster and the advertiser should exercise special caution with the content and presentation of commercials placed in or near programs designed for children. Exploitation of children should be avoided. Commericals directed to children should in no way mislead as to the product's performance and usefulness.

5. Appeals involving matters of health which should be determined by physicians should be avoided.

6. Reference to the results of research, surveys or tests relating to the product to be advertised shall not be presented in a manner so as to create an impression of fact beyond that established by the study. Surveys, tests or other research results upon which claims are based must be conducted under recognized research techniques and standards.

C. *Acceptability of Advertisers and Products*

In general, because radio broadcasting is designed for the home and the entire family, the following principles shall govern the business classifications listed below:

1. The advertising of hard liquor shall not be accepted.

2. The advertising of beer and wines is acceptable when presented in the best of good taste and discretion.

3. The advertising of fortune-telling, occultism, astrology, phrenology, palm-reading, numerology, mind-reading, character-reading, or subjects of a like nature, is not acceptable.

4. Because the advertising of all products of a personal nature raises special problems, such advertising, when accepted, should be treated with emphasis on ethics and the canons of good taste, and presented in a restrained and inoffensive manner.

5. The advertising of tip sheets, publications, or organizations seeking to advertise for the purpose of giving odds or promoting betting or lotteries is unacceptable.

6. The advertising of cigarettes shall not state or imply claims regarding health and shall not be presented in such a manner as to indicate to the youth of our country that the use of cigarettes contributes to individual achievement, personal acceptance, or is a habit worthy of imitation.

7. An advertiser who markets more than one product shall not be permitted to use advertising copy devoted to an acceptable product for purposes of publicizing the brand name or other identification of a product which is not acceptable.

8. Care should be taken to avoid presentation of "bait-switch" advertising whereby goods or services which the advertiser has no intention of selling are offered merely to lure the customer into purchasing higher-priced substitutes.

9. Advertising should offer a product or service on its positive merits and refrain from discrediting, disparaging or unfairly attacking competitors, competing products, other industries, professions or institutions. Any identification or comparison of a competitive product or service, by name, or other means, should be confined to specific facts rather than generalized statements or conclusions, unless such statements or conclusions are not derogatory in nature.

10. Advertising testimonials should be genuine and reflect an honest appraisal of personal experience.

11. Advertising by institutions or enterprises offering instruction with exaggerated claims for opportunities awaiting those who enroll, is unacceptable.

D. *Advertising of Medical Products*

Because advertising for over-the-counter products involving health considerations are of intimate and far-reaching importance to the consumer, the following principles should apply to such advertising:

1. When dramatized advertising material involves statements by doctors, dentists, nurses or other professional people, the material should be presented by members of such profession reciting actual experience, or it should be made apparent from the presentation itself that the portrayal is dramatized.

2. Because of the personal nature of the advertising of medical products, the indiscriminate use of such words as "Safe," "Without

Risk," "Harmless," or other terms of similar meaning, either direct or implied, should not be expressed in the advertising of medical products.

3. Advertising material which offensively describes or dramatizes distress or morbid situations involving ailments is not acceptable.

E. *Time Standards for Advertising Copy*

1. The amount of time to be used for advertising shall not exceed eighteen minutes within any single clock hour; provided, however, that in no event shall any thirty-minute segment of such clock hour exceed ten minutes of advertising time.

2. The maximum time to be used for advertising allowable to any single sponsor regardless of type program shall be:

5 minute	programs	1:30
10 minute	programs	2:10
15 minute	programs	3:00
25 minute	programs	4:00
30 minute	programs	4:15
45 minute	programs	5:45
60 minute	programs	7:00

3. Any reference to another's products or services under any trade name, or language sufficiently descriptive to identify it, shall, except for normal guest identifications, be considered as advertising copy.

4. For the purpose of determining advertising limitations, such program types as "classified," "swap shop," "shopping guides," and "farm auction" programs, etc., shall be regarded as containing one and one-half minutes of advertising for each five-minute segment.

F. *Contests*

1. Contests shall be conducted with fairness to all entrants, and shall comply with all pertinent laws and regulations.

2. All contest details, including rules, eligibility requirements, opening and termination dates, shall be clearly and completely announced or easily accessible to the listening public; and the winners' names should be released as soon as possible after the close of the contest.

3. When advertising is accepted which requests contestants to submit items of product identification or other evidence of purchase of products, reasonable facsimiles thereof should be made acceptable. However, when the award is based upon skill and not upon chance, evidence of purchase may be required.

4. All copy pertaining to any contest (except that which is required by law) associated with the exploitation or sale of the sponsor's product or service, and all references to prizes or gifts offered in such connection should be considered a part of and included in the total time limitations heretofore provided. (See Time Standards for Advertising Copy.)

G. *Premiums and Offers*

1. The broadcaster should require that full details of proposed offers be submitted for investigation and approval before the first announcement of the offer is made to the public.

2. A final date for the termination of an offer should be announced as far in advance as possible.

3. If a consideration is required, the advertiser should agree to honor complaints indicating dissatisfaction with the premium by returning the consideration.

4. There should be no misleading descriptions or comparisons of any premiums or gifts which will distort or enlarge their value in the minds of the listeners.

Appendix D

CODE OF SELF-REGULATION—MOTION PICTURE ASSOCIATION OF AMERICA

The Code of Self-Regulation of the Motion Picture Association of America shall apply to production, to advertising, and to titles of motion pictures.

The Code shall be administered by an Office of Code Administration, headed by an Administrator.

There shall also be a Director of the Code for Advertising, and a Director of the Code for Titles.

Nonmembers are invited to submit pictures to the Code Administrator on the same basis as members of the Association.

DECLARATION OF PRINCIPLES OF THE CODE OF SELF-REGULATION OF THE MOTION PICTURE ASSOCIATION

This revised Code is designed to keep in closer harmony with the mores, the culture, the moral sense and the expectations of our society.

The revised Code can more completely fulfill its objectives, which are:

1. To encourage artistic expression by expanding creative freedom and

2. To assure that the freedom which encourages the artist remains responsible and sensitive to the standards of the larger society.

Censorship is an odious enterprise. We oppose censorship and classification-by-law (or whatever name or guise these restrictions go under) because they are alien to the American tradition of freedom.

Much of this nation's strength and purpose is drawn from the premise that the humblest of citizens has the freedom of his own choice. Censorship destroys this freedom of choice.

It is within this framework that the Motion Picture Association continues to recognize its obligation to the society of which it is an integral part.

In our society the parents are the arbiters of family conduct.

Parents have the primary responsibility to guide their children in the kind of lives they lead, the character they build, the books they read, and the movies and other entertainment to which they are exposed.

The creators of motion pictures undertake a responsibility to make available pertinent information about their pictures which will enable parents to fulfill their function.

An important addition is now being made to the information already provided to the public in order to enable parents better to choose which motion pictures their children should see.

As part of the revised Code, there is a provision that producers in cooperation with the Code Administration, will identify certain pictures as suggested for mature audiences.

Such information will be conveyed by advertising, by displays at the theatre and by other means.

Thus parents will be alerted and informed so that they may decide for themselves whether a particular picture because of theme, content or treatment, will be one which their children should or should not see, or may not understand or enjoy.

We believe self-restraint, self-regulation, to be in the tradition of the American purpose. It is the American society meeting its responsibility to the general welfare. The results of self-discipline are always imperfect because that is the nature of all things mortal. But this Code, and its administration, will make clear that freedom of expression does not mean toleration of license.

The test of self-restraint . . . the rule of reason . . . lies in the treatment of a subject for the screen. The SEAL of the Motion Picture Association on a film means that the picture has met the test of self-regulation.

All members of the Motion Picture Association, as well as many independent producers, cooperate in this self-regulation. Not all motion pictures, however, are submitted to the Production Code Administration of the MPA, and the presence of the Seal is the only way the public can know which pictures have come under the Code.

We believe in and pledge our support to these deep and fundamental values in a democratic society:

Freedom of choice . . .

The right of creative man to achieve artistic excellence . . .

The role of the parent as the arbiter of the family's conduct.

The men and women who make motion pictures under this Code value their social responsibility as they value their creative skills. The Code, and all that is written and implied in it, aims to strengthen both those values.

STANDARDS FOR PRODUCTION

In furtherance of the objectives of the Code to accord with the mores, the culture, and the moral sense of our society, the principles stated above and the following standards shall govern the Administrator in his consideration of motion pictures submitted for Code approval:

The basic dignity and value of human life shall be respected and upheld. Restraint shall be exercised in portraying the taking of life.

Evil, sin, crime and wrong-doing shall not be justified.

Special restraint shall be exercised in portraying criminal or anti-social activities in which minors participate or are involved.

Detailed and protracted acts of brutality, cruelty, physical violence, torture and abuse, shall not be presented.

Indecent or undue exposure of the human body shall not be presented.

Illicit sex relationships shall not be justified. Intimate sex scenes violating common standards of decency shall not be portrayed. Restraint and care shall be exercised in presentations dealing with sex aberrations.

Obscene speech, gestures or movements shall not be presented. Undue profanity shall not be permitted.

Religion shall not be demeaned.

Words or symbols contemptuous of racial, religious or national groups, shall not be used so as to incite bigotry or hatred.

Excessive cruelty to animals shall not be portrayed and animals shall not be treated inhumanely.

STANDARDS FOR ADVERTISING

The principles of the Code cover advertising and publicity as well as production. There are times when their specific application to advertising may be different. A motion picture is viewed as a whole and may be judged that way. It is the nature of advertising, however, that it must select and emphasize only isolated portions and aspects of a film. It thus follows that what may be appropriate in a motion picture may not be equally appropriate in advertising. This must be taken into account in applying the Code standards to advertising. Furthermore, in application to advertising, the principles and standards of the Code are supplemented by the following standards for advertising:

Illustrations and text shall not misrepresent the character of a motion picture.

Illustrations shall not depict any indecent or undue exposure of the human body.

Advertising demeaning religion, race, or national origin shall not be used.

Cumulative overemphasis on sex, crime, violence and brutality shall not be permitted.

Salacious postures and embraces shall not be shown.

Censorship disputes shall not be exploited or capitalized upon.

STANDARDS FOR TITLES

A salacious, obscene, or profane title shall not be used on motion pictures.

PRODUCTION CODE REGULATIONS

I. *Operations*

A. Prior to commencement of production of a motion picture, the producer shall submit a shooting, or other, script to the Office of Code Administration. The Administrator of the Code shall inform the producer in confidence whether a motion picture based upon the script appears to conform to the Code. The final judgment of the Administrator shall be made only upon reviewing of the completed picture.

B. The completed picture shall be submitted to the Code Office and if it is approved by the Administrator, the producer or distributor shall upon public release of the picture place upon an introductory frame of every print distributed for exhibition in the United States the official Seal of the Association with the word "Approved" above the Seal, and below, the words "Certificate Number," followed by the number of the Certificate of Approval. All prints bearing the Code Seal shall be identical.

C. The Administrator, in issuing a Certificate of Approval, shall condition the issuance of the Certificate upon agreement by the producer or distributor that all advertising and publicity to be used for the picture shall be submitted to and approved by the Director of the Code for Advertising.

D. The Administrator, in approving a picture under the Code, may recommend that advertising for the picture carry the informational line Suggested for Mature Audiences. If the Administrator so determines, the distributing company shall carry the line Suggested for Mature Audiences in its advertising. The Administrator shall notify the Director of the Code for Advertising of all such pictures.

E. The title of an approved motion picture shall not be changed without prior approval of the Director of the Code for Titles.

F. Nonmembers of the Association may avail themselves of the services of the Office of Code Administration in the same manner and under the same conditions as members of the Association.

G. The producer or distributor, upon receiving a Certificate of Approval for a picture, shall pay to the Office of Code Administration a fee in accordance with the uniform schedule of fees approved by the Board of Directors of the Association.

II. *Motion Picture Code Board*

A. A Motion Picture Code Board is established with these two principal functions:

To hear appeals from decisions of the Code Administrator.

To act as an advisory body on Code matters.

1. The Code Board shall be composed of the following:

(a) The President of the Motion Picture Association of America, and nine other directors of the Association appointed by the President;

(b) Six exhibitors appointed by the President upon nomination by the National Association of Theatre Owners; and

(c) Four producers appointed by the President upon nomination by the Screen Producers Guild.

2. The President of the Motion Picture Association of America shall be Chairman of the Code Board, and the Association shall provide the secretariat.

3. The President may designate not more than two pro tempore members for each category as substitutes for members unable to attend a particular Board meeting or a hearing.

4. The presence of ten members shall constitute a quorum of the Board for meetings and hearings.

5. The members of the Board required to travel to attend a meeting shall be reimbursed for transportation and subsistence expenses, which shall be paid to them from funds of the Office of Code Administration.

B. Advisory

The procedures governing meetings of the Board in its advisory function shall be as follows:

1. The Board shall meet upon call of the Chairman at a time and place he may designate.

2. Members may submit suggestions for an agenda, which shall be prepared and circulated by the Chairman in advance of meetings. Upon majority vote, additional items may be submitted and brought up for discussion at meetings.

3. The Board through the Chairman may request the presence of the Code Administrator at meetings; may request oral and written reports from its distributor, exhibitor and producer members on the status of the Code; may call for advice and reports upon others in a position to contribute to a better understanding and more efficacious operation of the system of self-regulation; and may perform such other functions of an advisory nature as may redound to the benefit of the Code.

C. Appeals

1. Any producer or distributor whose picture has not been approved by the Code Administrator may appeal the decision to the Motion Picture Code Board by filing a notice of appeal to the Chairman of the Board.

2. The procedures governing appeals before the Code Board shall be as follows:

(a) The Board, upon being called into meeting by the Chairman, shall view an identical print of the picture denied a Certificate of Approval by the Code Administrator.

(b) The producer or the distributor and the Code Administrator, or their representatives, may present oral or written statements to the Board.

(c) The Board shall decide the appeal by majority vote of the members present and its decision shall be final.

(d) No member of the Board shall participate in an appeal involving a picture in which the member has a financial interest.

3. The jurisdiction of the Board is limited to hearing the appeal and it is without power to change or amend the Code.

4. The Code Board, if it authorizes the issuance of a Certificate of Approval, may do so upon such terms and conditions as it may prescribe.

ADVERTISING CODE REGULATIONS

1. These regulations are applicable to all members of the Motion Picture Association of America, and to all producers and distributors of motion pictures with respect to each picture for which the Association has granted its Certificate of Approval.

2. The term "advertising" as used herein shall be deemed to mean all forms of motion picture advertising and exploitation, and ideas therefor, including the following: pressbooks; still photographs; newspaper, magazine and trade paper advertising; publicity copy and art intended for use in pressbooks or otherwise intended for general distribution in printed form or for theatre use; trailers; posters, lobby displays, and other outdoor displays; advertising accessories, including heralds and throwaways; novelties; copy for exploitation tieups; and all radio and television copy and spots.

3. All advertising shall be submitted to the Director of the Code for Advertising for approval before use, and shall not be used in any way until so submitted in duplicate with the exception of pressbooks, which shall be submitted in triplicate.

4. The Director of the Code for Advertising shall proceed as promptly as feasible to approve or disapprove the advertising submitted.

The Director of the Code for Advertising shall stamp "Approved" on one copy of all advertising approved by him and return the stamped copy to the Company which submitted it. If the Director of the Code for Advertising disapproves of any advertising, the Director shall stamp the word "Disapproved" on one copy and return it to the Company which submitted it, together with the reasons for such disapproval; or, if the Director so desires, he may return the copy with suggestions for such changes or corrections as will cause it to be approved.

5. All pressbooks approved by the Director of the Code for Advertising shall bear in a prominent place the official seal of the Motion Picture Association of America. The word "Approved" shall be printed under the seal. Pressbooks shall also carry the following notice:

"All advertising in this pressbook, as well as all other advertising and publicity materials referred to therein, has been approved under the

Standards for Advertising of the Code of Self-Regulation of the Motion Picture Association of America. All inquiries on this procedure may be addressed to: Director of Code for Advertising, Motion Picture Association of America, 522 Fifth Avenue, New York, New York 10036.

6. When the Code Administrator determines that any picture shall carry the informational line "Suggested for mature audiences," the Director of the Code for Advertising shall require this line to appear in such advertising for that picture as the Director may specify. When the advertisement is limited in size, the Director may authorize the initials SMA to stand for "Suggested for mature audiences."

7. Appeals. Any Company whose advertising has been disapproved may appeal from the decision of the Director of the Code for Advertising, as follows:

It shall serve notice of such appeal on the Director of the Code for Advertising and on the President of the Association. The President, or in his absence a Vice President designated by him, shall thereupon promptly and within a week hold a hearing to pass upon the appeal. Oral and written evidence may be introduced by the Company and by the Director of the Code for Advertising, or their representatives. The appeal shall be decided as expeditiously as possible and the decision shall be final.

8. Any Company which uses advertising without prior approval may be brought up on charges before the Board of Directors by the President of the Association. Within a reasonable time, the Board may hold a hearing, at which time the Company and the Director of the Code for Advertising, or their representatives, may present oral or written statements. The Board, by a majority vote of those present, shall decide the matter as expeditiously as possible.

If the Board of Directors finds that the Company has used advertising without prior approval, the Board may direct the Administrator of the Code to void and revoke the Certificate of Approval granted for the picture and require the removal of the Association's seal from all prints of the picture.

9. Each Company shall be responsible for compliance by its employees and agents with these regulations.

Appendix E

PUBLIC RELATIONS CODE

DECLARATION OF PRINCIPLES

Members of the Public Relations Society of America acknowledge and publicly declare that the public relations profession in serving the legitimate interests of clients or employers is dedicated fundamentally to the goals of better mutual understanding and cooperation among the diverse individuals, groups, institutions and elements of our modern society.

In the performance of this mission, we pledge ourselves:

1. To conduct ourselves both privately and professionally in accord with the public welfare.

2. To be guided in all our activities by the generally accepted standards of truth, accuracy, fair dealing and good taste.

3. To support efforts designed to increase the proficiency of the profession by encouraging the continuous development of sound training and resourceful education in the practice of public relations.

4. To adhere faithfully to provisions of the duly adopted Code of Professional Standards for the Practice of Public Relations, a copy of which is in the possession of every member.

CODE OF PROFESSIONAL STANDARDS FOR THE PRACTICE OF PUBLIC RELATIONS

This Code of Professional Standards for the Practice of Public Relations is adopted by the Public Relations Society of America to promote and maintain high standards of public service and conduct among its members in order that membership in the Society may be deemed a badge of ethical conduct; that Public Relations justly may be regarded as a profession; that the public may have increasing confidence in its integrity; and that the practice of Public Relations may best serve the public interest.

1) A member has a general duty of fair dealing towards his clients or employers, past and present, his fellow members and the general public.

2) A member shall conduct his professional life in accord with the public welfare.

3) A member has the affirmative duty of adhering to generally accepted standards of accuracy, truth and good taste.

4) A member shall not represent conflicting or competing interests without the express consent of those concerned, given after a full disclosure of the facts.

5) A member shall safeguard the confidences of both present and former clients or employers and shall not accept retainers or employment which may involve the disclosure or use of these confidences to the disadvantage or prejudice of such clients or employers.

6) A member shall not engage in any practice which tends to corrupt the integrity of channels of public communication.

7) A member shall not intentionally disseminate false or misleading information and is obligated to use ordinary care to avoid dissemination of false or misleading information.

8) A member shall not make use of any organization purporting to serve some announced cause but actually serving an undisclosed special or private interest of a member or his client or his employer.

9) A member shall not intentionally injure the professional reputation or practice of another member. However, if a member has evidence that another member has been guilty of unethical, illegal or unfair practices, including practices in violation of this Code, he should present the information to the proper authorities of the Society for action in accordance with the procedure set forth in Article XIII of the Bylaws.

10) A member shall not employ methods tending to be derogatory of another member's client or employer or of the products, business or services of such client or employer.

11) In performing services for a client or employer a member shall not accept fees, commissions or any other valuable consideration in connection with those services from anyone other than his client or employer without the express consent of his client or employer, given after a full disclosure of the facts.

12) A member shall not propose to a prospective client or employer that his fee or other compensation be contingent on the achievement of certain results; nor shall he enter into any fee agreement to the same effect.

13) A member shall not encroach upon the professional employment of another member unless both are assured that there is no conflict between the two engagements and are kept advised of the negotiations.

14) A member shall, as soon as possible, sever his relations with any organization when he believes his continued employment would require him to conduct himself contrary to the principles of this Code.

15) A member called as a witness in a proceeding for the enforcement of this Code shall be bound to appear unless, for sufficient reason, he shall be excused by the panel hearing the same.

16) A member shall co-operate with fellow members in upholding and enforcing this Code.

Notes

1. The Impact of Mass Communication

1. David Riesman *et al., The Lonely Crowd* (New Haven: Yale University Press, 1950), especially Chap. I.
2. Claude E. Shannon, "The Mathematical Theory of Communication," *Bell System Technical Journal,* July and October, 1948. Reprinted as a book: Shannon and Weaver, *The Mathematical Theory of Communication* (Urbana: University of Illinois Press, 1949).
3. Adapted from the manuscript of a lecture, 1968.
4. Standard sources of these figures are *Editor & Publisher Yearbook* and N. W. Ayer's *Directory of Newspapers and Periodicals.*
5. Standard sources of these figures are *Broadcasting Yearbook* and *Motion Picture Almanac.*
6. C. E. Osgood, G. Suci, and P. Tannenbaum, *The Measurement of Meaning* (Urbana: University of Illinois Press, 1957).
7. This research was done by N. Maccoby and G. Comstock. For a summary, see W. Schramm, P. H. Coombs, F. Kahnert, and J. Lyle, *The New Media: Memo to an Educational Planner* (Paris: International Institute for Educational Planning, 1967), pp. 78–79.
8. Schramm, *et al., op. cit.,* pp. 57 ff.
9. E. Cooper and M. Jahoda, "The Evasion of Propaganda," *Journal of Psychology,* 23 (1947), pp. 15–25.
10. I. L. Janis and S. Feshbach, "The Effects of Fear-Arousing Communications," *Journal of Abnormal and Social Psychology,* 48 (1953), pp. 78–92.

2. Four Concepts of Mass Communication

1. Much of this chapter grows from memoranda prepared especially for the first edition of this book: "The Authoritarian Theory of the Press," by Fred S. Siebert; "The Libertarian Theory of the Press," by Fred S. Siebert; "The Social Responsibility Theory of the Press," by Theodore B. Peterson; "The Soviet Communist

Theory of the Press," by Wilbur Schramm. These were gathered and published as *Four Theories of the Press* (Urbana: University of Illinois Press, 1956) by Siebert, Peterson, and Schramm.

2. See Alfred Zimmern, ed., *Modern Political Doctrines* (New York: Oxford University Press, 1939), p. 3.

3. Robert MacIver, *The Web of Government* (New York: Macmillan, 1947), p. 322.

4. Zimmern, *op. cit.*, p. 3.

5. Fernand Terrou and Lucien Solal, *Legislation for Press, Film, and Radio* (Paris: UNESCO, 1951), pp. 127–128.

6. Ernst Cassirer, "The Enlightenment," in *Encyclopedia of the Social Sciences* (New York: Macmillan, 1935), Vol. 5, p. 547.

7. Robert L. Heilbroner, *The Worldly Philosophers* (New York: Simon & Schuster, 1953), pp. 13–14.

8. Thomas B. Howells, compiler, *A Complete Collection of State Trials* (London: 1704), Vol. 22.

9. A. A. Lipscomb, ed., *The Writings of Thomas Jefferson* (Washington: Thomas Jefferson Memorial Association, 1904), Vol. II, pp. 32–34.

10. John Stuart Mill, *On Liberty*, ed. Alburey Castell (New York: Crofts, 1947), p. 16.

11. Joseph Pulitzer, "The College of Journalism," *North American Review*, Vol. 178 (May, 1904), pp. 641–680.

12. See Siebert, Peterson, and Schramm, *op. cit.*, p. 107.

13. Crane Brinton, *The Shaping of the Modern Mind* (New York: New American Library, 1953), p. 204.

14. Karl Marx, *Das Kapital* (Chicago: University of Chicago Press, 1909), p. 25.

15. V. I. Lenin, *Collected Works* (New York: International Publishers, 1927), Vol. 4, p. 114.

16. Statements by Lenin, in the following pages, if not otherwise credited, are quoted from Antony Buzek, *How the Communist Press Works* (New York: Praeger, 1964), *passim*.

17. Terrou and Solal, *op. cit.*, p. 51.

18. Margaret Mead, *Soviet Attitudes Toward Authority* (New York: McGraw-Hill, 1951), p. 21.

19. Buzek, *op. cit.*, p. 59.

20. Will Irwin, "The American Newspaper," fifteen articles in *Collier's* from the issue of January 21 through the issue of July 29, 1911.

21. Commission on Freedom of the Press, *A Free and Responsible Press* (Chicago: University of Chicago Press, 1947).

22. Siebert, Peterson, and Schramm, *op. cit.*, pp. 78–79.

23. John Merrill, *The Press and Social Responsibility*, Freedom of Information Center Publication No. 001 (Columbia, Missouri: School of Journalism, University of Missouri, 1965), p. 2.

24. Charles A. Beard in *St. Louis Post-Dispatch Symposium on Freedom of the Press* (St. Louis, 1938).

3. Freedom and Government

1. William O. Douglas, *The Right of the People* (New York: Doubleday, 1958), p. 21.
2. *Schenck v. United States*, 249 U.S. 47 (1919).
3. Leonard W. Levy, *Legacy of Suppression* (Cambridge, Massachusetts: The Belknap Press of Harvard University Press, 1964), p. 237.
4. Morris Ernst and Alan Schwartz, *Censorship: The Search for the Obscene* (New York: Macmillan, 1964), p. 8.
5. J. Edward Gerald, "Freedom in Mass Communication," in *Social Science and Freedom: A Report to the People* (Minneapolis: University of Minnesota, 1955), p. 3.
6. *Hannegan v. Esquire*, 327 U.S. 146 (1946).
7. Rozanne Knudson, "Censorship in English Programs of California's Junior Colleges," unpublished dissertation (Stanford University, 1967).
8. Robert Lasch, "For a Free Press," *Atlantic Monthly,* Vol. 173 (June, 1944), p. 6.
9. 333 U.S. 507 (1948).
10. Walter Lippmann, *The Public Philosophy* (Boston: Little, Brown, 1955), p. 127.
11. Quoted in Ruth Inglis, *Freedom of the Movies* (Chicago: University of Chicago Press, 1947), p. 17.
12. *Ibid.,* pp. 19–20.
13. Walter Lippmann, address in *Problems of Journalism* (proceedings of the American Society of Newspaper Editors, 1936), pp. 154–156.
14. *Ibid.,* p. 157.
15. *Ibid.,* p. 158.
16. Quoted in *Editor and Publisher,* March 13, 1954, p. 84.
17. Quoted in *Editor and Publisher,* November 20, 1954, p. 10.
18. Quoted in *The Quill,* July, 1966, p. 37.
19. "ASNE Gets Plan to Avoid Guerrilla War with Courts," *Editor and Publisher,* April 22, 1967.
20. See *Editor and Publisher,* October 9, 1954, p. 62.
21. "Defendant Subjected to Electronic Scrutiny," *Editor and Publisher,* June 12, 1965.
22. *Ibid.*
23. Quoted in William L. Rivers, *The Opinionmakers* (Boston: Beacon Press, 1965), p. 2.
24. Paul L. Ford, ed., *The Writings of Thomas Jefferson* (New York: Putnam, 1892–99), Vol. II, p. 69.

25. "Press-Endorsed Info Act Restrictive, Frustrating," *Editor and Publisher,* November 12, 1966, p. 11.
26. *Ibid.*
27. *Ibid.*
28. *Ibid.*
29. Report of Sigma Delta Chi Committee on Freedom of Information, 1953, in *Quill,* January, 1953, p. 7.
30. Harold L. Cross, *The People's Right to Know* (New York: Columbia University Press, 1953), pp. 12 ff.
31. Robert W. Sink, Champaign-Urbana (Illinois) *Courier,* March 14, 1955.
32. James S. Pope, Address to the American Society of Newspaper Editors, in *Problems of Journalism,* 1951, p. 175.
33. Printed in the San Francisco *Chronicle,* February 27, 1967, p. 1.
34. Associated Press, printed in the San Francisco *Chronicle,* March 19, 1967, p. 1.

4. Freedom and Society

1. Commission on Freedom of the Press, *A Free and Responsible Press* (Chicago: University of Chicago Press, 1947), p. 59.
2. Robert Lasch, "For a Free Press," *Atlantic Monthly,* Vol. 173 (June, 1944), p. 6.
3. Quoted in Commission on Freedom of the Press, *op. cit.,* pp. 60–61.
4. William L. Rivers, *The Opinionmakers* (Boston: Beacon Press, 1965), pp. 174–175.
5. *Ibid.,* p. 177.
6. *Ibid.,* p. 178.
7. Ben Bagdikian, "Wilmington's 'Independent' Newspapers," *Columbia Journalism Review,* Vol. 3 (Summer, 1964), pp. 13–17.
8. A. J. Liebling, *The Wayward Pressman* (New York: Doubleday, 1947), p. 103.
9. Donald I. Rogers, "Businessmen: Don't Subsidize Your Enemies," *Human Events,* August 11, 1962, pp. 599–600.
10. Quoted in *Editor and Publisher,* November 6, 1954, pp. 13 ff.
11. Herbert R. Mayes, "Freedom of Information in the Market Place," in *Freedom of Information in the Market Place* (Fulton, Missouri: Ovid Bell Press, 1967), pp. 2 ff.
12. Quoted in *Editor and Publisher,* March 19, 1966.
13. Quoted in Theodore Peterson *et al., The Mass Media and Modern Society* (New York: Holt, Rinehart and Winston, 1965), p. 191.
14. Ben Bagdikian, "Journalist Meets Propagandist," *Columbia Journalism Review* (Fall, 1963), pp. 29 ff.
15. *Ibid.*
16. *Editor and Publisher,* April 24, 1954.
17. Quoted in *Editor and Publisher,* April 17, 1954.
18. Unpublished manuscript, 1968.

19. Nika Hazelton, "Feeding the Food Editor," *National Review,* November 15, 1966, p. 1164.
20. *Ibid.*
21. Quoted in *Newsweek,* January 3, 1966, p. 14.
22. Daniel J. Boorstin, *The Image* (New York: Harper & Row, 1964), pp. 11–12.
23. James F. Fixx, "When Extremists Attack the Press," *Saturday Review,* February 13, 1965, pp. 72–73.
24. Hortense Powdermaker, *Hollywood, the Dream Factory* (Boston: Little, Brown, 1950), p. 71.

5. Truth and Fairness

1. George Hunt, "1938: Birth of the Baby; 1965: Drama of Life," *Life,* May 21, 1965, p. 3.
2. Joseph Fletcher, *Situation Ethics* (Philadelphia: Westminster Press, 1965), pp. 17–31.
3. *Ibid.,* p. 31.
4. Wilbur Lewis, "The Prevalence of Error," *Columbia Journalism Review,* Winter, 1965, pp. 48–49.
5. *Ibid.*
6. Quoted in *Nieman Reports,* Vol. 5 (October, 1951), p. 5.
7. Quoted in *Congressional Record,* April 17, 1967, pp. H 4248–H 4249.
8. *Nieman Reports, loc. cit.*
9. From the *AP Log;* quoted in *Editor and Publisher,* March 13, 1954, p. 66.
10. Address to the 1955 convention of the National Association of Radio and Television Broadcasters; quoted in *Editor and Publisher,* May 28, 1955, p. 9.
11. Quoted in William L. Rivers, *The Mass Media: Reporting, Writing, Editing* (New York: Harper & Row, 1964), p. 178.
12. *Ibid.,* p. 180.
13. Quoted in *Nieman Reports,* Vol. 9 (October, 1955), p. 8.
14. Rivers, *op. cit.,* p. 181.
15. Elmer Davis, *But We Were Born Free* (Indianapolis: Bobbs-Merrill, 1954).
16. Jack Gould, "TV and McCarthy," *New York Times,* March 4, 1954.
17. *Ibid.*
18. L. N. Flint, *The Conscience of the Newspaper* (New York: Appleton, 1925), p. 154.

6. The Negro and the News: A Case Study

1. Governor's Commission on the Los Angeles Riots, *Violence in the City—an End or a Beginning?* (Los Angeles: Governor's Commission, 1965), pp. 84–85.

2. P. F. Lazarsfeld and R. K. Merton, "Mass Communication, Popular Taste, and Organized Social Action," in W. Schramm, ed., *Mass Communication* (Urbana: University of Illinois Press, 1960), p. 498.
3. Leslie Sargent, Wiley Carr, and Elizabeth McDonald, "Significant Coverage of Integration by Minority Group Magazines," *Journal of Human Relations,* Vol. 14, No. 4 (Fourth Quarter, 1965).
4. Bayard Rustin, "The Watts 'Manifesto' & the McCone Report," *Commentary,* March, 1966, p. 30.
5. *Ibid.,* p. 31.
6. Anonymous, "A Case for News Suppression," *Columbia Journalism Review,* Vol. II, No. 3 (Fall, 1963), pp. 11–12.

7. Popular Art

1. Alexis de Tocqueville, *Democracy in America.*
2. Dwight Macdonald, "A Theory of Mass Culture," in Bernard Rosenberg and David Manning White, eds., *Mass Culture* (Glencoe, Illinois: The Free Press, 1957), p. 70.
3. *Ibid.,* p. 61.
4. Clement Greenberg, "Avant-Garde and *Kitsch," Partisan Review,* Fall, 1939, p. 38.
5. Macdonald, *op. cit.,* p. 65.
6. Walt Whitman, "Democratic Vistas," in *Mass Culture* (see note 2), pp. 35 ff.
7. *Ibid.,* p. 38.
8. Gilbert Seldes, "The People and the Arts," in *Mass Culture* (see note 2), p. 78.
9. Ernest van den Haag, "Of Happiness and Despair We Have No Measure," in *Mass Culture* (see note 2), p. 516.
10. Seldes, *op. cit.,* p. 74.
11. Macdonald, *op. cit.,* p. 64.
12. *Report of Royal Commission on the Press, 1947–49* (London: His Majesty's Stationery Office, 1949), p. 108.
13. Ben Hibbs, "You Can't Edit a Magazine by Arithmetic," *Journalism Quarterly,* Vol. 27 (1950), pp. 369–377.
14. Lyman Bryson, *The Communication of Ideas* (New York: Harper, 1948), chapter on "Popular Art," pp. 227 ff. See also the *Saturday Review of Literature,* May 30, 1940, p. 14.
15. Dan Lacy, "Freedom and Books," *Nieman Reports,* Vol. 8 (January, 1954), p. 29.
16. Coulton Waugh, *The Comics* (London: Macmillan, 1947), p. 352.
17. George Orwell, *Dickens, Dali, and Others* (London), pp. 90–91.
18. Herta Herzog, "What Do We Know About Daytime Serial Listeners?" in Paul F. Lazarsfeld and Frank Stanton, eds., *Radio Research, 1942–43* (New York: Duell, Sloan & Pearce, 1941), pp. 24–25.

19. *Ibid.*
20. Orwell, *op. cit.,* pp. 214–215.
21. Hortense Powdermaker, *Hollywood, the Dream Factory* (Boston: Little, Brown, 1950), p. 74.
22. Martha Wolfenstein, *Movies: A Psychological Study* (Glencoe, Illinois: The Free Press, 1950), p. 300.
23. *Ibid.*
24. Wolcott Gibbs in the *Saturday Review of Literature,* quoted in Ruth Inglis, *Freedom of the Movies* (Chicago: University of Chicago Press, 1947), p. 8.
25. Powdermaker, *op. cit.,* p. 72.
26. Wolfenstein, *op. cit.,* pp. 293–307.
27. William E. Hocking, *Freedom of the Press: A Framework of Principle* (Chicago: University of Chicago Press, 1947), pp. 44–45.
28. Hollis Alpert, "Sexual Behavior in the American Movies," *Saturday Review,* June 23, 1956, p. 10.
29. Mimeographed copy in the possession of the authors.

8. Responsibilities: the Government, the Media, the Public

1. William E. Hocking, *Freedom of the Press: A Framework of Principle* (Chicago: University of Chicago Press, 1947), *passim.*
2. *To Secure These Rights,* Report of the President's Committee on Civil Rights (Washington: Government Printing Office, 1947), pp. 8–9.
3. 341 U.S. 494 (1951).
4. Commission on Freedom of the Press, *A Free and Responsible Press* (Chicago: University of Chicago Press, 1947), p. 83.
5. Morris Ernst, *The First Freedom* (New York: Macmillan, 1946).
6. Commission on Freedom of the Press, *op. cit.,* p. 83.
7. Quoted in *FoI Digest,* Vol. 8 (May–June, 1967), p. 5.
8. *Ibid.*
9. Roy Lewis and Angus Maude, *Professional People* (London: Phoenix House, 1952), p. 289.
10. *Ibid.,* p. 266.

Suggested Readings

(In order to keep this list within usable bounds, only books and monographs have been included. A very large number of journal articles and essays are also relevant. Some of them are suggested in the reference notes.)

1. The Impact of Mass Communication

Background in history

Gramling, Oliver. *AP: The Story of the* News. New York: Farrar, 1940. (Lively story of beginnings of news agencies, with spotlight on the Associated Press.)

Hogben, Lancelot. *From Cave Painting to Comic Strip*. London: Oxford, 1948. (One of few studies dealing broadly with the development of human communication *before* the mass media.)

Morris, Joe Alex. *Deadline Every Minute: The Story of the United Press*. Garden City: Doubleday, 1957. (Lively, anecdotal history.)

Mott, Frank Luther. *American Journalism: A History, 1690–1960*, third edition. New York: Macmillan, 1962. (Much-used text.)

Peterson, Theodore B. *Magazines in the Twentieth Century*, second edition. Urbana: University of Illinois Press, 1964. (Social and economic history.)

Ramsaye, Terry. *A Million and One Nights: A History of the Motion Picture*. New York: Simon and Schuster, 1964. (Readable history.)

White, Llewellyn. *The American Radio*. Chicago: University of Chicago Press, 1946. (Interesting material on early days of broadcasting.)

Introduction to the media

Barnouw, Erik. *Mass Communications*. New York: Holt, Rinehart and Winston, 1956. (Emphasis on broadcasting.)

Berelson, Bernard, and Morris Janowitz (eds.). *Reader in Public Opinion and Communication,* new edition. New York: The Free Press, 1963. (General scholarly readings.)

Emery, Edwin, Phillip H. Ault and Warren K. Agee. *Introduction to Mass Communications*. New York: Dodd, Mead & Co., 1960. (General introductory text.)

Hohenberg, John. *The News Media: A Journalist Looks at His Profession*. New York: Holt, Rinehart and Winston, 1968. (Informed account of newsmen and newsgathering.)

International Encyclopedia of the Social Sciences. *Communication* (a series of articles by well known scholars on structure, control, audiences, and effects, of mass and interpersonal communication). New York: Academic Press, 1968.

Peterson, Theodore, Jay W. Jensen and William L. Rivers. *The Mass Media and Modern Society*. New York: Holt, Rinehart and Winston, 1965. (The media in their social context.)

Rivers, William L. *The Mass Media: Reporting, Writing, Editing*. New York: Harper & Row, 1964. (General introduction.)

Schramm, Wilbur (ed.). *Mass Communications: A Book of Readings*, second edition. Urbana: University of Illinois Press, 1960. (General readings.)

Yu, Frederick T. C. (ed.). *Behavioral Sciences and the Mass Media*. New York: Russell Sage Foundation, 1968. (Collection of readings.)

Effects of the media

Handbook of Social Psychology (Gardner Lindzey, ed.). *Effects of Mass Media* (by Walter Weiss) and *Attitude Change* (by William J. McGuire). Boston: Addison Wesley, 1969. (Excellent summaries.)

Klapper, Joseph T. *The Effects of Mass Communication*. New York: The Free Press, 1960. (Summary of what was known in late '50s of effects of the mass media.)

Schramm, Wilbur (ed.). *The Process and Effects of Mass Communication*. Urbana: University of Illinois Press, 1954. (Readings and original papers on the structure, function, and effect of the media.)

2. Four Concepts of Mass Communication

Buzek, Antony. *How the Communist Press Works*. New York: Praeger, 1964. (A study of the theory behind it, as well as the way it operates.)

Davis, Elmer. *But We Were Born Free*. Indianapolis: Bobbs-Merrill, 1954. (Thoughtful treatment of freedom and responsibility by a great journalist and newscaster.)

Inkeles, Alex. *Public Opinion in Soviet Russia: A Study in Mass Persuasion*. Cambridge: Harvard University Press, 1950. (Authoritative study of Soviet use of the mass media.)

Markham, James Walter. *Voices of the Red Giants: Communications in Russia and China*. Ames: Iowa State University Press, 1967. (Organization and performance of these mass media systems.)

Mill, John Stuart. *On Liberty*, many editions. (Classic statement of libertarian theory of press freedom.)

Siebert, Fred S., Theodore B. Peterson, and Wilbur Schramm. *Four Theories of the Press.* Urbana: University of Illinois Press, 1956. (Good starting place for reading about different kinds of mass media systems.)

Terrou, Fernand, and Lucien Solal. *Legislation for Press, Film, and Radio.* Paris: UNESCO, 1951. (Analyzes different national systems of mass communications and their bases in law.)

3. Freedom and Government

Associations of the Bar of the City of New York (Harold R. Medina, chairman). *Freedom of the Press and Fair Trial.* New York: Columbia University Press, 1967. (Significant case study.)

Carmen, Ira H. *Movies, Censorship, and the Law.* Ann Arbor: University of Michigan Press, 1966.

Cater, Douglass. *The Fourth Branch of Government.* Boston: Houghton Mifflin, 1959. (The news media in Washington.)

Chafee, Zechariah. *Government and Mass Communication.* Chicago: University of Chicago Press, 1947. (Classic study from the Commission on Freedom of the Press, dealing with the interrelation of press and government.)

Cohen, Bernard. *The Press and Foreign Policy.* Princeton: Princeton University Press, 1963. (Impact of the press in the making and interpreting of foreign policy.)

Conant, Michael. *Antitrust in the Motion Picture Industry: Economic and Legal Analysis.* Berkeley: University of California Press, 1960.

Cross, Harold L. *The People's Right to Know.* New York: Columbia University Press, 1953. (The case for the right of the press to publish news freely, by long-time legal counsel to publishers.)

Ernst, Morris, and Alan Schwartz. *Censorship: The Search for the Obscene.* New York: Macmillan, 1964. (Discussion of obscenity cases.)

Franklin, Marc A. *The Dynamics of American Law.* Mineola, N.Y.: The Foundation Press, 1968. (Excellent overview.)

Gerald, J. Edward. *The Press and the Constitution, 1931–1947.* Minneapolis: University of Minnesota Press, 1948. (Relations of press to government regulation and court decisions.)

Gillmor, Donald M. *Free Press and Fair Trial.* Washington: Public Affairs Press, 1966. (One of best treatments of this issue.)

Grey, David L. *The Supreme Court and the News Media.* Evanston: Northwestern University Press, 1968. (Readable description of the flow of Supreme Court news through the media.)

Hachten, William A. *The Supreme Court on Freedom of the Press: Decisions and Dissent.* Ames: Iowa State University Press, 1968. (Reader of significant cases, with commentaries.)

Johnson, Gerald W. *Peril and Promise: An Inquiry into Freedom of the Press.* New York: Harper & Row, 1958. (Warnings about threats to civil liberties.)

Konvitz, Milton Ridvas. *Expanding Liberties: Freedom's Gains in Postwar America*. New York: Viking Press, 1966. (Legalistic view of civil liberties.)

Macneil, Robert. *The People Machine*. New York: Harper and Row, 1968. (Readable description of the interplay of TV and politics.)

McGaffin, William, and Erwin Knoll. *Anything but the Truth: The Credibility Gap: How the News Is Managed in Washington*. New York: Putnam, 1968. (Two veteran Washington correspondents discuss the problem.)

Randall, Richard S. *Censorship of the Movies: The Social and Political Control of a Mass Medium*. Madison, University of Wisconsin Press, 1968. (How free should the movies be?)

Rivers, William L. *The Opinionmakers*. Boston: Beacon Press, 1965. (Study of the Washington press corps. See also the earlier study in this pattern by Leo Rosten, *The Washington Correspondents*, New York, 1937).

4. Freedom and Society

Agee, Warren Kendall (ed.). *The Press and the Public Interest*. Washington: Public Affairs Press, 1965. (Readings in the performance of the press.)

Dexter, Lewis Anthony, and David Manning White (eds.). *People, Society, and Mass Communications*. New York: The Free Press, 1964. (General readings on mass communication in society.)

Gerald, J. Edward. *The Social Responsibility of the Press*. Minneapolis: University of Minnesota Press, 1953. (Broad consideration of press in its social and governmental context.)

Mayer, Martin. *Madison Avenue, U.S.A.* New York: Harper & Row, 1958. (The advertising industry.)

Rucker, Bryce W. *The First Freedom* (Introduction by Morris L. Ernst). Carbondale, Illinois: Southern Illinois Press, 1966. (Second-generation book following Morris L. Ernst's hard-hitting defense of civil liberties in *The First Freedom*. This one is especially interesting in its treatment of the dangers of corporate take-over.)

Seldes, Gilbert V. *The New Mass Media: Challenge to a Free Society*. Washington: American Association of University Women, 1957. (Consideration of the freedom and responsibility to be expected of the media.)

5. Truth and Fairness

Boorstin, Daniel J. *The Image*. New York: Harper & Row, 1964. (An historian's view of pseudo-events.)

Flint, L. N. *The Conscience of the Newspaper*. New York: Appleton. 1925. (Early casebook on journalism ethics.)

Gross, Gerald (ed.). *The Responsibility of the Press*. New York: Fleet Publishing Corporation, 1966. (Reader on press ethics.)

Liebling, A. J. *The Wayward Pressman.* New York: Doubleday, 1947. (Urbane criticism of press performance.)

Lippmann, Walter. *Public Opinion.* New York: Harcourt, Brace & World, 1922. (Classic book on public opinion from viewpoint of a journalist.)

Westin, Alan F. *Privacy and Freedom.* New York: Atheneum, 1967. (Warning of dangers in massive collection of personal and social data.)

6. The Negro and the News: A Case Study

Cohen, Jerry, and William S. Murphy. *Burn, Baby, Burn!.* New York: E. P. Dutton, 1966. (Vivid and detailed account by staff members of Los Angeles *Times.*)

Conot, Robert. *Rivers of Blood, Years of Darkness.* New York: Morrow, 1960. (Paperback, Bantam, 1967.) (Vivid background for racial violence.)

Fiske, Paul L., and Lowenstein, Ralph. *Race and the News Media.* University of Missouri, 8th Freedom of Information Conference. New York: Frederick A. Praeger, 1967. (Discussions of news coverage of racial matters.)

Governor's Commission on the Los Angeles Riots. *Violence in the City—an End or a Beginning?.* Los Angeles: Governor's Commission, 1965. (Brief report on causes and steps toward prevention of Los Angeles riots.)

Lyle, Jack. *The News in Megapolis.* San Francisco, Chandler, 1967. (How the media in a large city handle the news.)

National Advisory Commission on Civil Disorders (Kerner). *Report of the National Advisory Commission on Civil Disorders.* New York: Bantam Books, 1968. (Valuable analysis.)

National Commission on the Causes and Prevention of Violence (Walker Report). *Rights in Conflict.* New York: New American Library, 1968. (Important official report.)

University of Missouri, Freedom of Information Center. *Race and the News Media.* Columbia: University of Missouri. (Symposium.)

7. Popular Art

Casty, Alan (ed.). *Mass Media and Mass Man.* New York: Holt, Rinehart and Winston, 1968. (Reader.)

Inglis, Ruth. *Freedom of the Movies.* Chicago: University of Chicago Press, 1947. (How the movie industry worked in the 1940s, and what the public has a right to expect of it.)

McLuhan, H. Marshall. *Understanding Media: The Extensions of Man.* New York: McGraw-Hill, 1964. (McLuhan's best known book, especially relevant here because of its comparison of social and psychological effects of oral culture, print culture, and audiovisual culture.)

Powdermaker, Hortense. *Hollywood, the Dream Factory*. Boston: Little, Brown, 1950. (Anthropologist's view of the movie industry.)

Rosenberg, Bernard, and David Manning White (eds.). *Mass Culture: The Popular Arts in America*. Glencoe: The Free Press, 1957. (A collection of essays and papers on art produced for the masses.)

Schramm, Wilbur, Jack Lyle, and Edwin B. Parker. *Television in the Lives of Our Children*. Stanford: Stanford University Press, 1961. (Chief American study on the effects of television. See also chief English study of this type: Hilde Himmelweit, A. N. Oppenheim, and Pamela Vince, *Television and the Child*, London, Oxford, 1958.)

Seldes, Gilbert. *The Great Audience*. New York: Viking, 1950. (Comments on successes and shortcomings of mass media.)

White, David Manning, and Robert H. Abel (eds.). *The Funnies: An American Idiom*. New York: The Free Press, 1963. (Readings that interpret and criticize the American comic strip.)

8. Responsibilities: the Government, the Media, the Public

Becker, Carl L. *Freedom and Responsibility in the American Way of Life*. New York: Alfred A. Knopf, 1945. (Excellent background in the history of ideas.)

Commission on Freedom of the Press. *A Free and Responsible Press*. Chicago: University of Chicago Press, 1947. (Summary report with recommendations.)

Hocking, William E. *Freedom of the Press: A Framework of Principle*. Chicago: University of Chicago Press, 1947. (Commission on Freedom of the Press book by philosopher member of Commission.)

Levy, Herman Phillip. *The Press Council: History, Procedure, and Cases*. New York: Macmillan, 1967. (Study of the institution created in the United Kingdom to examine the performance of the press.)

Lippmann, Walter. *The Public Philosophy*. Boston: Little Brown, 1955. (Mature conclusions of a great journalist.)

Royal Commission on the Press. *Reports*. London: H. M. Stationery Office. (Several volumes since 1947 dealing with separate inquiries into the performance and responsibility of the mass media.)

Svirsky, Leon (ed.). *Your Newspaper: Blueprint for a Better Press*. New York: Macmillan, 1948. (Nieman Fellows writing about responsible journalism.)

Index

75 76 77 9 8 7 6